Narrative and Consciousness

Narrative and Consciousness

Literature, Psychology, and the Brain

EDITED BY
Gary D. Fireman
Ted E. McVay, Jr.
Owen J. Flanagan

OXFORD
UNIVERSITY PRESS
2003

OXFORD
UNIVERSITY PRESS

Oxford   New York
Auckland   Bangkok   Buenos Aires   Cape Town   Chennai
Dar es Salaam   Delhi   Hong Kong   Istanbul   Karachi   Kolkata
Kuala Lumpur   Madrid   Melbourne   Mexico City   Mumbai   Nairobi
São Paulo   Shanghai   Taipei   Tokyo   Toronto

Copyright © 2003 by Oxford University Press, Inc.

Published by Oxford University Press, Inc.
198 Madison Avenue, New York, New York 10016

www.oup.com

Oxford is a registered trademark of Oxford University Press

Library of Congress Cataloging-in-Publication Data
Fireman, Gary D.
   Narrative and consciousness : literature, psychology, and the brain /
edited by Gary D. Fireman, Ted E. McVay, Jr., and Owen J. Flanagan.
      p.   cm.
Includes bibliographical references and index.
   ISBN 0-19-514005-2; 0-19-516172-6 (pbk.)
   1. Consciousness—Congresses.   2. First person narrative—Congresses.
3. Autobiographical memory—Congresses.   I. Fireman, Gary D.   II. McVay,
Ted E.   III. Flanagan, Owen J.
   BF311 N26 2003
   153—dc21   2002011745

9 8 7 6 5 4 3 2 1

Printed in the United States of America
on acid-free paper

Acknowledgments

This volume would not have been possible without the generous financial support of various Texas Tech University colleges, departments, and programs given to the conference from which this collection is taken. Most especially, we would like to thank the Program in Comparative Literature for allowing us to organize the conference under the rubric of its annual symposium, Provost John Burns, dean of the Graduate School David Schmidley, and Jane Winer, dean of the College of Arts and Sciences, for their most generous financial support. Additional support was provided by the Center for Interaction of the Arts and Sciences, the Departments of Psychology, Classical and Modern Languages and Literatures, English, and Philosophy, the College of Human Sciences and its Department of Human Development and Family Studies, and the Women's Studies Program.

The editors would also like to thank the contributors, not only for their essays that make this book what it is but also for their patience.

Contents

Contributors   ix

1. Introduction   3
    Gary D. Fireman, Ted E. McVay Jr. and Owen Flanagan

    PART I: THE ROLE OF NARRATIVE IN THE
    DEVELOPMENT OF CONSCIOUS AWARENESS

2. Narrative and the Emergence of a Consciousness of Self   17
    Katherine Nelson
3. The Development of the Self   37
    Valerie Gray Hardcastle

    PART II: NARRATIVE AND AUTOBIOGRAPHICAL
    MEMORY

4. The Role of Narrative in Recollection: A View from Cognitive
    Psychology and Neuropsychology   53
    David C. Rubin and Daniel L. Greenberg
5. Material Selves: Bodies, Memory, and Autobiographical
    Narrating   86
    Sidonie A. Smith

PART III: AUTOBIOGRAPHICAL NARRATIVE, FICTION, AND THE CONSTRUCTION OF SELF

6. Rethinking the Fictive, Reclaiming the Real: Autobiography, Narrative Time, and the Burden of Truth   115
    Mark Freeman

7. Dual Focalization, Retrospective Fictional Autobiography, and the Ethics of *Lolita*   129
    James Phelan

PART IV: NARRATIVE DISRUPTIONS IN THE CONSTRUCTION OF SELF

8. The Pursuit of Death in Holocaust Narrative   149
    Lawrence L. Langer

9. Community and Coherence: Narrative Contributions to the Psychology of Conflict and Loss   166
    Robert A. Neimeyer and Finn Tschudi

PART V: THE NEURAL SUBSTRATE OF NARRATIVE AND CONSCIOUSNESS REALIZATION (OR THE NATURALIST MODEL)

10. Empirical Evidence for a Narrative Concept of Self   195
     John Bickle

11. Sexual Identities and Narratives of Self   209
     Gillian Einstein and Owen Flanagan

Index   233

Contributors

John Bickle is Professor and Head of the Department of Philosophy and Professor in the Neuroscience Graduate Program at the University of Cincinnati. He is the author of *Psychoneural Reduction: The New Wave* and *Philosophy and Neuroscience: A Ruthlessly Reductive Account* and is Editor-in-Chief of *Brain and Mind: A Transdisciplinary Journal of Neuroscience and Neurophilosophy.*

Gillian Einstein is Scientific Review Administrator for Molecular, Developmental and Cellular Neurosciences at the National Institutes of Health. She moved to NIH from the Neurobiology Department at Duke University, where in addition to teaching and research she initiated an on-going multidisciplinary curricular program across the cognitive sciences.

Gary D. Fireman is Associate Professor of Psychology and Director of the Psychology Clinic at Texas Tech University. He has written articles on clinical and developmental psychology and has co-edited special issues of the journal *Intertexts* and the *Journal of Constructivist Psychology* that treat narrative and consciousness.

Owen Flanagan is James B. Duke Professor of Philosophy, Professor of Psychology-Experimental, Professor of Neurobiology, Core Member of the Graduate Faculty in Cognitive Neuroscience, and Affiliated Faculty, Graduate Program in Literature at Duke University. He is the author of *The Science of the Mind; Consciousness Reconsidered; Self Expressions: Mind, Morals, and the Meaning of Life; Dreaming Souls: Sleep, Dreams, and the Evolution of the Conscious Mind.*

Mark Freeman is Professor of Psychology at the College of the Holy Cross where he also serves as the W. Arthur Garrity, Sr. Professor in Human Nature Ethics and Society. He is the author of *Rewriting the Self: History, Memory, and Narrative* and *Finding the Muse: A Sociopsychological Inquiry into the Conditions of Artistic Creativity.*

Daniel L. Greenberg earned his BA and MA from Duke University and is currently working toward his Ph.D. in Duke's Department of Psychological and Brain Sciences. His research focuses on the neuroanatomical basis of autobiographical memory and he has published articles on this and other topics in *Biological Psychiatry, Cortex,* and the *Proceedings of the National Academy of Sciences.*

Valerie Gray Hardcastle is Professor of Philosophy and Director of Science and Technology Studies at Virginia Tech Polytechnic Institute and State University, and author of *Locating Consciousness; How to Build a Theory in Cognitive Science* and *The Myth of Pain* and editor of *Where Biology Meets Psychology: Philosphical Essays.*

Lawrence L. Langer is Professor of English emeritus at Simmons College in Boston. In the fall of 2002 he was the Strassler Distinguished Visiting professor in the Center for Holocaust and Genocide Studies at Clark University. His *Holocaust Testimonies: The Ruins of Memory* won the National Book Critics Circle Award for criticism in 1991. Other works include *The Holocaust and the Literary Imagination, Preempting the Holocaust and Other Essays,* and *Admitting the Holocaust: Selected Essays.*

Ted E. McVay Jr. is Associate Professor of Spanish at Texas Tech University. He has co-edited special narrative-related issues of the comparative literature journal *Intertexts* and the *Journal of Constructivist Psychology.* His research centers on the relation between visual images and metaphors and visual epistemology in Renaissance and baroque Spanish poetry.

Robert A. Neimeyer holds a Dunavant Chair in Psychology at the University of Memphis and edits both the *Journal of Constructivist Psychology* and *Death Studies.* His most recent books include *Lessons of Loss: A Guide to Coping, Meaning Reconstruction and the Experience of Loss* and *Disorders of Construction.*

Katherine Nelson, Distinguished Professor Emerita of Psychology, The Graduate School of City University of New York, is the author of *Language in Cognitive Development: The Emergence of the Mediated Mind,* editor of *Narratives from the Crib* and co-editor of *Socio-Cultural Psychology: Theory and Practice of Doing and Knowing.*

James Phelan, Professor of English, The Ohio State University, is the author of *Narrative as Rhetoric: Technique, Audiences, Ethics, Ideology; Reading People, Reading Plots: Character, Progression, and the Interpretation of Narrative;* and *Worlds from Words: A Theory of Language in Fiction,* and editor of the award-winning journal *Narrative.*

David C. Rubin is Professor of Psychological and Brain Sciences at Duke University and author of *Memory in Oral Tradition: The Cognitive Psychology of Epic, Ballads, and Counting-Out Rhymes* (William James Award from APA,

American Association of Publishers Best New Professional Scholarly Book in Psychology). He also edited *Remembering Our Past: Studies in Autobiographical Memory.*

Sidonie A. Smith is the Martha Guernsey Colby Collegiate Professor of English and Women's Studies at the University of Michigan. She is the author of *Reading Autobiography: A Guide to Interpreting Life Narratives, Moving Lives: Twentieth Century Women's Travel Narratives, Subjectivity, Identity and the Body: Women's Autobiographical Practices in the Twentieth Century, Marginality and the Fictions of Self-Representation,* and co-editor of *Getting a Life: Everyday Uses of Autobiography.*

Finn Tschudi is retired Professor of Psychology from the University of Oslo, Norway. He is a member of Johan Galtung's TRANSCEND network (www.transcend.org) and has co-authored *Crafting Peace: On the Psychology of the TRANSCEND Approach.* He has worked to introduce conferencing in Norway and is a consultant to various agencies dealing with conflicts. He is also working to perfect computer programs for studying homo/heterogeneity in how different groups of people construe social and personal issues by using repertory grids.

Narrative and Consciousness

1   Introduction

Gary Fireman
Ted McVay
Owen Flanagan

The daughter of one of the editors, upon entering the fifth grade, was given the assignment of learning about a child in the class whom she did not know well. Specifically, she was instructed to develop an interview that would answer the question "Who are you?" Of course, her collaborator was to do the same. Thus, one evening during the first week of class, in attempting to respond to her classmate she asked, "Dad, where was my favorite vacation?" After *his telling* her where *they* went and *discussing* what *they* did on *her* favorite vacation, she then asked, "What is my most frightening memory?" Unable to answer the second question, he came to the awkward realization of how quickly and thoughtlessly he was willing to answer the first. She wanted to provide stories to answer questions about who she is, and initially it seemed perfectly reasonable to both of them that he help construct them. The stories we tell to ourselves and others, for ourselves and others, are a central means by which we come to know ourselves and others, thereby enriching our conscious awareness. Narrative pervades our lives—conscious experience is not merely linked to the number and variety of personal stories we construct with each other within a cultural frame but is also consumed by them.

The claim, however, that narrative constructions are essential to conscious experience is not that informative unless we can also begin to provide a distinct explanation for narrative in relation to consciousness. The method we propose to use in this pursuit, the "natural method" (Flanagan, 1992), examines the relations among the findings, concepts, and methods of phenomenological, psychological, and neurobiological analyses of narrative and consciousness recognizing that each line of analysis has legitimate aims. Such an analysis demands a constant vigilance against privileging or diminishing the value of any one approach: findings from each perspective inform the others with an aim to explain our everyday beliefs about narrative and consciousness. It strives both to be sensitive to the particular case and to maintain a degree of general integrity and coherence within the cultural, interpersonal, and biological contexts.

The natural method was designed originally to corral consciousness by paying attention to how it seems (its phenomenology), what mental labor it does (its psychology), and how it is realized (its neurobiology). Recent work on the problems associated with self-consciousness, personal identity, self-representation, and dream narrative and interpretation have resulted in an expansion of the method, now dubbed the "expanded natural method" (Flanagan, 1996, 2000). The expanded method requires looking to anthropology, history, sociology, religion, literature, and even popular culture to explain the construction of different types of narrative as well as the norms that govern narrative expression and narrative concealment.

The concept of narrative has been called "one of the more prominent currents in late 20th-century intellectual life" (Neisser & Fivush, 1994, p. vii), and a number of philosophers of mind have argued that the portions of human consciousness beyond the purely somatic—self-awareness, self-understanding, and self-knowledge—are products of personal narratives (e.g., Dennett, 1991). It is "because of the nature of our minds," as Dan P. McAdams (1993) claims, that "we are impelled as adults to make sense of our lives in terms of narrative" (p. 134). This powerful role for narrative is realized by the linking of personal memories to present conditions and future hopes, by organizing, translating, and providing continuity and coherence to experience. Self-awareness and self-knowledge are constructed, to a significant degree, through narrative as we compose and assemble stories for ourselves and our world. In a complex interplay between the experience that makes for the personal story and the personal story that structures the experience, the narrator discovers the meaning and significance of the experience. It is through narrating that we learn about our selves, our community, and the social world (Bruner, 1986, 1990).

The attempt to explain the process has resulted in a proliferation of discriminating approaches. As Russell and Lucariello (1992) comment, "Some of the best minds in literary scholarship and in cognitive and developmental psychology have spent years attempting to get hold of the essential and distinguishing characteristics of narrative" (p. 671). Literary theorists have long studied narrative form in various rhetorical transactions and have provided rich descriptions of its sophistication and complexity, closely examining such things as narrative form, the narrator's language, and generic conventions and their relation to content. In the study of psychology, the analysis of self-narrative and consciousness is so compelling and important that it has formed an integral part of the discipline since its inception (James, 1890/1983). Personal narratives are the basis for introspective reports in cognitive research (Nelson, T. O., 1996), the database for work in autobiographical memory and psychotherapy (Freeman, 1993; Neimeyer, 1994; Rubin, 1996), a learned skill that emerges from and belongs to the community with a specific developmental history (Nelson, K., 1989), and one manner by which a person comes to know him- or herself (Neisser, 1988).

The recent prominence of a narrative approach to understanding mind and human consciousness has led some to argue that narrative is present in practically all human activity (Howard, 1991). Although some may see such a sweeping proclamation as problematic in that (for example) events can be chronicled without explicitly being narrated, we would argue that human culture always provides an implied, underlying, or overarching narrative context. Given that personal narrative and self-representation exist as human experience, are spontaneous and recurrent by early childhood, and give meaning to experience, they are therefore central to a conception and examination of human consciousness. Narrative does not merely capture aspects of the self for description, communication, and examination; narrative constructs the self.

As the various chapters in this book demonstrate, personal stories are jointly constructed through social relations, are shaped by our nature and culture, and are logically compatible with the naturalistic scientific method of investigation. If yesterday's model of positivist naturalism (with the constraints of causal explanation, prediction, and control) is surrendered, then a plurality of methodological approaches are available and may be used to understand the meaning that informs a person's action in the world as lived. Narratives are available for observation; they are public and shared, and as a result their examination does not of necessity result in subjectivism and relativism. Narratives are governed by culturally embedded formal rules—character roles, time and plot structure, and so forth—that define whether they are recognized as coherent and cogent. Personal narration gives continuity to self and meaning to action as it locates and values present activity in the context of past experience and projected outcomes. Narrative is also tied to the development of signs and language and as such is constrained by and consistent with developmental biology and human neurobiology as well as linguistic structures and narrative traditions. But the necessary link of narrative to signs and language raises important questions about truth and accuracy as conveyed in personal narrative (e.g., see Freeman, 1993; Jopling, 2000; McAdams, 1993). The telling of a personal story, as a selective and imaginative process, is also powerfully influenced by the audience one has or anticipates having: an inevitable and necessary tension results as the fictive (ultimately from Latin *fingere*, "to form or fashion") process is imposed on real events in an effort to re-present the self to others with a suasory purpose. As the line between the imagined and the factual blurs, the difficult question of how to determine what makes a "good" (e.g., coherent, organized, meaningful, compelling) personal narrative becomes crucial.

This book is the outcome of an interdisciplinary conference titled Narrative and Consciousness: Literature, Psychology, and the Brain, held at Texas Tech University in February 1999. While most of the chapters are expanded versions of papers presented by the invited speakers, additional chapters were solicited in an effort to broaden the interdisciplinary nature of the book. The primary focus of the collection is on the interplay among biological, psychological, philosophical, and literary approaches to examining the role of narrative in the formation and function of consciousness. Following from the work of Owen Flanagan (1991a, 1991b, 1992, 1996), our intent is to engender a collaborative examination of narrative and consciousness that is sensitive to "phenomenological seeming" yet constrained by empirical findings in psychology and cognitive science, and thereby to "deliver the concept from its ghostly past and provide it with a credible naturalistic analysis" (Flanagan, 1991a, p. 364).

With the natural method providing the framework, the following chapters demonstrate how insight about the link between narrative and consciousness may result from the coordination of phenomenological and scientific approaches. Surprisingly, this naturalistic method has rarely been used, as the conventional wisdom (espoused by many philosophers and psychologists who have thought long and hard about the problem) has maintained the incommensurability of phenomenology and science. We suggest that the conventional view has been a significant contributor to the increasingly more fragmented, insular, and diminished position of the social sciences and humanities than that of the "hard sciences." This volume aims to challenge the conventional wisdom by presenting information that cuts across conceptual levels and disciplines. The book is divided into five areas of inquiry whose importance is evident in many fields of investigation into the human condition. They are coordinated to illustrate the viability of the naturalistic method for examining narrative and consciousness. They include: (1) the role of narrative in the development of conscious awareness, (2) narrative and autobiographical memory, (3) autobiographical narrative, fiction, and the construction of self, (4) narrative disruptions in the construction of self, and (5) the neural substrate of narrative and consciousness realization. This interdisciplinary effort is of particular importance as it provides a counterpoint to the movement toward increasing insularity of academic disciplines by introducing empirical rigor into the literary discourse of understanding experience while challenging scientific discourse to recognize that an explanation of narrative and conscious awareness must include value and meaning.

Part I: The Role of Narrative in the Development of Conscious Awareness

In this section the authors address the emergence of consciousness as related to self and critically examine the role that narrative plays in its development. Katherine Nelson emphasizes a dynamic "self-organizing developing system" approach and argues that the expansion of the child's consciousness occurs by way of multiple social realities, communicative discourse, and the human disposition to narrativize events and impose meaning on people's actions. Her view sets narrative not as some special human gift but as part and parcel of the range of developments during the years when the child enters fully into the linguistic world. These developments include awareness of self and other, of the wider world beyond self, and of past and future. She goes on to tell the story of the emerging levels of narrative from intentional babble, to the telling of stories about action, to the stories a child tells with a specific, personal past and a recognition of a generalized world. For Nelson, narrative emerges from and belongs to the community, but in the individual lives of children it is a vehicle through which consciousness of both self and the wider social and temporal world becomes manifest and gradually emerges as a new subjective level of conscious awareness.

Valerie Gray Hardcastle takes a different approach to understanding the role of narrative in the emergence of self and conscious awareness. Hardcastle opposes what she views as the dominant developmental paradigm: "Once we master language, understand causal efficacy, interpret our desires, and recognize the intentions of others, then we get a self as a sort of cognitive bonus." In contrast, she argues that a drive for selfhood pushes us along in our linguistic and cognitive development and that children's earliest affective expressions demonstrate that they narrate all the time. Hardcastle suggests that from the beginning children try to understand the world and self as meaning something, as stories with plot and temporal sequence. She states that "language and reason are only tacked on at the end as useful additions in completing this enterprise." Hardcastle takes a meaning-making and affective approach to understanding the development of narrative, self, and conscious awareness. In the child's efforts to construct meaning in experience, the affective dimension serves to structure reasoning, guide thoughts, and anchor autobiographical memory.

Part II: Narrative and Autobiographical Memory

The authors examine the role of narrative in autobiographical memory from two traditionally opposing points of view in these two essays. David C. Rubin and Daniel L. Greenberg start from a neurobiological and cognitive science perspective, while Sidonie A. Smith starts from the position of a social constructivist. Interestingly, the authors from each tradition use the experience of special subjects whose bodily structure has been damaged (individuals with specific neurological impairment and individuals with autism) to articulate the complex relationship between the material and the cultural. Rubin and Greenberg review extensive empirical data to demonstrate that the adult's conscious recall of personal events involves narrative along with other forms of reasoning, (e.g., language, as distinct from narrative, and imagery) and is supported by multiple neural systems spread throughout the brain. They examine what is needed for and what is gained by having a "full-blown" autobiographical recollection, integrating factors across neurological and psychological levels of analysis. To illustrate the connection across these levels, they present material from the autobiographical memory of adults who suffer damage to the various neural systems involved in recollection. In doing so, they demonstrate the complexity of functions required for narrative and suggest that narrative reasoning may not be one process but a constellation of processes. In understanding the relations between narrative and the other modes of reasoning required for autobiographical memory they caution against the temptation to reify and reduce autobiographical memory to neural systems.

Sidonie A. Smith, however, is concerned that the probing of science into the interior of persons at the neural, connectionist, or even subatomic quantum level in order to understand autobiographical memory too often misses the impact of the sociocultural, historical, and political context. She frames the current search "to map, track, and heal the remembering subject" in terms of current Western politics or "memoro-politics." For Smith, this shifts the focus to the uses of autobiographical memory and the conceptions of self that are engendered by current scientific (material) studies of autobiographical memory. Specifically, she presents the complex relationship of the material to the autobiographical in the personal narrative of an autistic woman. Given the unique constellation of social interactions, communicative patterns, and behavioral repertoires manifest in autistic persons, Smith explores what she takes to be the constituent aspects of autobiographical subjectivity (e.g., experience, language, embodiment, identity, culture, and agency) and confronts important questions about consciousness, selfhood, and the implications of constructing a life story. Throughout she underscores "the cultural situatedness of the storied selves we become."

Part III: Autobiographical Narrative, Fiction, and the Construction of Self

The essays in this section examine the extent to which autobiographical narrative blurs the distinction between fiction and nonfiction in the process of giving more form and meaning to life than occurs in life itself, a process that results from the need to construct and the allure to examine both self and other situated in a world.

Mark Freeman questions the position that autobiographies, even when based on factually accurate information, inevitably falsify experience by virtue of their literary character. Freeman recognizes that autobiographical narrative does not re-present past experience. Instead the past is reconstructed from the vantage point of the present and provided with increased connectedness and coherence. However, Freeman maintains that this reconstruction does not obviate the possibility of autobiographical narrative's depicting reality or attaining historical truth. Specifically, he argues that there is a need to rethink the idea of the fictive and, by extension, to reclaim the idea of the real in the context of theorizing about autobiographical reflection and writing. For Freeman, the notion of narrative time, as addressed by Paul Ricoeur, is of particular value in reconsidering the categories of the fictive, the real, and the notion of truth.

James Phelan begins by addressing the blur between fiction and nonfiction and examines technique and ethics in the representation of consciousness in fictional autobiographical narrative. Phelan examines a retrospective pseudoautobiography, one of the most familiar forms in the Western literary tradition, Vladimir Nabokov's Lolita. In this text Phelan focuses on the dual nature of the "I" of the protagonist Humbert Humbert, both as the representing narrator and as the represented character, and the techniques by which the reader is made aware of these different "I"s. Phelan demonstrates that the retelling of events in order to construct a personal story typically occurs with the author highly cognizant of the audience. That is, narrative is constructed with an, often conscious, agenda. This is exemplified through Nabokov's effort to make the reader uncomfortably aware of Humbert's retelling or refashioning his story in order to persuade his audience to be sympathetic. This refashioning of the events into a story with an agenda is manipulated by Nabokov in such a way to show the conflict within the protagonist as both character and narrator as to the truth and ethics of his actions. Phelan goes on to consider the reader's "ethical engagement and response, . . . in conjunction with the narrative's technique, [his or her] . . . cognitive understanding, and [his or her] . . . emotional response."

Part IV: Narrative Disruptions in the Construction of Self

The authors in this section explore instances of disruption in personal narrative and the concomitant breakdown of narrative form in the construction of self. Lawrence L. Langer examines the oral and written testimony of Holocaust survivors as to how their agonizing life in the midst of German atrocities impacted autobiographical narrative. He sees embedded in the story of survival a darker chronicle that continues to infect a portion of the victim's memory as the victim continues on a journey that has not yet reached an end. It is the theme of death, and a particular kind of dying, that menaces the victim's memory. Langer questions whether it is possible to come back to life when still walking the path toward death. It is a paradox he sees enshrined in one survivor's statement: "I died in Auschwitz but no one knows it." Langer draws on vivid testimony of literal encounters with the dead to explore the legacy left in the survivors' construction of self and, in particular, "their missed destiny of death."

Robert A. Neimeyer and Finn Tschudi begin their chapter by highlighting the function of personal narrative and articulating various forms of narrative disruption evident among people who are troubled or in conflict. Pulling from the applied clinical setting, they articulate the critical role of increasing personal coherence and reworking personal meaning of one's narrative(s) in contributing to improved well-being. After establishing the utility of a narrative framework within the clinical setting, the main thrust of the chapter is the extension of therapeutic techniques for narrative repair and elaboration to the Western criminal system. They write: "It strikes us that similar processes of narrative disintegration and domination occur at this broader social level, particularly in the context of conflict and its 'resolution' by the state." This extension raises a provocative challenge to the dominant narrative in the Western criminal system that suggests a shift from a "retributive paradigm" to a "restorative paradigm." Further, they suggest that the power for determining the substance and outcome of the criminal proceeding (establishing the setting, characterization, plot, goals, and conclusion of the story) should shift from the state to the protagonists, especially the victims. They ground their argument for a shift to a restorative paradigm in the novel working justice practices referred to as Transformative Justice Australia. Neimeyer and Tschudi demonstrate how such novel justice practices empower the protagonists to avoid the ignominy of being characterized as offender and victim by the state and provide them with the opportunity to co-author narratives of themselves as complex moral agents within a community.

Part V: The Neural Substrate of Narrative and Consciousness Realization (or The Naturalist Model)

In this section the authors examine the relation between narrative and neurobiological functioning. John Bickle presents convincing empirical evidence from images of the functioning brain for the neural basis of personal narratives. Citing the biophysics of positron emission tomography (PET), Bickle briefly explains both the method by which brain activity (blood flow and glucose metabolism) can be spatially localized to a high degree of specificity and the analytic techniques for achieving adequate temporal resolution. He utilizes the PET evidence of brain areas activated during inner speech to establish neurobiological support for the theory of a narrative concept of self. Bickle goes on to examine the crucial question about the causal efficacy of a narrative self from the neurobiological point of view. Does the narrative self initiate (control) cognition and behavior or does the narrative self make sense (create meaning) of cognition and behavior after they occur? Bickle presents research about the neural regions' subserving cognition and behavior as evidence to support a conclusion that narrative-self-control is narrative fiction. He states: "Activity in the brain's language regions, and hence the neurally realized narrative self, neither accurately reflects *nor causally affects* very much of what is really going on." Bickle concludes by examining the implications of his position for the practical activity of moral training. Presenting traditional instruction (abstract verbal discussion or discussion of hypothetical scenarios) versus practice (actually planning and executing moral behaviors), Bickle finds in favor of the later.

Gillian Einstein and Owen Flanagan put forward the idea that the narrative of self is strongly influenced by the body (including the brain). Extending William James's (1890–1983) notion that personal narrative depends on early somatic input, they highlight how personal stories about the self as a sexual being (sexual self-consciousness) are related to biology. Einstein and Flanagan argue that biology, along with culture, plays a powerful role in our sense of ourselves as gay, straight, transsexual, eager, or asexual. Through outlining the permutations and combinations possible for genes, hormones, receptors, and enzymes they demonstrate that there is enough variation in the development of the sexual phenotype of both the brain and the rest of the body to account for the continuum of sexual selves and that nonalignment of phenotype with early developmental pathways can lead to views of oneself that are in contrast to the culture's expectations. Narratives from an XYY male, an XY individual born with ambiguous genitalia who was shaped into a female phenotype, and a female-to-male transsexual illustrate the power that early development has in shaping one's personal narrative and the tension and distress that exists in one's personal narrative when biology and culture are not aligned.

Conclusion

As can be seen from the preceding descriptions, the essays in this volume address many important issues that arise when examining narrative and consciousness: the question regarding the necessity of narrative; the form and function of narrative and its role in the emergence of conscious awareness; the relation of the self to the body (not limited to the brain); the interplay of culture, memory, and body in the construction of personal narrative; the distinction between the real and the fictive in personal narrative; the development of narrative and its function in the emergence of selfhood; and the role of trauma and discourse in shaping personal narratives. By approaching these problems from the diverse perspectives of contributors from across disciplines, we hope to demonstrate our claim for the efficacy of the natural method in approaching the question of narrative, in its form and its function in general and its specific role in the emergence of conscious awareness. While such an approach may seem like merely good sense, we recognize that the placement of contributions from such diverse disciplines next to one another in one volume will raise questions about the coherence of concepts and stability of language use across the chapters. And in fact, using the natural method can be dangerous if one tries—by constructing overly inclusive, incoherent categories that contain incongruous elements—to see heterogeneity when there is evidence for only a hodgepodge. When examining the concept of narrative across levels of analysis (or across disciplines) we must strive to avoid making arbitrary connections that would result in meaningless combinations of form and function of no use in addressing the problem of narrative.

While the lack of coherence among the various concepts that treat the same phenomenon presents frustrating obstacles to communication between disciplines, it is that very lack that cries out for an inclusive approach, making it clear that the study of the nature of narrative is too big for any one of these disciplines alone, as they are currently defined. Just as Spanish Baroque poets would present two very different metaphors for one object and hold them in a tension that called the reader to appreciate both while recognizing that neither was adequate, so must we hold our theoretical models (which, after all, are metaphors). The question for the reader, then, is not which approach might be his or her cup of tea, as no single perspective can adequately represent all we know about narrative. Rather, the reader must ask to what extent the various points of view might be woven together and what are points of agreement and disagreement across disciplines. The search for potential relations across such disparate disciplines as literary theory, philosophy, psychology, and neuroscience requires an appreciation of the interpretive as well as the definitive and an interest in making sense of the stories we tell as well as in explaining how personal narrative supervenes on certain neural processes. This broadened approach gives us the potential to move toward an understanding of personal narratives and their role in conscious awareness.

We spoke earlier in this introduction about the problem of the "insularity" of disciplines that share a common goal, and the island analogy is apt. It is our hope that this collection will contribute to the reconception of the current state of inquiry into narrative and consciousness as an archipelago—a group of related and interdependent islands—and cause us to look for the submerged (and currently unseen) structures that connect them.

References

Bruner, J. (1986). *Actual minds, possible worlds.* Cambridge, MA: Harvard University Press.

Bruner, J. S. (1990). *Acts of meaning.* Cambridge, MA: Harvard University Press.

Dennett, D. C. (1991). *Consciousness explained.* Boston: Little, Brown.

Flanagan, O. (1991a). *The science of the mind.* Cambridge, MA: MIT Press.

Flanagan, O. (1991b). *Varieties of moral personality.* Cambridge, MA: Harvard University Press.

Flanagan, O. (1992). *Consciousness reconsidered.* Cambridge, MA: MIT Press.

Flanagan, O. (1996). *Self expressions: Mind, morals, and the meaning of life.* New York: Oxford University Press.

Flanagan, O. (2000). *Dreaming souls: Sleep, dreams, and the evolution of the conscious mind.* New York: Oxford University Press.

Freeman, M. (1993). *Rewriting the self: History, memory, and narrative.* London: Routledge.

Howard, G. S. (1991). Culture tales: A narrative approach to thinking, cross-cultural psychology, and psychotherapy. *American Psychologist, 46,* 187–197.

James, W. (1983). *The principles of psychology.* Cambridge, MA: Harvard University Press. (Original work published 1890)

Jopling, D. A. (2000). *Self-knowledge and the self.* New York: Routledge.

McAdams, D. P (1993). *The stories we live by: Personal myths and the making of the self.* New York: Guilford.

Neimeyer, R. (1994). The role of client-generated narratives in psychotherapy. *Journal of Constructivist Psychology, 7,* 229–242.

Neisser, U. (1988). Five kinds of self-knowledge. *Philosophical Psychology, 1,* 35–59.

Neisser, U., & Fivush, R. (1994). *The remembering self: Construction and accuracy in the self-narrative.* Cambridge: Cambridge University Press.

Nelson, K. (Ed.) (1989). *Narratives from the crib.* Cambridge, MA: Harvard University Press.

Nelson, T. O. (1996). Consciousness and metacognition. *American Psychologist, 51,* 102–116.

Rubin, D. C. (Ed.) (1996). *Remembering our past: Studies in autobiographical memory.* Cambridge: Cambridge University Press.

Russell, R. L., & Lucariello, J. (1992). Narrative, yes; narrative as infinitum, no! *American Psychologist, 47,* 671–672.

PART I

*The Role of Narrative in the
Development of Conscious Awareness*

2   Narrative and the Emergence of a Consciousness of Self

Katherine Nelson

In this chapter I explore the hypothesis of a new level of consciousness that emerges in early childhood together with a new sense of self situated in time and in multiple social realities. It is proposed that this level is made possible by human communicative discourse, specifically linguistic and especially narrative. Essential parts of this proposal are the constructs of developing systems, emerging levels, the expansion of the child's consciousness, and the concurrent related sense of self in the social world.

The Problem of Conscious Awareness and the Consciousness of Self

In developmental psychology the issue of conscious awareness has not been successfully addressed. Issues of cognitive development have been approached from the perspective of positing internal mechanisms that can explain changes in behavior with age. The phenomenology of the individual and the experiential perspective of the child, which are essential to the issue of conscious awareness, have been systematically ignored. It is my belief that this is a prime weakness in explanations of early developmental change in such currently puzzling areas as theory of mind and self-and-other understanding. Taking the perspective of the child's experience in the world is, I think, essential to understanding these developments. Such an approach takes us beyond the simplistic assumptions of the mind as a well-formed information-processing system unchanging in development to an awareness of radical change in both structure and function of mind over developmental time, influenced throughout by uniquely human capacities for affiliation, communication, social relations, cultural conventions, and linguistic genres. This understanding and approach to the problem are supported by new emphases on the importance of postnatal neurological development and organization that last into the childhood years.

The standard epistemic model of cognitive development, which rests on the conception of a fully finished brain equipped at birth with the mechanisms for constructing theories to explain the world and solve logical problems, can no longer be accepted. (Note that this was not Piaget's epistemic model; rather, modern cognitive development in rejecting stages and structural change has implicitly incorporated these assumptions.) In place of the epistemic or theory-constructing child I propose to substitute the *experiential child*. The child in this view is not seeking truth or a coherent explanation of the world (at least not at the outset) but understanding of phenomena relevant to his or her own experience of events in a particular circumscribed world, which includes the people and objects significant within those events. In this framework, I believe it is possible not only to address the problem of the development of consciousness but also to make headway toward its explication, if not its solution.

The approach I am taking is broadly compatible with that of nonlinear dynamic systems theories that have come to prominence in developmental psychology since the 1980s, but with a provenance that reaches back to earlier systems principles established by Bertalanffy (1968). Experimental designs and mathematical analyses that could handle complex interplays among sets of variables that operated in dynamic systems have been proposed by a number of advocates of this approach (Thelen & Smith, 1998; van Geert, 1998). Like others who applaud the systems idea in the abstract, I recognize that it is often difficult to apply in the concrete world of experimental science, especially in an area as ill-defined as consciousness is at the present time. Because of the nature of the problem, a systems approach to the development of consciousness is necessarily conceptual.

Yet a radical shift in perspective is gained by turning from the search for the single unique cause of some development to recognizing that we are dealing with an *ongoing self-organizing developing system*, within which small changes in some variables may affect the organization of the system in important ways, which sometimes result in the emergence of a new variable or a new level of behavior or cognition. Variable pathways to a common end point, and variable end points from a common starting point, such as are observed in cognitive domains, are important indications of developing systems. The concept of *emergent levels*, a construct that appears necessary to the explanation of developing biological systems, becomes understandable within this conceptual framework, and its importance can be given due weight (see MacWhinney, 1998, for examples in the area of language).

Lacking the construct of emergence, it appears that the child must *begin with* the materials and the tools by which to construct, or to change, concepts, beliefs, the knowledge base, logic, or theory (or whatever structure seems appropriate to the discourse). Interaction between organism and environment—Piaget's (1970) solution—has come to seem inadequate to the complexity and abstractness that contemporary researchers have identified as the necessary mental basis for the infant's and child's behaviors. Internalization—posited by both Piaget and Vygotsky—has come into question as being both vacuous and too dependent on external knowledge sources for current cognitive theories.

It is my belief that the principles, if not the empirical practices, of systems thinking will help us to move beyond these origin-seeking dead ends and the innatist origins to which they seem to point (see Gottlieb, 1997). In particular, to take the insights of both Piaget and Vygotsky (1963) into account in modeling development in a social, linguistic, cultural, communicative world, it is essential to see the individual child as a self-organizing intelligent system that incorporates and responds to varied sources of information and challenge. The metaphor of *making sense* captures the process of succeeding levels and spirals of knowing within different domains, each with vertical positive feedback effects and horizontal reverberations across the system as a whole.

The image is not so much of bootstrapping as of ratcheting up; each new level of understanding reached reveals new sources of knowledge and evokes a new effort at organization within and across domains. An analogy can be invoked with the acquisition of succeeding levels of visual perspective made possible with the achievement of new levels of locomotion, with first sitting up, then crawling (new vistas appear), then cruising (again, new perspectives on old scenes and newly viewed objects), then walking freely (no longer tied to secure supports). The world was there all along, but the view from the infant's eyes was constrained by locomotor possibilities and thus the sources of knowledge of the physical world were only gradually made accessible (see Adolph, 1997; Campos, Bertenthal, & Kermoian, 1992). The analogy can be both applied and extended to the knowledge that is available at each step of the sequence. The crawling child has knowledge of the room at a 16" distance from the floor but has only a fleeting view of anything higher, thus has no reliable memory/knowledge of levels above. But the existence of supporting structures in view provides the motivation for boosting the self to the cruising level, where such knowledge is accessible and where it can scaffold further excursions to new boundaries, which again makes new views and subsequent knowledge of the scene available.

Problem of Consciousness

How can we address the problem of consciousness, then, within the framework of the experiential child? The sketch of the growing awareness of the world

available as succeeding stages of locomotion are achieved suggests an accompanying awareness of the possibilities of self-movement within the world. Such
awareness in all likelihood is no different in kind from the awareness of other
primates and, indeed, of other mammals. That is, it is awareness of self-
movement in the world and of aspects of the world previously encountered
or similar to other encounters. The same may be said of awareness of other
people and their movements.

Many researchers agree that a new level of conscious awareness, call it
social awareness or social consciousness, ensues when the infant is about nine
months old and develops further over the next three or four months (Tomasello, 1995). This level is characterized by the onset of joint attention between adult and child. The infant follows the adult's gaze to fix attention on
what the adult is looking at, follows the adult's use of a finger-point to direct
attention, and begins to use finger-pointing on his or her own in the expectation
that the adult will attend to the infant's target. These developments appear
crucial to the onset of word learning and further language development. Some
observers consider this level of social awareness to be uniquely human and
uniquely suited to establishing communication in language.

Yet at this point in development infants do not even pass the mirror recognition test, which suggests a limited level of self-awareness. In the mirror
recognition test a mark is surreptitiously placed on the child's nose or forehead
and the question is whether the child, seeing his or her image in a mirror, will
attempt to touch or rub out the mark visible there on own face (passing) or
on the mirror image (failing). In tests with other primates, chimpanzees typically pass this test, although monkeys do not. Thus children below the age
of about 18 months appear not yet to have reached the level of self-awareness
exhibited by (adult) chimpanzees.

Many people, however, believe that when children pass the mirror test
they have reached an important milestone that indicates a level of self-
consciousness, which is also evidenced in symptoms of shyness, embarrassment,
and shame. Howe and Courage (1993) believe on the basis of this and other
evidence that the 2-year-old has achieved a "cognitive self," a characterization
that implies an objective sense of self, an object that can be represented mentally and thought about. Is this then the onset of or the maturation of a characteristic level of human consciousness or is there more to be described and
explained?

In the experiential view put forth here this level of self-awareness, while
a real achievement in comparison with the earlier, more limited, social awareness, is only another ratcheting up toward a new view of self, other, and the
world, equivalent perhaps, in the earlier analogy to the stage of cruising with
support. Indeed the metaphor of cruising with support during the preschool
years seems particularly apt. In the case of consciousness the support is pro-

vided by parents, peers, and other adults who, using language, provide a verbal support for children to explore their experience in a new way, with new perspectives borrowed from those offered by others. With these introductory remarks we reach the central part of this essay on the role of narrative in the emergence of consciousness, and in the following sections I consider this issue from the point of view of levels of representation, which rather nicely fit the levels of social and self-awareness sketched thus far and extend to the levels not yet reached.

Beginnings of Narrative

The origins of narrative in human life and its implications for human conscious awareness have been considered from several perspectives in the psychological, anthropological, and developmental literatures. As already noted, the idea of origins is elusive at best within a systems framework where new levels of competences, skills, or knowledge systems may emerge over time from the recombination of earlier appearing elements. Some of the contrasting views of narrative emphasize the point.

Bruner (1990) has written persuasively about the importance of narrative in human lives, and the beginnings of narrative in the life of the child. In the course of this discussion he implicated an innate disposition to narrativize events and to impose meaning on people's actions, to attribute mental states, that is, to have a theory of mind. Bruner views this general claim as a radical turn away from the computational mind of contemporary cognitive science by emphasizing human meaning making as the essential cognitive characteristic of the species.

But we may ask: Why innate? The implicit answer accepted by a number of social-cultural theorists seems to be that there is no *identifiable origin or source* for how children of two or three years come to interpret others' intentions, to form canonical scripts, to understand and compose stories of their own. Thus it seems to Bruner and others that there must be a disposition that is built into the human mind, ready to be triggered by the social world, in infancy or at latest when language becomes available. There is surely something to this story, but it leaves us hanging. What is the nature of this disposition? Is it located somewhere in the brain? How did it get there? Is there an evolutionary story to be told about this? And for those of us who resist the proliferation of innate *content* knowledge, an innate theory of mind or narrative frame does not seem much preferable to an innate language of thought. But what is the alternative?

Building on the evolutionary story proposed by Merlin Donald (1991), I have adopted the idea of *levels* of representation that compose the hybrid modern adult mind. (I will explicate this at greater length in following sections.) Here let me note that Donald's third tier of memory or representation emerged with the language capacity to form narratives, a capacity that is tied also to the formation of large social groups and cultural complexes (see also Dunbar, 1993). Narratives emerge as *social forms*, which include explanatory myths, among other genres that support the coherence and cohesiveness of the community. In this framework narrative making is a specifically human characteristic. However, it is *not an individual capacity* but a social-cultural one. It results from a long historical process of the development of social communicative skills at different levels (motoric and linguistic) and of concurrent development of group construction of communities. These are complex system developments that go beyond individual participants, wherein narrative emerges as an *explanatory format* of the cultural group. Carrithers (1991) provides a similar explanatory framework, which situates story within the complex of social institutions that are essential to human culture, although he does not provide the same evolutionary dynamic that Donald's theory does.

Hendriks-Jansen (1996) goes further within a systems framework of individual development, wherein he sees the infant embedded in and surrounded by cultural narratives, narratives that underlie the ways that parents view their roles and the role of the child within the family and larger community. The child then "grows into" these narratives; our contemporary cultural narratives and myths serve in this way, just as those of other eras and places do. There is no special need for the child to be innately disposed to make stories, although of course among the human potentials that develop in the early years of life must be those that make it possible to enter into and adopt others' stories as one's own. These potentials are revealed in the study of how young children adapt in their social worlds.

Examining what we know about the development of narrative making by parents and young children, I am led inexorably to a systems view compatible with those of Donald, Carrithers, and Hendriks-Jansen. Moreover, it is a developmental view that sets narrative not aside as some kind of special individual human gift but as part and parcel of the wide-ranging developments that take place during the critical years when the child can enter fully into the linguistic world but is not yet a participant in formal schooling. These developments include awareness of self and other, of the wider world beyond self, of past and future; in traditional cognitive developmental terms, they include theory of mind, perspective taking, autobiographical memory, and self-concept. This view then suggests the close connection between narrative and the emergence of a specifically human level of consciousness. It is possible, I believe, to draw these connections more tightly.

Hybrid Levels

The idea of levels of knowing is not novel in cognitive psychology; it is found in notions of implicit and explicit learning, of implicit and explicit memory, and of episodic and semantic memory, among other cognitive domains. In evolutionary epistemology (Campbell, 1974/1982; Oakley, 1983; Plotkin, 1982) the idea is elaborated further. Not all of these theorists are speaking to the same issues. For example, Campbell attempts to conceptualize all levels of knowledge in terms of a Darwinian evolutionary model of generate-select-replicate, although the selective forces differ at different levels. In contrast, Plotkin views different forms of knowledge gathering and storing as emerging at different points in evolutionary history, with evolution "handing on" the knowledge-gaining-and-preserving process from genes to learning at later points that involves more complex organisms.

Donald's model is related to Plotkin's, but he sees the sequence differently. He starts from the general primate level of cognition, which he views as "episodic." The point here is that the nonhuman primate is tied to the *here-and-now individual experiential level* of memory. Albeit living in a social community, individual primates at this level do not learn significantly from one another (according to Tomasello [1990] they engage in emulation, not true imitation). They do not call up memory at will, but rather memory is evoked by environmental conditions. The specifics of this description may not hold up as we learn more about primate group living, but we may accept the general picture. The state Donald described for the nonhuman primate is not unlike the cognitive state of the human infant, who, however, is more helpless and more dependent upon adult caretakers than other primate infants (and dramatically more so than adult primates for whom the description is meant to apply). In addition, the human child is surrounded from birth by cultural artifacts and linguistic discourse, which makes any analogy from primate to human infant somewhat questionable. For example, it was noted earlier that chimpanzees typically pass the mirror recognition test, while it is not until 2 years of age that most toddlers have passed it.

Donald projects a novel emergent level of learning, knowing, communicating, and transforming representations within the evolutionary history of hominids, namely, the level that he calls *mimesis* or mimetic representation. This level began with the capacity for motoric imitation and for self-cued memory and carried the hominid line far in the direction toward symbolization, by enabling the learning and practice of skills, recall and recombination of motoric activities, the use of motor gestures as shared communicative forms, and the capacity for both synchronous and complementary roles in activities. Donald sees this as a necessary preliminary stage to that of language itself.

The next transition to symbolic language, with the central function of narrative making, emerged only with *Homo sapiens* about thirty-five thousand years ago and was accompanied by a rapid acceleration of cultural growth. (The date for modern human morphology is well established, although controversy rages about the exact dating of different levels of speech and language evolution.) The growing capacity for rapid speech processing during this period of evolution made possible the much broader communication of information within a community of language users. The social-cultural function of speech and its primary product at this point, narrative, contributed to the cohesive and coherent structure of the group. We can project a newly emerging *cultural consciousness* on this basis, incorporating within it a new consciousness of time contained within narrative.

Finally, with the invention of written language forms in historical times the knowledge-spreading possibilities became infinitely greater, across civilizations and aeons of time, with repercussions for individuals in terms of storing knowledge not in individual minds but in external forms that can be consulted as prosthetic memory and representation devices. According to Donald's theory, it is only in this most recent stage that logic and scientific theorizing have been or could have been developed. Thus, in this theory, narrative precedes and perhaps structures theorizing and logic making.

In many ways Donald's theory dovetails rather nicely with the early stages of cognitive and linguistic development in human infancy and early childhood (as suggested in Nelson [1996]). What I would like to emphasize here is a point that applies to both the evolutionary and developmental versions of the levels hypothesis: that the different levels of knowing and remembering each continue to exist for individual knowers as one kind emerges from another. Event representations and mimetic representations both support and are independent of linguistic representations. These earlier levels may be changed in function and form as they interact with other levels and as each succeeding level takes on some of the functions previously served by a preceding one.

The eventual emergent adult mind is, in Donald's terms, *hybrid*, a layered construction of different ways of learning, communicating, and problem solving via different representational types. It is easily demonstrated both informally and through empirical research that humans employ all of these representational modes, simultaneously or as complementary sources of information. The hybrid mind is capable of representing simultaneous composites in everyday life or in attending to performances such as the opera, where visual scenes, action, music, and language all combine to produce a singular effect. Of course one may selectively attend to a single level, a practice called concentration, whether on text or tennis, where distractions from other representational modalities are screened out of awareness.

Setting the Stage for Narrative in Childhood

I turn now to the central question addressed in this chapter: the relation of narrative, self, and consciousness as they emerge in the life of the child. As Bruner (1990) has emphasized, one can conceive of narrative as incorporating two dimensions—in his terms the *landscape of action* and the *landscape of consciousness*. The former landscape is equivalent to the event sequence in Labov and Waletsky's (1967) analysis of narrative and the latter to their idea of the importance of evaluation in the narrative. One can also distinguish along similar lines between plot and the motivations that inspire and devolve from the actions within the plot. Other similar divisions have been made in the narrative literature. However, the divisions are not neat; plot involves motivations and assessments of actions; evaluations may be revealed in the language used to describe the action as well as in a summing up of its meaning. But for our purpose we can think of the landscape of action as the sequencing of actions to make a coherent and cohesive event. And we can think of the landscape of consciousness as the revealing of the mental states of the actors that are associated with the action, including their goals, their perspectives, their beliefs, their emotions, and so on.

In addition to these two understandings, Carrithers (1991) has claimed that understanding a cultural narrative requires knowledge of the culture's institutions, history, and social organization (one could add its geography and numerous other cultural knowledge aspects). Further, time enters as essential to narrative understanding not only in terms of the order of events—its sequencing—but also in terms of the location of the event itself in social-cultural or individual time. These are all basic to the foundation of the simplest narratives of self and other, as well as to the culture's myths and stories, from *Cinderella* or *The Cat in the Hat* to *Oedipus Rex*. When and how do these constituents become part of the child's understanding of the world, and when and how might they come together to establish the beginnings of narrative competence? And how, if at all, do they bear on the emergence of a new level of consciousness or self-understanding?

We have good evidence that children can understand and represent the sequence of familiar repeated events, which involves several related actions, by 1 year of age. They understand the scripts of their own worlds, in terms of general event representation, and will protest if an action is omitted. Experimental evidence (e.g., Bauer & Mandler, 1990) has shown that at about one year children can remember brief sequences of novel events (two or three actions) over several days. By 3 years of age they can verbalize a number of familiar scripts in reliable sequence (Nelson & Gruendel, 1981). These event representations derived from personal experience then may form the basis for the *canonical events* from which narratives are made; they are not themselves real narratives but only event sequences. They are the way things are and should be, but thereby no explanation or evaluation is expected or required. Thus at some time between 1 and 3 years of age we can assume that the basics of the *landscape of action* are understood, although the specifics of temporal location and perspective remain in doubt. The relation of this level of event knowledge, based on direct experience, to the level of knowledge about events relayed only through language is an area that is little understood but that may provide an important key to understanding language and cognition, in both development and evolution.

How the landscape of consciousness enters into the child's representations and narratives is much more obscure than the landscape of action. When in the course of infancy and childhood children become cognizant of intentionality, that is, of their own and others' mental states, is a topic that has been studied intensely over the past 15 years under the rubric of children's "theory of mind." Some theorists (e.g., Trevarthen, 1980) claim that infants have the same capacity as anyone to express and interpret emotions and goals of others. Others (e.g., Tomasello, 1995) see a turning point at 9 months, when infants begin to tune in to another's attentional state and to share attention, thus becoming launched into the world of interpreting others' actions in terms of their mental states. Still others (e.g., Gopnik & Meltzoff, 1996) view the child as operating with a primitive kind of theory of mind from birth and engaging in a series of reconstructions over the next four years until a mature theory that matches that of the cultural environment is in place. However, there is room for skepticism regarding the degree to which young children are reading other people's minds rather than their behavior, as well as the extent to which children are aware of their own mental states (Nelson, 1996). Such awareness would seem to mark a new level of consciousness beyond the social and self levels of the earlier periods, described previously.

Other mechanisms have been proposed to explain an emerging awareness of mind on the part of the child, but to review them all would take us beyond our present concerns. What seems important is that the infant is embedded in a social world from the outset of extrauterine life, and the evidence indicates that there is a slow awakening over the succeeding years to the perspectives of other people. This evidence, briefly summarized earlier, is considered here in relation to the development of narrative understanding. The shared attention that Tomasello notes at 9 months (and that he sees as a critical causal mechanism of specifically human cognition) is an indication that the infant is newly aware of a class of social signals (gazing, pointing) to which he or she was previously indifferent. Other evidence of growing *awareness of sharing the world of others* follows closely: intentional babble and then first words modeled on adult forms; games with reciprocal roles; primitive kinds of symbolic play modeled after the adult's real or play actions; and attempts to take on the adult's role in bathing and feeding, for examples. These are all primitive forms of intersubjectivity and provide the necessary basis for the interpretation and acquisition of language, but they remain on the *level of action*. They appear as good evidence of an *emerging* level of mimesis, as described by Donald. Mimesis enables learning to produce forms modeled by others and form an internalized model so that it may be recalled (mentally or in action) and used for future productions, transformations, and recombinations. These abilities do not require taking a perspective on events that is not one's own and that is not confined to the here and now of present activity.

Although the research on memory, categorization, and language use from 1 to 2 years of age indicates growing abilities in these cognitive functions, there is also persuasive evidence (Nelson, 1989) that for the child of 2 years the only *temporal differentiation* is that of the present activity and everything else that has been entered into memory as a representation of the experienced world. These "temporally unfixed" representations may consist of sequences of events, of people and their routines, or of places and their associated objects. Others may be less organized, consisting of scraps of this and that, the kind of thing we all have noodling around in our heads, recognizable when encountered but not part of our easily accessible world knowledge or episodic memory. An important part of this claim is that the young child's view is *singular*—there is only one perspective on the world, his or her own. There is only one reality, that of the directly experienced world (Nelson, 1999). This is a very difficult perspective for us as adults to take, given our multiply experienced and representational worldviews. It is, however, essential to understanding how a different level of conscious awareness may emerge as narratives of the social and cultural community become accessible to the child.

The Emergence of Narrative in Childhood

The description just offered, based on my best reading of the developmental literature, implies that at 2 years of age the child has only a few of the rudiments that enter into narrative, mainly the landscape of action, the child's own perspective on canonical events. Lacking are temporal perspective and location, the cultural background of events not one's own, awareness of the internal states that motivate action, and the capacity for understanding the "trouble" in events that requires interpretation and problem solving (although children themselves of course experience motivations of desire, love, sadness, happiness, anger, and so on, and recognize the symptoms of these in intimate others); understanding remains on the level of action. During this early developmental period language is being learned and used but is not yet a *vehicle for conveying the representation of narrative* either from the child him- or herself or from another to the child so that the child can represent the representation in his or her own mental space. These moves require further development of the rudiments of narrative as well as their integration into a whole genre. Children's first narrative productions occur in action, in episodes of symbolic play by groups of peers, accompanied by—rather than solely through—language. Play is an important developmental source of narrative, through which children may become accustomed to transforming scripts into narratives with semiplots, plots that present "trouble" but unfold in real time without prior planning. The landscape of consciousness may also emerge dramatically in play in the form of expression of emotion and differing perspectives on the same action.

The most studied sources of children's grasp of narrative structure are conventional stories (read or told) and personal narratives told around, to, or with young children. Miller (Miller, Potts, Fung, Hoogstra, Mintz, 1990) has documented the extensive exposure of very young children in low-income families to the narratives of adults with adults about their personal lives, as well as about the children's experiences. Engel (1986), Fivush (1994), Hudson (1990), and others have documented the ways in which parents and children construct narratives of past experiences that they have shared, emphasizing the different styles of talking in these accounts from more elaborative and narrative to more repetitive. The researchers have found that children move from contributing one or two bits of information about an experience to more equal co-construction of the narrative about it. Yet, as Fivush has emphasized, throughout the preschool years the vast majority of the evaluative comments or information contributed comes from the parent, not from the child. This accords with studies of children's story productions during the same period (2½ to 5 years) that show that when asked to tell a "made up story," many children produce what looks like a script, without either motivation or problem, or may insert some anomalous element into the "story" without otherwise altering it (Seidman, Nelson, & Gruendel, 1986). When given practice in storytelling, however, children tend to settle on a familiar gender-specific format (Nicolopoulou & Weintraub, 1998). In many ways, then, throughout the preschool period children seem to remain focused on the landscape of action even as a narrativelike genre is emerging in the form of the ability to sequence episodes based on experience or on other people's relatings.

Three essential components of narrative discussed previously remain weak or nonexistent in most of the narrative productions of the 3- to 5-year-old preschooler: temporal perspective, the mental as well as physical perspective of self and of different others, and essential cultural knowledge of the unexperienced world. It is these aspects, not the simple sequencing of episodic events, that incorporate the power of narrative for both personal and cultural growth. How then do the skeletal kinds of emerging narrative skills lead into the fuller and more enriching and "humanizing" aspects of the mature genre, in the process establishing a new consciousness of self, of others, and of self in time, place, and society? An *emerging new conscious awareness of self and world*, like narrative itself, is neither an either/or thing nor dependent upon one causal element in the developmental scheme, but evidence suggests that experience with forms of narrative contributes importantly to this new level of consciousness.

A possible alternative to the role of narrative is children's achievement of a theory of mind, an achievement that has been measured primarily in terms of understanding that beliefs (one's own and others') can be false and that typically is found at about four and one-half years of age. This understanding is important to comprehension of many narratives from real life as well as from fiction, which raises the question of the direction of the causal relations. Preceding this achievement (as standardly measured), naturalistic home-based family studies show that children are attuned to other people's states of ignorance, their emotions and desires, and will demonstrate understanding that other people's likes and desires may be different from the child's own (e.g., Dunn, 1988). Such observations indicate a gradually emerging understanding of different perspectives on the world of experience, perspectives that are revealed especially in narrative discourse and that are not discernible in actions alone. It appears that narrative and theory of mind are intimately intertwined in development.

Then and Now, Self and Other

One of the most striking inferences to be made about the cognitive status of the very young child is his or her isolation from other times and others' worlds of experience. By "other times" I mean the time of the specific past and the envisioned future beyond the now of the present activity space. It is not that the child is not aware of the not-now; the implication is that for the child there are but two temporal spaces—the present and the nonpresent. As for experiences other than one's own, when action is the only realm of communication and representation these are necessarily blocked out. Piaget calls this egocentrism, but it is an egocentrism that simply lacks perspective because there is no possible alternative view but one's own. There are no insights into another's life because there is no vehicle except shared actions through which experience can be shared. The claim here is that shared experiential narratives are the symbolic vehicles, available only to humans, through which such insights are gained, including the important insight that the other has a past and a present that differ from one's own, as well as the accompanying insight that one's own past is unique to oneself.

This last-named important insight rests on the critical role of contrast in establishing conceptual awareness. The point here is a variation on the developmental process of differentiation and subsequent integration posited by Werner (1957). A state of consciousness of self-as-actor in activities shared with others does not require an awareness of self with a unique status, unless and until it is represented as differentiated from the others' experience of the activities. Only then can the child view the self as having a specific experiential history that is different from others and thus a specific personal past and possible specific future. When this conceptual contrast is made between self and other it opens up a new level of conscious awareness beyond the locked-in *self-in-the-now world* that began in infancy and expanded in only limited ways in the subsequent two or three years. To the extent that this analysis is right these are indeed profound developmental changes.

Let me examine these interrelated propositions more closely by sketching how this widening of temporal, social, and cultural-spatial perspective might proceed in the context of narrative experience. Consider a very simple example of a 2-year-old looking at photographs with his mother. This example is part of one from Nelson (1996, pp. 166–167; original data from Engel's 1986 study of mother-child talk about the past):

C: Mommy, the Chrysler Building.
M: The Chrysler Building?
C: The Chrysler Building?
M: Yeah, who works in the Chrysler Building?
C: Daddy.
M: Do you ever go there?
C: Yes, I see the Chrysler Building/picture of the Chrysler Building.
M: I don't know if we have a picture of the Chrysler Building. Do we?
C: We went to . . . my Daddy went to work.
M: Remember when we went to visit daddy? Went in the elevator, way way up in the building so we could look down from the big window?
C: big window.
M: mmhm
C: (pause) When . . . we did go on the big building . . .
C: mmhm, the big building. Was that fun? Would you like to do it again? Sometime.
C: I want to go on the big building.

In this example Mother was bringing out pictures of past events (visiting grandmother, etc.) and attempting to get the child to talk about these "memories," without much success. Something in the situation, however, evoked in the child a memory of an expedition and he said, "Mommy, the Chrysler Building." Mother responds that they don't have a picture of the Chrysler Building but reminds him of the trip they took to the Chrysler Building. She then puts the events in order (plot), including the scraps proffered by the child (e.g., "Daddy"), and gives it an evaluation (fun). She also suggests they might do it again in the future. She has made it into a specific event, a narrative, with a high point and an evaluation. True, it lacks much in the way of intentionality and repeats the child's own experience, rather than providing a new event or point of view, but it makes a whole of the bits and pieces and sets the child's vaguely offered remembrance into a specific episode.

This kind of recalling provides a narrative structure for the child's own remembered past. In my study of crib monologues (Nelson, 1989) I found that Emily at 2½ years had begun to master the forms for recalling the experience of a day past in a narrative format. Even earlier Emily had begun to verbally repeat parts of routines on the format of "what will happen tomorrow." The landscape of action to fit narrative has begun to emerge by this age, at least for many children. It is notable that it emerges, at least as far as the evidence thus far indicates, with respect to the child's own experience, which is forecast and rehearsed with him or her by parents. These stories are not, however, located in any specific past. The not-now begins to be filled with specific semiplots, but they are not ordered among themselves.

These semiplot episodic reports have given rise to the claims that children of 2 years have autobiographical memory or, at the least, that they have episodic memories (Howe & Courage, 1993). Other evidence, however, documented particularly by Miller and colleagues (1990), has shown that children of 2 to 4 years often "appropriate" someone else's story as their own. Miller provides observations of appropriation by a child from a parent's account. For example, one small boy who was told by his mother in a cautionary way about having fallen off a stool when she was young retold this story later as his "when I fell off the stool." Miller also reports children in preschool freely appropriating another child's story as their own. These cases provide suggestive evidence that children's stories may be undifferentiated as to whose stories they are, that is, whose experiences they are. The conclusion follows that these verbal retellings are not personal or autobiographical, because they are not differentiated from a nonspecific past and a social generalized world. They are stories based on the child's life experiences, but they are no more personal than are any other stories.

But don't young children know the difference between their own experience and others'? Don't we all know whether something happened to ourselves or to someone else? There are many indications that children do not and that, indeed, we adults need to work hard to make this distinction. False memories provide the most dramatic evidence. Recent research indicates that children will report some quite outlandish events as having happened to them if they have been given narratives about these events or even hints of narratives (Ceci & Bruck, 1993). Piaget (1968) reported a vivid memory of his own from early childhood, of a dramatic event that never happened. In this case he "remembered" his nursemaid "rescuing" him from an attempted kidnapping when he was less than 3 years of age, only to find out as an adolescent that the story had been made up by the nurse to impress his parents. His "memory," which he retained throughout life, included many specific details of the visual scene that never happened. How can this be?

Note that all the material noted here with which children work or on which adults rely comes from a verbal source. Narrative is the vehicle of communicating representations of events between people by verbal means. By Donald's theory and by the developmental account being set out here, the verbal-narrative representation is on a different level from the direct-experience-activity level. The verbal level becomes newly activated as the child becomes able to engage in narrativizing with others. But then what was first an actively experienced episode by the child has been turned into a verbal report, and verbally reported and exchanged narratives accumulate to form a store of stories, some mine, some yours, at first not differentiated as to source.

At some point then, it becomes important to differentiate mine from yours and, in so doing, to establish that there are different perspectives on the world, different specific pasts, and different specific futures. An example of this movement comes from Emily's monologues at 32 months (Nelson, 1996, p. 198). Here Emily reports an episode from her father, who cannot run in a marathon although he wants to, and she puzzles about why that is.

> Today Daddy went, trying to get into the race but the people said no so he, he has to watch it on television. I don't know why that is, maybe 'cause there's too many people. I think that's why, why he couldn't go in it. . . . So he has to watch it on television . . . on Halloween day, then he can run a race and I can watch him. I wish I could watch him. But they said no no no. Daddy Daddy Daddy! . . . No no, no no. Have to watch on television. But on Halloween Day he can run, run a race. Tomorrow (he'll) run (???) He says yes. Hooray! My mom and dad and a man says "you can run in the footrace," and I said "that's nice of you. I want to." So next week I'm going to . . . run to the footrace and, and run in the footrace 'cause they said I could.

Emily's life has begun to expand beyond her own experience and into a world that she does not know and cannot predict or explain. Yet she still lives primarily in the here and now of her own understood routines. There is a growing awareness that not only do other people have feelings and thoughts like one's own, but also these feelings and thoughts may be different from one's own. Indeed, it is this *contrast* (as suggested previously) that makes one's own feelings and thoughts visible and conceptualizable as such to oneself. Then the consciousness of self emerges as a unique entity, as a specific person different from other persons, with a continuity from babyhood to adulthood. Then the child can lay claim to his or her own stories and mark them with the markers of "I did that at that time" or "it happened to me." Other people's stories belong to them and not to oneself, and these stories can be seen as based on different intentionalities and different subjectivities.

Conclusion

A new level of consciousness emerges in the early childhood years that is based on the differentiation of the self-awareness of the early years and the self-and-other awareness of the transition period. The first is consciousness of the here and now, informed by previous experience but without conscious reflection on that experience. The strong hypothesis that emerges from this perspective is that the new level of consciousness is dependent upon language used to exchange views of self and other, primarily through narratives but also through commentary on the self by others, as well as on their own feelings, thoughts, and expectations of what might happen (Nelson, 1993). This new kind of consciousness is a different kind of *self-consciousness* that brings the self into the observed world where others have been playing out their roles in the child's view of the experiential world. This is James's or Mead's *ME* rather than the Experiencing *I* (Nelson, 2001). The I of the transition period can be self-aware and therefore bashful and embarrassed but is not yet capable of both acting and observing at the same time. Perhaps this sketchily presented development (see Nelson, 1997, 2001), with such profound implications, seems too weighty to place on the vehicle of narrative. Yet it is worth the effort to see how far such a proposal can take us in understanding the early development of self, language, and cultural consciousness.

In brief, the account here is that narrative emerges from and belongs to the community, but in the individual lives of children it is a vehicle through which consciousness of both self and the wider social and temporal world becomes manifest and gradually emerges as a new subjective level of conscious awareness, with a sense of a specific past and awareness of a possible future, as well as with new insight into the consciousness of other people.

References

Adolph, K. E. (1997). Cognitive-motor learning in infant locomotion. *Monographs of the Society for Research in Child Development, 62*(3), 1–140.
Bauer, P. J., & Mandler, J. M. (1990). Remembering what happened next: Very

young children's recall of event sequences. In R. Fivush & J. A. Hudson (Eds.), *Knowing and remembering in young children* (pp. 9–29). New York: Cambridge University Press.

Bertalanffy, L. von (1968). *General systems theory.* New York: Braziller.

Bruner, J. S. (1990). *Acts of meaning.* Cambridge, MA: Harvard University Press.

Campbell, D. T. (1982). Evolutionary epistemology. In H. C. Plotkin (Ed.), *Learning, development and culture: Essays in evolutionary epistemology* (pp. 73–107). New York: Wiley. (Original work published 1974)

Campos, J. J., Bertenthal, B. I., & Kermoian, R. (1992). Early experience and emotional development: The emergence of wariness of heights. *Psychological Science, 3,* 61–64.

Carrithers, M. (1991). Narrativity: Mindreading and making societies. In A. Whiten (Ed.), *Natural theories of mind: Evolution, development and simulation of everyday mindreading* (pp. 305–318). Oxford: Blackwell.

Ceci, S. J., & Bruck, M. (1993). Suggestibility of the child witness: A historical review and synthesis. *Psychological Bulletin, 113,* 403–439.

Donald, M. (1991). *Origins of the modern mind.* Cambridge, MA: Harvard University Press.

Dunbar, R. I. M. (1993). Coevolution of neocortical size, group size, and language in humans. *Brain and Behavioral Sciences, 16,* 681–735.

Dunn, J. (1988). *The beginnings of social understanding.* Cambridge, MA: Harvard University Press.

Engel, S. (1986). *Learning to reminisce: A developmental study of how young children talk about the past.* Unpublished doctoral dissertation, City University of New York Graduate Center.

Fivush, R. (1994). Constructing narrative, emotion, and self in parent-child conversations about the past. In U. Neisser & R. Fivush (Eds.), *The remembering self: Construction and accuracy in the self-narrative* (pp. 136–157). New York: Cambridge University Press.

Gopnik, A., & Meltzoff, A. (1996). *Words, thoughts and theories.* Cambridge, MA: MIT Press.

Gottlieb, G. (1997). *Synthesizing nature-nurture: Prenatal roots of instinctive behavior.* Mahwah, NJ: Erlbaum.

Hendriks-Jansen, H. (1996). *Catching ourselves in the act: Situated activity, interactive emergence, evolution, and human thought.* Cambridge, MA: MIT Press.

Howe, M. L., & Courage, M. L. (1993). On resolving the enigma of infantile amnesia. *Psychological Bulletin, 113,* 305–326.

Hudson, J. A. (1990). The emergence of autobiographic memory in mother-child conversation. In R. Fivush & J. A. Hudson (Eds.), *Knowing and remembering in young children* (pp. 166–196). New York: Cambridge University Press.

Labov, W., & Waletzky, J. (1967). Narrative analysis. In J. Helm (Ed.), *Essays on the verbal and visual arts* (pp. 12–44). Seattle: University of Washington Press.

MacWhinney, B. (Ed.) (1998). *The emergence of language.* Mahwah, NJ: Erlbaum.

Miller, P. J., Potts, R., Fung, H., Hoogstra, L., & Mintz, J. (1990). Narrative practices and the social construction of self in childhood. *American Ethnologist, 17,* 292–311.

Nelson, K. (Ed.) (1989). *Narratives from the crib.* Cambridge, MA: Harvard University Press.

Nelson, K. (1993). Events, narratives, memories: What develops? In C. Nelson (Ed.), *Minnesota Symposium on Child Psychology: Vol. 26* (pp. 1–24). Memory and affect in development Hillsdale, NJ: Erlbaum.

Nelson, K. (1996). *Language in cognitive development: The emergence of the mediated mind.* New York: Cambridge University Press.

Nelson, K. (1997). Finding oneself in time. In J. G. Snodgrass & R. I. Thompson (Eds.), *The self across psychology: Self-recognition, self-awareness, and the self-concept, Annals of the New York Academy of Sciences, 818,* 103–118.

Nelson, K. (1999). Memory and belief in development. In D. Schacter & E. Scarry (Eds.), *Memory, brain, and belief* (pp. 259–289). Cambridge, MA: Harvard University Press.

Nelson, K. (2001). From the Experiencing I to the Continuing Me. In C. Moore & K. Lemmon (Eds.), *The self in time: Developmental issues* (pp. 15–34). Mahwah, NJ: Erlbaum.

Nelson, K., & Gruendel, J. (1981). Generalized event representations: Basic building blocks of cognitive development. In M. Lamb & A. Brown (Eds.), *Advances in developmental psychology* (vol. 1, pp. 131–158). Hillsdale, NJ: Erlbaum.

Nicolopoulou, A., & Weintraug, J. (1998). Individual and collective representations in social context: A modest contribution to resuming the interrupted project of a sociocultural developmental psychology. *Human Development, 41,* 215–235.

Oakley, D. A. (1983). The varieties of memory: A phylogenetic approach. In A. Mayes (Ed.), *Memory in animals and humans* (pp. 20–82). Workingham, England: Van Nostrand Reinhold.

Piaget, J. (1968). *On the development of memory and identity.* Barre, MA: Clarke University Press.

Piaget, J. (1970). Piaget's theory. In P. H. Mussen (Ed.), *Carmichael's handbook of child development* (3d ed., vol. 1, pp. 703–732). New York: Wiley.

Plotkin, H. C. (Ed.) (1982). *Learning, development, and culture: Essays in evolutionary epistemology.* New York: Wiley.

Seidman, S., Nelson, K., & Gruendel, J. (1986). Make believe scripts: The transformation of ERs in fantasy. In K. Nelson (Ed.), *Event knowledge: Structure and function in development* (pp. 161–187). Hillsdale, NJ: Erlbaum.

Thelen, E., & Smith, L. (1998). Dynamic system theories. In W. Damon Series (Ed.) R. M. Lerner (Vol. Ed.), *Handbook of child psychology: Vol 1. Theoretical models of human development* (5th ed., pp. 563–634). New York: Wiley.

Tomasello, M. (1990). Cultural transmission in the tool use and communicatory signaling of chimpanzees? In S. T. Parker & K. R. Gibson (Eds.), *"Language" and intelligence in monkeys and apes* (pp. 274–311). New York: Cambridge University Press.

Tomasello, M. (1995). Understanding the self as social agent. In P. Rochat (Ed.),

The self in infancy: Theory and research (pp. 449–460). Amsterdam: Elsevier.

Trevarthen, C. (1980). The foundations of intersubjectivity: Development of interpersonal and cooperative understanding in infants. In D. R. Olson (Ed.), *The social foundations of language and thought* (pp. 316–342). New York: Norton.

van Geert, P. (1998). A dynamic systems model of basic developmental mechanisms: Piaget, Vygotsky, and beyond. *Psychological Review, 104*, 634–677.

Vygotsky, L. (1963). *Thought and language* (E. Hanfmann & G. Vakar, Trans.). Cambridge, MA: MIT Press.

Werner, H. (1957). *Comparative psychology of mental development.* New York: International Universities Press.

3   The Development of the Self

Valerie Gray Hardcastle

Thursday, March 26, 1998
Tonight I am going to a march with over 200 people and we
are going around streets and sing songs and yell WE'RE NOT
AFRAID OF YOU!! We're doing that to show people that
we're not afraid of you but you need a flashlight to see and
[your] hair pulled back.

Friday, March 27, 1998
The march was great and we walked a mile. We walk through
town and we yelled:
  We're women
  We're angry
  We're not going shopping.
And we yell for fair[ness]. Lots of people heard us.
                                    —Diary entries of Kiah, then 7 years old

Perhaps only because I am her mother, I am impressed with
Kiah's journal descriptions of the evening I took her and her siblings to a Take
Back the Night rally. But do notice the sophistication in her narrative. In her
first entry, she anticipates a forthcoming event, using a future expectation to
define her current moment. Not only does she understand the mechanics of
the activity she is about to be engaged in, but she also appreciates its social
significance. In the next entry, she describes what happened, reacting to her
past and judging it worthwhile, appropriating it as now part of her self. She
has immortalized this event as one of a string of defining features for Kiah

Hardcastle. Kiah is the 7-year-old girl who participated in the Take Back the Night rally in Blacksburg, Virginia, 26 March 1998.

We are all engaged in similar self-constructive exercises, all the time. What drives us to do so? Where does this narrative self come from?

The dominant research paradigm in developmental psychology answers that the self is one end product of some more-or-less universal developmental stages. Once we master language, understand causal efficacy, interpret our desires, and recognize the intentions of others, then we get a self as a sort of cognitive bonus.

But what if the dominant tradition is wrong about how we unfold? In this essay, I argue for just this conclusion. It makes more sense—theoretically and empirically—to hold that a drive for selfhood pushes us along in our linguistic, cognitive, and mnemonic development instead of the other way around. By paying attention to the affective dimensions of children's lives and what it is they are doing outside the laboratory, in their own homes and schools, we can see that they narrate all the time. First and foremost they and we want to understand our world and our selves as meaning something, as stories, as things with plots, with beginnings, middles, and ends. Language and reason are only tacked on at the end as useful additions in completing this enterprise.

Piaget's Legacy

Jean Piaget's constructivist epistemology, the forerunner of modern developmental theory in psychology, holds that all learning is domain-general. As children develop and grow, they repeatedly change the ways they represent the world to themselves. These globally occurring alterations follow a biologically determined stepwise progression. The minds of all human babies develop and grow in the same way: they all assimilate their experiences to the most suitable mental structure or scheme for coping with them and, at the same time, they also accommodate their schemes to the inputs in order to reach cognitive equilibrium. Over time, the schemes become better and better integrated with one another until (ideally) we have complex, coherent mental structures (see discussion in Abrahamsen, 1998, for a brief overview of Piaget's theory).

More important for our purposes, Piaget (1929) believed that children under the age of 7 could not distinguish thoughts from the rest of the world. Young children, he believed, confuse thinking, dreaming, and remembering with speaking, sensing, and acting. This "childhood realism," once viewed as gospel in developmental psychology, has now fallen in disfavor, as scientists realized what most parents had already known, that 3-year-olds can tell their mental lives apart from the environment and that even infants act differently toward humans and other intentional agents than the rest of their world (Carey, 1985; Chandler & Boyes, 1982; Estes, Wellman, & Woolley, 1990; Leslie, 1984; Premack, 1990).

Still, Piagetian theory has far from "collapsed," as Alison Gopnik and Andrew N. Meltzoff (1997) have asserted (see also Abrahamsen, 1998, p. 155). Piaget's legacy continues to reign strong. His core assumptions that cognitive failure, conflict, and competition push along intellectual development, that development proceeds along a common pathway for normal children, and that there is a rich interaction between child and environment remain as fundamental features in many contemporary developmental theories (see, e.g., Bates & MacWhinney, 1987; Gopnik & Meltzoff, 1997; Johnson & Morton, 1991; and Thelen & Smith, 1994). In addition, Piaget's view of children as rational agents in the making remains an important background assumption in contemporary developmental psychology (see, e.g., Carey, 1985, 1988; Gelman & Wellman, 1991; Gopnik & Meltzoff, 1997; Karmiloff-Smith, 1992; Keil, 1989; Perner, 1991; Wellman, 1990; Wellman & Gelman, 1992). It is this last assumption that I wish to challenge here.

In his research, Piaget differentiated cognitive development from the emotions, understanding them as two separate though interrelated systems. He sought only to explain the intellectual side of children, leaving the affective for others to pursue at some other time. This division of labor and the emphasis on rationality continue largely intact today.

Gopnik and Meltzoff (1997), for example, argue that the best way to understand the evolution of children's cognition is by analogy to (an idealized version of) scientific methodology. For them, children are little scientists. They seek to understand their world by producing hypotheses, making predictions, testing these ideas through observation and experimentation, and then revising their hypotheses to better fit the world. Children occupy themselves by trying to "outline the causal relations among existing abstract conceptual structures, input from the outside world, and new abstract conceptual structures" (pp. 221–222).

Annette Karmiloff-Smith (1992) also sees the child as scientist. In particular, she writes,

> young children are spontaneous psychologists. They are interested in how the mind can have thoughts and theories and in how representations mediate between the mind and the world. In order to engage in human interaction, . . . to understand their intentions/beliefs/desires, to interpret their statements/gestures/actions . . . each of us relies on . . . a folk theory that enables us to ascribe mental states to ourselves. (p. 117)

According to Karmiloff-Smith, children use proto-scientific theories to understand themselves and others. They develop theories of mind to explain human action just as we developed theories in chemistry to explain the properties of substances.

It is like other theory-building activities; it involves inferences based on unobservables

> (mental states, such as belief), a coherent set of explanations and causal links between mental states and behavior which are predictive of future actions . . . , a growing distinction between evidence and theory . . . , and a clearly defined mentally represented domain over which the causal explanations operate. (p. 138)

I maintain that these quotations misdescribe children and scientists alike. Perhaps we all do wish to understand the world and our role in it and we alter our beliefs as a result of what we see and do. But we also live in a world rich in meaning and affect, and it is these two aspects of our environment that motivate us to act, explore, describe, and redescribe. Neither children nor scientists would pursue their activities if they did not feel that what they were doing was somehow important, and important in a deeply personal way. As we shall see later, highlighting the meaning-giving aspects of life changes how we should interpret what children are doing when they are creating their selves.

Nor do we pursue these cognitive-affective activities outside of a social context. Science is a shared activity. So is childhood. We explain our world to ourselves and to others as part of a communal pastime. Emphasizing the social aspects of life also changes how we should understand the development of mind. In sum, I claim that the purely cognitive point of view leaves out important components of childhood development, components fundamental to any child developing any sort of self.

A Different Interpretation

Though champions of a purely cognitive approach and I disagree about much, we both nevertheless do agree that the beginning of children's understanding of their mental lives starts with proto-declarative statements (see, e.g., Baron-Cohen, 1989, 1991; Karmiloff-Smith, 1992). It is here on this common ground I shall start building my defense of a meaning-making approach to understanding psychological development.

Preverbal gesturing takes two forms. Children can issue imperatives. "Give me sustenance!" says a glare and a five-fingered point to the bottle. They can also simply assert facts to the world. "That is food over there," says the smile and the gentle hand waving toward the dinner table. These nonverbal assertions or proto-declaratives seem to be the one form of communication that sets humans apart from all other animals. We are not communicating with one another to satisfy some immediate bodily need, nor are we alerting others to danger, food, shelter, or mates. We are talking merely to share the world together.

This drive to talk just to talk shows up as early as infants can begin to express it. (Some would claim that it is therefore an innate or inborn drive. I am not going to worry about that issue here. Suffice it to say, that for whatever reason, it starts as early as we do.) As children become more proficient in communicating, their declaratives, not surprisingly, become more sophisticated as well. Nonetheless, the basic message behind their utterances remains largely the same. And it remains largely unchanged throughout adulthood, too.

Consider the example of my son, Quinn. One of his first words was "Moke!" which means "milk." He spent a great deal of his first two years of life pointing out to me all instances of "moke" in the world. The refrigerator section in the grocery store was a particular thrill. Milk was an important part of his life, since that was about all he would consume for his first thirty months, and he took glee in sharing his delight with me or with anyone one else who would listen. Then, when he moved from uttering single words to more complex constructions, he would say, "Wook, Mommy, moke! See dat?" Even though his sentences were much more complicated, most of what he said was verbal icing on his original message: "milk is important to me." By 3 he would say, "I like moke. Bot don't like beg'tables." He identified his love of milk with who he was and contrasted that with things he didn't like. For Quinn, he is what he eats. Now, at 4 and quite the chatterbox, he says, "I used to like milk when I was a baby, but I don't like it anymore. I like chocolate milk, but not plain milk. I like Sprite. I like V8 Splash. But I don't like plain milk."

The message that underlies all of Quinn's declarations is the same: "Milk is meaningful in my world. It is significant to me. My relationship to milk is part of who I am." Though Quinn can now express his personal preferences more effectively and his preferences have in fact changed over time, the framework in which he emotes remains unaltered. His likes and dislikes are fundamental to how he understands himself and how he presents himself to others. He defines himself in terms of what he cares about, what appeals to him, and what does not.

But children are not just intent on sharing what they prize about themselves to others. They are working just as hard to discern the essential components of others and what those essential components are like. They want to share your life with you as much as they want you to participate in theirs.

It is not by accident that at the same time children begin to express themselves declaratively they also begin to imitate others. All my children, from the time they could wriggle, would pull books out of the bottom shelf of the nearest bookcase and then flip through the pages intently, pausing only to giggle to themselves every once in a while. As they were the offspring of academics, their behavior was transparent. They were doing, to the best of their ability, what their parents did.

From my perspective, children imitating their parents are doing more than practicing self-expression, though they do that as well. But they are also sharing their parents' selves back to them. Their message is "I understand you. This is what you do. This is who you are." It is their version of my pointing out instances of moke to little Quinn as my way of saying to him, "I understand you and what is important in your life."

Certain things matter to children. These things matter to how they understand the world and their lives in it. These are also the things children spend their time talking about. It isn't quite fair to characterize their conversations, declarations, and imitations as "hypothesis testing." Nor are they merely practicing leading a life just in case they will need to do so for real later. Of course, they do learn about their world and people as a result of their activities, but they are also doing much more; they are already leading emotionally rich and vibrant lives. They are connecting emotionally with their friends and neighbors. From the time infants start to show preferences, they react to the world in terms of their predilections. What they take to be the good, the bad, and the ugly colors their interactions with others. It affects how and what they think of themselves and then how they describe themselves to the world.

The Importance of Emotional Attachment

Unlike Piaget and the neo-Piagetians, I hold that we code our experiences in a dual fashion. Our experiences, the ones we remember anyway, are those that have both sensory and affective dimensions. In some respects, the emotional side of our experiences is the more important, for it allows us to structure our world. It provides the backbone for our ideas, thoughts, and patterns of reasoning (see also Damasio, 1994; Greenspan with Benderly, 1997).

We can see the primacy of the emotions in infants as young as only a few days old. They prefer the smell and taste of their mother over other women; they prefer sweet liquids to sour, bitter, or neutral ones. Once they can track objects with their eyes, they will visually pursue their favorite people. These preferences are highly individual and idiosyncratic, as our emotional reactions to all the world are (Greenspan, 1989; Greenspan with Benderly, 1997; Hardcastle, 2000).

Piaget discusses how an infant learns about causality from sensorimotor interactions with the world. In what is now a standard experimental paradigm in psychology, he showed how an infant can learn to pull a string in order to ring a bell or move a mobile. However, way before infants are physically coordinated enough to perform that task, they understand that smiling at their caregivers results in a hug or a smile back (Greenspan with Benderly, 1997). They routinely manipulate their environment emotionally before they do it physically.

Emotional interaction is the fundamental touchstone for both infants and parents. It is no surprise that crying is contagious in day care, but clumsiness is not. Parents are much more aware of whether their children are cranky on a particular day than if they are more forgetful than usual. From a very early age, we are sensitive to the emotional states of our peers. The emotions and moods of those around us affect both how we feel and how we behave around them.

Another and perhaps more revealing way in which we can see how emotions guide our thoughts is through how children learn to classify things in their environment. Again using what are now standard benchmark tests in developmental psychology, Piaget demonstrated how and when children carve up their world using the size, color, shape, or function of objects. However, well before children can sort blocks they can recognize and classify members of their own family. They understand their family as a unit through emotional affiliation; divvying up the world in terms of other characteristics comes later.

Preschoolers' lives are ruled by who is their friend for the day (or the hour) and who hurt whose feelings. They move with ease in a remarkably complicated social structure that they track with little difficulty. Ask them what they did or learned on some day and the response is invariably some version of "nuthin'." Ask them who got a time-out—who angered the teacher or disturbed another child—and the verbal dam is broken.

These early emotional experiences form a "core" around which we structure our views of ourselves and the world (Eder, 1994, p. 180; see also Emde, 1983; Stern, 1985). We use our emotions cognitively, in other words. Just as Quinn now understands himself in terms of his previous beverage preferences, so, too, do the rest of us categorize and regiment our perceptions and thoughts in terms of what has moved us. When learning about numbers in preschool, children quite often will cheer the "evens" and boo the "odds" (Coghill, 1978, as discussed in Walkerdine, 1988). Being odd has negative connotations, and children are quite sensitive to this dimension. They use it to learn about and then later remember abstract numeric properties. In spite of what the followers of Piaget presume, we cannot divorce how we feel about things from how we think about them.

The deep connection between cognition and emotion cannot be glossed over or subtracted out of our psychological equations, for it infects all aspects of our mental lives. Indeed, the deep connection helps explain away some of the more puzzling developmental phenomena. For example, the usual story in development is that children learn first to apply concepts to concrete familiar objects and then later to more abstract and less familiar ones. D. W. Hamlyn is merely reporting folk wisdom when he notes that "the priority of the concrete to the abstract is something that all normal human beings could discover by reflection on what they know about the nature of human development, of human learning" (1973, p. 42, as quoted in Code, 1998).

However, this pattern of increasing abstraction does not always occur in children. Sometimes we see the reverse. For example, some children appear to have the comparative concepts of big, medium, and small correct for abstract objects, such as cups or circles, but will still nonetheless insist that Momma Bear of the Three Bears is bigger than Poppa Bear (cf. Walkerdine, 1998). This sort of data usually gets coded as the concepts not yet having been mastered and so is swept under the empirical carpet. However, as Valerie Walkerdine shows, there is more to the story than mere confusion on the part of the children. When she looked at the structure of their individual families, she discovered that the children's real mothers were in fact bigger than their real fathers, usually literally but sometimes figuratively (as some fathers were absent). The way these children understood the relationship of bigger and smaller was entirely correct after all. Indeed, it was quite sophisticated. Important for our purposes, it was their emotional affiliations that keyed their generalizations.

Hamlyn (1973) is wrong. We do not move from the concrete to the abstract in our generalizations. Affective ties are the most fundamental relationships and we build from there. Development entails learning to perceive the world apart from our emotions. We don't become more abstract thinkers as we age; we just become less emotionally involved.

Life Stories

Given how children especially use emotional reactions to divide up the environment, it is not surprising that they and we would use the same tack in appreciating and remembering ourselves. We understand ourselves in terms of what we like and what we dislike, what was good and what was bad, what was exciting, and what was important. We don't know how else to do it.

Cheshire, my middle child, has a journal in which she just lists everything she loves ("I love Sam. . . . I love Tyler. . . . I love Mom. . . . I love my house. . . . I love [the] Spice Girls. . . . I love bubbles. . . . I love skeletons. . . ."), everything she likes ("I like Ceeanna. . . . I like Maddie. . . . I like Cece. . . . I like the book *Box Turtle*. . . . I like the dinosaurs. . . . I like Oreo [her pet rat]. . . ."), and everything she hates ("I hate T.J. . . . I hate Alex D. . . . I hate Darrolyn. . . . I hate Sarah. . . . I do not like Greta. . . ."). This goes on for about twenty pages; I've only given you the highlights. Admittedly, Cheshire may be a bit extreme here, as she is in everything she does, but her message is certainly unambiguous. Her life consists of her likes and her dislikes.

So much of our time, both as children and as adults, is spent communicating back and forth with our kith and kin who we all are in terms of how we feel and under what circumstances. We impart this information to others by telling stories about ourselves regarding the things in our world that are exciting, different, novel, or otherwise important. Robyn Fivush (1994) argues that our narratives about self structure the events in our lives both linearly and causally. She describes them as "emotionally meaningful, causally connected sequences of actions that provide both temporal and evaluative cohesion to life events" (p. 136).

But not only do we share what in our present circumstances is important; we also spend a great deal of time recalling the meaningful events of yore. Children begin talking about their past almost as soon as they begin talking at all (Eisenberg, 1985; Hudson, 1990; Miller & Sperry, 1988; Nelson, 1988), and their backward looks continue through adulthood. And it is the evaluative and emotional ingredients of our narratives that link our past experiences to a developing sense of self, for they give a framework in which to appreciate the present and by which to anticipate the future.

It would be another essay to describe precisely how children learn to create canonical historical narratives. Let me just say briefly here that children are socialized into using particular narrative formulas through adult-guided conversations about the past (Fivush, 1994; Miller, 1994). Parents spend much of their time talking to and around their children about what has happened in their lives, giving them templates for how to talk and think about their past history as a chain of significant events (Fivush, 1994; Miller, 1994).

As early as 2 years of age, children begin participating in adult versions of self-narratives. Consider the conversation between a mother and her 32-month-old daughter recorded by Fivush:

M: Remember when Mommy and Daddy and Sam [baby brother] went in the car for a long time and we went to Memaw's house?

C: (nods head yes)

M: Yeah. What did we see when we were in the car? Remember Daddy was showing you outside the car. What was it?

C: I don't know.

M: Do you remember we saw some mountains and we went to that old house, and what did we do? We took off our shoes and we walked on the rocks. What did we do? What was there?

C: I don't know.

M: Mommy and Noel [the child] took off our shoes and walked in the water.

C: (nods head yes)

M: Yeah, was that fun? (1994, p. 140)

The mother is providing a model for how the child should interpret her experience and is giving a personal example of the strategy for how her culture and community would understand the child's life. She picks out from the myriad of events the ones that would be considered important—going to Me-maw's house, seeing the mountains, walking in the stream—and she provides the culturally appropriate affective reaction: it was fun.

Children appear naturally responsive to this approach. Miller and her colleagues have shown that toddlers as young as 2½ were 4 times more likely to contribute successfully to stories that their mothers were telling about them than stories their mothers told them that did not have them as a character (Miller, Potts, Fung, Hoogstra, & Mintz, 1990). Children are naturally interested in themselves, what others think about them, and how to use what others think to redescribe their own experiences in narrative form.

For example, William, a 2½-year-old, tells and retells a sledding adventure, with each version becoming more sophisticated and more laden with affect. His first rendition is fairly minimal: "Sledding! I hold on! . . . I hold on to sled." In the second version, his mother steps in to help him elaborate the important event from the adventure. William begins: "I go sled. I go on," and then his mother interrupts with, "Tell Lisa what happened to your face. Who did that." William replies, "I felled on you—. I cut mine." In the third version, William structured the story around his accident, as his mother had wanted him to, and added further evaluative details: "I-I didn't hurt my face. [He] did. Eddie [his brother]—and Eddie said I am fraidy cat. [She] was supposed to catch me, um— . . . I didn't get catched." His mother then suggested that he had been afraid after all, which he vigorously denied. (This example comes from Miller, 1994, pp. 173–174.) William moves from a brief assertion of an event, to an adventure with a point, as modeled by his mother, and then finally to a genuine, action-packed narrative, punctuated by his own evaluation of the episode. This pattern of elaborative affective retelling exemplifies how we construct our self-narratives.

Most of our life stories will be forgotten over time, but some will continue to be told and retold, forming a core around which we can hang our other life events. But at the heart of any story about self is the expression of some emotional reaction of the person talking. Miller (1994) concludes that "remembering in the service of personal storytelling is inherently evaluative" (p. 175). She is correct. Children's life stories may conform to emblematic patterns defined by their culture, their community, their neighbors, and their families (Bruner, 1987; Labov, 1982; Spence, 1982), but their affective responses are all their own. (By the way, this is one reason that Quinn's autobiography is so dull: he gives us a litany of life events, to be sure, but he omits the human reactions to them.)

To call this life activity theory building sells it short. That isn't enough. It is a way of caring about ourselves and others. It is a way of integrating and consolidating our affective reactions to the events around us, a way of making our life events meaningful, to us and to others. It is a way of living a life as well as a way of understanding it.

Cognition as Narrative Instrument

From this perspective, memory and cognition become instrumental processes in the service of creating a self. They are the means to that end. As we tell and retell stories of ourselves either to ourselves, as part of rehearsing our life events in memory, or to others, as part of our social nature, we are in effect shaping our memories of these events, making them more and more part of who we are. Remember little William and his sled. His story got progressively more elaborate and more laden with emotion with each telling. All of us are the same way. Telling our life stories is a two-way street. The more we tell, the greater our emotion attached to the event, and then the greater the memory (whether accurate or not) for that event. The greater the memory, then the more likely we are to retell the story, which means the greater the emotional salience will be. And so it goes.

Talking to one another, telling one another our personal stories, increases the emotions we feel about the happenings. Indeed, any sort of communal sharing increases the emotional impact. Movies seen with fellow humans provoke greater autonomic reactions than the same moves seen alone. Together we find funny stories funnier, sadder stories sadder, and scary stories scarier (Hess, 1998). We truly are social creatures who experience better, who experience more, when in groups.

In short, things aren't remembered just to be remembered or analyzed just to be understood, but they are remembered and analyzed so that we can later use them in stories about ourselves. Indeed, veridicality has never been particularly important in our conversations. In fact, we are notoriously bad at recording incidents accurately, as the recent spate of literature that surrounds false memories attests. It has always been easy to manipulate memory through leading questions or guided imagery, as prosecutors know full well. The social performance itself is what counts. For selves aren't static entities to be preserved in our stories. Instead they are created through the narrative process, and then they are revised and reworked as we tell and retell our life story.

Perhaps the best way to appreciate what I am claiming here is to remember the words of Henry James: "Adventures happen to people who know how to tell it that way." I would only add: "And we all know how to tell it that way."

Acknowledgments

I thank Cheshire and Kiah Hardcastle for permission to use their journal entries in my discussion of children's narratives. Even though their diaries are marked "privet," they made an exception for what they understood to be a good cause. Earlier and briefer versions of this essay were presented at a conference on the narrative self in Lubbock, Texas, to the Cognitive Science Program at the University of Arizona, and to the Philosophy Departments at the University of Cincinnati and Virginia Tech. My thanks to all the audiences for their very helpful, thoughtful, and thought-provoking comments. An expanded version of this essay was published in *Cognitive Systems Research*. This essay was completed while I was a Taft Fellow at the University of Cincinnati. I thank the university for its generous support.

References

Abrahamsen, A. (1998). Cognitive and linguistic development. In W. Bechtel & G. Graham (Eds.), *A companion to cognitive science* (pp. 146–156). New York: Blackwell.

Baron-Cohen, S. (1989). Perceptual role-taking and proto-declarative pointing in autism. *British Journal of Development Psychology, 7,* 113–127.

Baron-Cohen, S. (1991). Precursors to a theory of mind: Understanding attention in others. In A. Whiten (Ed.), *Natural theories of mind: Evolution, development, and simulation of everyday mindreading* (pp. 233–251). New York: Blackwell.

Bates, W., & MacWhinney, B. (1987). Competition, variation, and language learning. In B. MacWhinney (Ed.), *Mechanisms of language acquisition* (pp. 157–193). Hillsdale, NJ: Erlbaum.

Bruner, J. (1987). Life as narrative. *Social Research, 54,* 11–32.

Carey, S. (1985). *Conceptual change in childhood.* Cambridge, MA: MIT Press.

Carey, S. (1988). Conceptual differences between children and adults. *Mind and Language, 3,* 167–181.

Chandler, M. J., & Boyes, M. (1982). Social-cognitive development. In B. B. Wolman (Ed.), *Handbook of development* (pp. 290–310). New York: Prentice Hall.

Code, L. (1998). Naming, naturalizing, normalizing: "The child" as fact and artifact. In P. Miller & E. Scholnick (Eds.), *Toward a feminist developmental psychology* (pp. 215–237). New York: Routledge.

Coghill, V. (1978). *Infant school reasoning.* Teachers' Research Group, unpublished manuscript.

Damasio, A. R. (1994). *Descartes' error: Emotion, reason, and the human brain.* New York: G. P. Putnam's Sons.

Eder, R.A. (1994). Comments on children's self-narratives. In U. Neisser & R. Fivush (Eds.), *The remembering self: Construction and accuracy in the self-narrative* (pp. 180–190). Cambridge: Cambridge University Press.

Eisenberg, A. R. (1985). Learning to describe past experience in conversation. *Discourse Processes, 8,* 177–204.

Emde, R. N. (1983). The prerepresentational self and its affective core. *Psychoanalytic Study of the Child, 38,* 165–192.

Estes, D., Wellman, H. M., & Wooley, J. D. (1990). Children's understanding of mental phenomena. In H. Reese (Ed.), *Advances in child development and behavior* (pp. 41–87). New York: Academic Press.

Fivush, R. (1994). Constructing narrative, emotion, and self in parent-child conversations about the past. In U. Neisser & R. Fivush (Eds.), *The remembering self: Construction and accuracy in the self-narrative* (pp. 136–157). Cambridge: Cambridge University Press.

Gelman, S. A., & Wellman, H. M. (1991). Insides and essence: Early understandings of the non-obvious. *Cognition, 38,* 213–244.

Gopnik, A., & Meltzoff, A. N. (1997). *Words, thoughts, and theories.* Cambridge, MA: MIT Press.

Greenspan, S. I. (1989). *The development of the ego: Implications for personality theory, psychopathology, and the psychotherapeutic process.* Madison, CT: International Universities Press.

Greenspan, S. I., with Benderly, B. L. (1997). *The growth of mind: And the endangered origins of intelligence.* New York: Addison-Wesley.

Hamlyn, D. W. (1973). Logical and psychological aspects of learning. In R. S. Peters (Ed.), *The concept of education* (pp. 24–43) London: Routledge & Kegan Paul.

Hardcastle, V. G. (2000). It is okay to be complicated: The case of emotion. In R. D. Ellis & N. Newton (Eds.), *The caldron of consciousness: Motivation, affect and self-organization—An anthology* (pp. 19–131). Amsterdam: John Benjamins.

Hess, U. (1998). *The experience of emotion: Situational influences on the elicitation and experience of emotions.* Paper presented at the Emotions, Consciousness, Qualia workshop in Ischia, Italy, 19–24 October.

Hudson, J. A. (1990). The emergence of autobiographical memory in mother-child conversation. In R. Fivush & J. A. Hudson (Eds.), *Knowing and remembering in young children* (pp. 166–196). Cambridge: Cambridge University Press.

Johnson, M. H., & Morton, J. (1991). *Biology and cognitive development: The case of face recognition.* New York: Blackwell.

Karmiloff-Smith, A. (1992). *Beyond modularity: A developmental perspective on cognitive science.* Cambridge, MA: MIT Press.

Keil, F. C. (1989). *Concepts, kinds, and cognitive development.* Cambridge, MA: MIT Press.

Labov, U. (1982). Speech actions and reactions in personal narrative. In D. Tannen

(Ed.), *Analyzing discourse: Text and talk* (pp. 219–247). Washington, DC: Georgetown University Press.

Leslie, A. M. (1984). Infant perception of a manual pickup event. *British Journal of Developmental Psychology, 2,* 19–32.

Miller, P. J. (1994). Narrative practices: Their role in socialization and self-construction. In U. Neisser & R. Fivush (Eds.), *The remembering self: Construction and accuracy in the self-narrative* (pp. 158–179). Cambridge: Cambridge University Press.

Miller, P. J., & Sperry, L. L. (1988). Early talk about the past: The origins of conversational stories of personal experience. *Journal of Child Language, 15,* 292–315.

Miller, P. J., Potts, R., Fung, H., Hoogstra, L., & Mintz, J. (1990). Narrative practices and the social construction of self in childhood. *American Ethnologist, 17,* 292–311.

Nelson, K. (1988). The ontogeny of memory for real world events. In U. Neisser & E. Winograd (Eds.), *Remembering reconsidered: Ecological and traditional approaches to memory* (pp. 244–276). Cambridge: Cambridge University Press.

Perner, J. (1991). *Understanding the representational mind.* Cambridge, MA: MIT Press.

Piaget, J. (1929). *The child's conception of the world.* New York: Routledge & Kegan Paul.

Premack, D. (1990). Words: What they are, and do animals have them? *Cognition, 37,* 197–212.

Spence, D. P. (1982). *Narrative truth and historical truth: Meaning and interpretation in psychoanalysis.* New York: Norton.

Stern, D. (1985). *The interpersonal world of the infant: A view from psychoanalysis and developmental psychology.* New York: Basic.

Thelen, E., & Smith, L. B. (1994). *A dynamic systems approach to the development of cognition and action.* Cambridge, MA: MIT Press.

Walkerdine, V. (1988). *The mastery of reason: Cognitive development and the production of rationality.* New York: Routledge.

Wellman, H. M. (1990). *The child's theory of mind.* Cambridge, MA: MIT Press.

Wellman, H. M., & Gelman, S. A. (1992). Cognitive development: Foundational theories of core domains. *Annual Review of Psychology, 43,* 337–375.

PART II

Narrative and Autobiographical Memory

4   The Role of Narrative in Recollection:
      A View from Cognitive Psychology
      and Neuropsychology

      David C. Rubin
      Daniel L. Greenberg

          In this chapter, we investigate the role that narrative plays when
people recollect their past—that is, when they provide a report of their own life
anywhere in length from a single event to an entire life story. First, we outline a
collection of processes, which include narrative reasoning, that come into play
during recollection, noting that each appears to have a distinct neural substrate.
Second, we examine the effects of neural damage that disrupts these cognitive
processes. Based on this review, we conclude that narrative reasoning is one process among many used in recollection but probably the least well understood.
          At the 32nd Annual Comparative Literature Symposium on Narrative and
Consciousness: Literature, Psychology, and the Brain, there was a roundtable
discussion at which I (DCR) sat on the stage with other speakers. I remember
the incident and could produce a coherent narrative account about it. I might
do this as if I were telling a story about someone else who participated in an
event that I did not witness or even as an account of a fictional character; or,
in contrast, I might do this with a sense of reliving my own past. For the latter
case, I might use the English word *recollection* (Baddeley, 1992; Brewer, 1996)
or, following Tulving (1983; Wheeler, Stuss, & Tulving, 1997), I might claim
that I am in a special state of consciousness, called *autonoetic consciousness*, in
which I am conscious now of a past conscious state. This chapter focuses on
this latter case of recollection, of conscious recall of actual events rather than
nonexperienced (Larsen, 1988) and fictive events. For now, to provide a hint
of the type of argument to be made here, we will claim that narrative per se
is not important to the difference between reliving a memory and not, although

narrative devices may be used to mark a sense of reliving explicitly in text; rather, this difference is more often caused by processes that involve visual imagery.

Prepostmodern psychologists like to define their terms, and so this paragraph might have been the place where we offered operational definitions of basic concepts. Instead, we use another solution to try to avoid solving our problems (and making new ones) through premature definition (Rubin, 1992). We will start with the most detailed and precise descriptions of our terms that capture what we believe is the essence of the processes at work, ones that are consistent with what we know about behavior and biology. If we are to benefit from evidence from different levels of analysis, we need to consider evidence from each level, usually in an iterative fashion. For example, one cannot look for the neural system or systems necessary to support narrative reasoning without some notion of what narrative reasoning is at the behavioral level. However, if one already knows fully what narrative reasoning is at the behavioral level, an investigation of the related biology can yield little useful information about behavior. If particular aspects of narrative reasoning were lost or damaged as a result of particular diseases or a particular kind of neural insult, we would want to try to group those aspects together in a description at the behavioral level. Similarly, if particular aspects of narrative reasoning appeared together at certain periods of development (Nelson, this volume), we might look for common neural development. There is no strict logic that suggests any relations will be present among the different levels; we are just attempting an iterative search for the most encompassing explanations. To begin this search (and for narrative reasoning it is just beginning) we provide a progress report on our attempt to describe the cognitive and neural basis of recollection, that is, the basis for the conscious recall of autobiographical memory into which the process of narrative reasoning must fit.

Systems Needed for Recollection: Behavioral Data

At least a handful of cognitive processes, each with a partially separable underlying neural system, are needed to provide a recollection (Rubin, 1995b, 1998). Here we consider an *explicit memory system* that encodes information in other systems, then later retrieves the separately stored information and integrates it into a memory; an *imagery system*, both because it is an important component in its own right and because it is a well-understood component to contrast with the less well understood narrative reasoning; a *language system*, because narrative reasoning is often considered a part of language and so distinguishing language from narrative is important if the independent effects of narrative are to be noted; and finally a *narrative reasoning system*. We use the term *narrative reasoning* to posit a process that results in the product of narrative (cf. Bruner, 1986; Fitzgerald, 1996). When its use is restricted to narratives that are autobiographical memories, narrative reasoning is similar to what Habermas and Bluck (2000) call autobiographical reasoning. We could also consider emotions and imagery in other senses, such as olfaction and audition, but do not; less is understood about these processes, and in any case we wish to preserve our focus on narrative. The change from *processes* to *systems* or *components* is a conscious choice to emphasize that we are making an activity into a thing so that it can have a location (actually a widely distributed location but a location nonetheless) to make it easier to combine the behavioral and the neuropsychological data.

Explicit Memory

We posit an explicit memory system that combines information from the other systems. Psychologists and neuropsychologists have traditionally assumed such a central system, and there is good evidence for it. In the past, they have usually concentrated on this system alone in their theories of autobiographical memory, excluding a detailed analysis of the way in which the system combines information from other systems. The basic metaphor of a central process that puts things into places in memory, stores them there, and then finds them later dates back to at least the ancient Greeks, but it has reached its most well defined, sophisticated, and useful form in the computer models of cognitive psychology. There are two main differences from this basic metaphor we wish to make here. First, we do not assume that each memory is in one place; rather, we assume that it is distributed in the brain. While the memory is encoded or retrieved, its various locations are active at the same time; at other times, the locations remains dormant or are active in other memories or tasks. Thus the memory as a whole exists at one time but not in one place (Damasio, 1989). This abstract idea will become more concrete and detailed as we specify some of the systems in which the memory is located.

The second difference is that like many others (Damasio, 1989; McClelland, McNaughton, & O'Reilly, 1995; Mishkin & Appenzeller, 1987, June; Moscovitch, 1995; Schacter, 1996; Schmajuk & DiCarlo, 1992; Squire, 1987, 1992; Wheeler et al., 1997), we wish to use a central process that is both behaviorally and biologically plausible. We therefore look for one in the brain and use it as our metaphor instead of a metaphor of a wax tablet, attic, file cabinet, telephone switchboard system, cow's belly, computer, or any of a host of other metaphors that each capture some useful aspects of human memory (Roediger, 1980). Once the brain, or anything else, is accepted as a metaphor used to understand human behavior, discourse often becomes confused as to whether it is about the behavior or the metaphor. This is certainly the case for the literature in cognitive psychology that accepts the computer as its metaphor. Here the confusion is worse. The brain is not only used as a metaphor, a conceptual nervous system invented to explain behavior; it is also the most likely physical location of the control of that behavior. For us, the substrate of recollection is the brain, and so in this chapter, having switched to terms such as *system* and *component*, we freely mix behavioral and neural evidence. The brain remains a metaphor to the extent we select freely from among its many properties or posit new properties to it in a way that is not strongly supported from studies of the brain itself. But the brain is more than a metaphor when the study of the brain provides an independent source of evidence. We include such evidence here.

One more observation about the explicit memory system will be noted now; others will be discussed later in the chapter when the biology of the system is considered. The processes performed by the central system in consciously retrieving, rather than encoding, a memory take a very long time. Undergraduates cued individually with words take about 10 seconds to produce an autobiographical memory; 70-year-old volunteers take almost twice as long (Fitzgerald & Lawrence, 1984; Robinson, 1976; Rubin & Schulkind, 1997). Undergraduates can begin pronouncing the same words used to cue the autobiographical memories or can decide whether a sequence of letters presented visually is a word or a pronounceable nonword in about a quarter of a second (Rubin, 1980), so retrieval in recollection may be very different in nature from other forms of retrieval psychologists have studied that take place on a much shorter time scale. On a cognitive level, cyclical retrieval (Conway, 1996; Conway & Pleydell-Pearce, 2000; Conway & Rubin, 1993), in which each successive retrieval serves as the cue for the next search, might produce such a delay; at a neural level, the delays are consistent with a nervous system that has closed-loop pathways among systems at some distance from each other that would take relatively long times to produce successive iterations. Thus the explicit memory system helps encode and integrate the information needed for recollection but does not store information itself.

Imagery

We describe the best understood of the remaining component systems needed for recollection, visual imagery, as a model of what might be done with narrative reasoning. Visual imagery is an analog system (Paivio, 1971; Rumelhart & Norman, 1986; Shepard, 1978) that shares many properties with visual perception. It can be broken down behaviorally and neurally into spatial and object components (see Rubin, 1995a, for a review).

Imagery has a central role in autobiographical memory for several reasons. First, it provides a powerful memory aid (Paivio, 1971, 1986, 1991), an observation that predates experimental psychological work on imagery by a millennium or two (Yates, 1966). Almost all mnemonic systems are based on visual imagery (Paivio, 1971; Yates, 1966). Most of the evidence for imagery's mnemonic role comes from its effects on long-term memory, but imagery can also be seen as an important aspect of our ability to manipulate visual information (Baddeley, 1986) and can even be seen as having most of its effects in this way rather than on long-term representations (Marschark, Richman, Yuille, & Hunt, 1987). That is, the imagery system should be viewed as a way not only to store information of a particular kind but also to consciously manipulate it.

Imagery is also important in autobiographical memory because of its role in increasing the specific, relived, personally experienced aspect of autobiographical memory. Specific, concrete details do more than improve memory. Concrete, easy-to-image details make stories seem more accurate, thoughtful, and believable (Pillemer, 1992, 1998; Pillemer, Desrochers, & Ebanks, 1998; Pillemer, Picariello, Law, & Reichman, 1996). Although vivid images do not guarantee accuracy (Winograd & Neisser, 1992), people act as if memory for details implies that the central points are remembered correctly. For instance, an eyewitness's testimony is more effective if details are included, even if they are irrelevant to the case (Bell & Loftus, 1989), and sensory details make people likely to judge that they did an action rather than just thought about it (Johnson, Hashtroudi, & Lindsay, 1993; Johnson & Raye, 1981). You are more likely to decide that you really did lock the door rather than just thought you did if you can image yourself doing it. Chafe (1982, 1990) notes that language varies along the dimension of *involvement*. Involvement is marked linguistically by the use of first person and of dialogue, the same traits that are present when one seems to others to be reliving an experience or seeing it in one's mind's eye (Pillemer et al., 1998). Thus, evidence that the remberer has an image is routinely taken as evidence for a relived, personally experienced, accurate autobiographical memory. In this role of increasing the specific, imagery interacts with language and narrative reasoning. The language of a journal article is abstract, general, low in imagery. A moving narrative usually is not. The experience of having an image is linguistically marked in narrative (Chafe, 1982, 1990; Pillemer et al., 1998) and has been at least from the time of Homer (Bakker, 1988, 1993).

In addition, imagery is central to two specific areas of the psychological literature on autobiographical memory. The first is the debate on flashbulb memories. The term *flashbulb memories* was coined by Brown and Kulik (1977) to talk about those memories for which your mind seems to take a permanent fixed picture of important events (see Conway, 1995; Winograd & Neisser, 1992, for reviews; Neisser, 1982, for a more constructivist view). Prototype flashbulb memories include knowing the details of where you were and what you were doing when you first heard that President Lincoln (Colegrove, 1899), President Kennedy, or Martin Luther King (Brown & Kulik, 1977) was assassinated, or that Pearl Harbor was attacked (Neisser, 1982), or the space shuttle *Challenger* exploded (Winograd & Neisser, 1992). Imagery is a part of the flashbulb metaphor of taking a picture and an attempt to rename it as *vivid memory* (Rubin & Kozin, 1984), and it has effects on memory. The best predictor of the narrative recall of when people heard about the verdict of the O. J. Simpson trial was reported imagery (Bluck & Li, in press). Second, imagery enters in the autobiographical memory literature in cognitive psychology in the distinction between *field* and *observer* points of view, that is, whether one sees oneself in the memory or sees it from the original observer's viewpoint, a distinction that dates back at least to Freud (see Robinson & Swanson, 1993, for a review). One can distance oneself; one can change perspective by manipulating the image to take a different view. Thus we have two metaphors of imagery: one as a static, accurate picture that is most common in the autobiographical memory literature and another as a fluid mental-model image that can be seen from different points of view (both literally and figuratively), which is more common when psychologists try to understand imagery and how it differs from language (Paivio, 1971; Rumelhart & Norman, 1986; Shepard, 1978). The contrast between the two metaphors is one reason that the classic conflict between the view of memories as fixed and memories as constructions (e.g., Neisser, 1967) becomes so heated when applied to the autobiographical memory of eyewitness testimony and of recovered memories of sexual abuse.

Psychologists have viewed visual imagery as one process or faculty and consciousness, with its sense of reliving or recollection, as another. In contrast, most philosophers of mind have noted that a sense of reliving comes with a visual image (Brewer, 1996). In a recent study, we made a direct assessment of the relationship between the sense of reliving and visual imagery (Rubin, Schrauf, & Greenberg, 2000). We cued each of 50 undergraduates with 30 words and asked them to think of an autobiographical memory for each. Of the resulting 1,500 possible memories, 521 were rated as 6 or 7 on a 7-point scale of the extent to which the undergraduates felt that they were reliving the original event. The scale ranged from "1—not at all" to "7—as if were happening right now." Of these 521 highly relived memories only 8 were rated below 5 on a 7-point scale that used the same descriptions for the end points but asked the undergraduates if they could see the event in their mind. Thus, with only 8 exceptions out of 521 memories that were rated highly on the reliving scale, a strong visual image was reported. Moreover, undergraduates who had a high average value of imagery calculated over all 30 of their memories also tended to have high average values of reliving, showing that this might be a general style of recall. The relationship between the sense of reliving and having a coherent narrative was much weaker. Consistent with this data is the strong sense of living (rather than reliving) that is present in dreams, often in the absence of a globally coherent narrative (Flanagan, this volume). Thus visual imagery appears to have a role in the conscious recollection of autobiographical memory that narrative reasoning does not have.

Language

By any linguistic, behavioral, or neuropsychological analysis, if language is considered as a thing it is not a unified, indivisible thing, but is understood in terms of components that can be identified. Usually these components include phonetics, syntax, semantics, and often some higher-level structure such as pragmatics or narrative. We first consider language to include structure at the level of the sentence and below and thus do not include narrative. We do this for three reasons. First, linguistics, which takes language as its object of study, tends to do so. Second, the study of aphasia, or language loss, usually makes this distinction as well. Third, there are many instances of narrative, such as mime and silent films, that do not use language in the usual sense. The first two reasons are for convenience. It is much easier to review and summarize a literature if one keeps the definitions of that literature. Later we will discuss the relationship of narrative reasoning and language.

One could easily claim that phonetics and syntax should have little effect on recollection. After all, on the one hand, phonetics and syntax might mainly help us decode and encode ideas for purposes of communication that are actually stored in some unspecified nonlinguistic form. On the other hand, there is a long tradition in philosophy and psychology from very different theoretical perspectives that claims we often (or always) think in words, that we talk to ourselves, and that this inner speech is equated with consciousness (Carruthers, 1996; Damasio, 1989; Ericsson & Simon, 1993; Skinner, 1974). Under this view, to have conscious, explicit memory we need phonetically and syntactically correct language. The argument for meaning is stronger. Semantics at the level of words and syntax plus semantics at the level of phrases and sentences have traditionally been seen as ways of interpreting and storing information about the world, at both a personal and a cultural level (e.g., Pavlov's second signal system [Popov & Rokhlin, n.d.]), with different languages fostering the formation of different realities (Lucy, 1992; Whorf, 1956). That is, from almost any perspective, language is a central aspect of our memory for events and its loss should have major effects on memory beyond the effects that must occur given the specific loss.

One way to look at the effect of language on autobiographical memory is to obtain autobiographical memories from people who know two or more languages, because they can provide information on how their different languages affect their memory. Most of the memories of the sequential bilinguals (i.e., people who learned one language after another) that we have tested come to the person in a particular language, much the way some people report that a dream comes to them in a particular language (Schrauf & Rubin, 1998, 2000). The language of the memory is often not the language in which the testing is done but is instead likely to be the language that was being used at the time of the event. For our current purposes, however, we are unable to assign this attribution to the phonetics, syntax, and semantics of the memory rather than to its narrative structure, the topic we turn to next.

Narrative Reasoning

Having provided a minimal description of the role of a central memory component, a visual imagery component, and a language component that operates at the level of the sentence and below, we turn to our main concern: narrative. Although there is no generally accepted definition of narrative in psychology (or perhaps anywhere else), psychologists generally agree on the properties of narrative. Schank and Abelson's (1995) view stresses the goal-directed nature of stories. Kintsch and Van Dijk (1975) note that a coherent narrative requires judgments of empathy, relevance, and theme. In cognitive psychological terms, Brewer (1980, p. 223) notes that "narrative discourse is discourse that attempts to embody in linguistic form a series of events that occur in time. . . . the cognitive structure underlying narrative is the mental representation of a series of temporally occurring events that are perceived as having a causal or thematic coherence."

Bruner (1986) views narrative as a mode of thought, a perspective that moves narrative from a description of text structure to a form of organization or process. In Bruner's words, the narrative mode of thought produces "good stories, gripping drama, believable (though not necessarily true) historical accounts. It deals in human or human-like intention and action and the vicissitudes and consequences that mark their course. It strives to put its timeless miracles into the particulars of experience, and to locate the experience in time and space" (p. 13). Brewer's idea of the cognitive structure that underlies narrative and Bruner's idea of a mode of thought, both of which move narrative from a structure present in language to the cognitive process of narrative reasoning, are most useful here.

Most researchers who have examined the form and content of autobiographical memory have focused on narrative structure; most claims for the importance of language in autobiographical memory have actually been claims for the importance of narrative. For example, Robinson (1981, 1996) integrated and extended theories of narrative from linguistics and folklore into cognitive psychology. Barclay (1986, 1996; Barclay & Smith, 1992) examined the schematic nature of autobiographical memory and its relation to the local and general culture in which the individual is located. This approach produces the "conversational nature of autobiographical remembering" (Barclay & Smith, 1992, p. 82). Fitzgerald (1988, 1992, 1996) uses concepts such as "narrative thought" and "self-narratives" to account for autobiographical memory and its changes with mood and age. Schank and Abelson (1995) claim that "the content of story memories depends on whether and how they are told to others, and these reconstituted memories form the basis of the individual's *remembered self*" (p. 1). Using a psychoanalytic framework, Schafer (1981) and Spence (1982) note the importance of narrative. In a more humanistic approach, Freeman (1993, this volume) tied narrative to autobiographical memory, and Gergen and Gergen (1988) use narrative structure and communication to stress the social nature of remembering and the self. Narrative structure is central in recollection in groups (Hirst & Manier, 1996) and in the shared memories that define them (Bruner & Feldman, 1996). Creating narrative structure in recollection is a skill taught to children (Fivush, Haden, & Reese, 1996; Miller & Sperry, 1988; Nelson, 1993, this volume).

Narrative establishes a major form of organization in autobiographical memory, providing temporal and goal structure. Autobiographical memories are usually recorded as narrative; they are told to another person and to oneself. Inclusions and exclusions depend in part on the narrative structures used. If information is not central to the narrative structure, it is less likely to be remembered. For example, Brown and Kulik (1977) observed that reports of flashbulb memories tend to have canonical categories, such as the place, ongoing event, informant, affect in others, affect in self, and aftermath. Neisser (1982) countered that these may not be properties of flashbulb memories at all but rather properties of the narrative genre used to report any news. Thus Neisser claimed that these autobiographical memories are shaped by narrative conventions of the culture.

Finally, Habermas and Bluck (2000) use the term *autobiographical reasoning* to define the process by which autobiographical memories are combined into a coherent life story and related to the current self. They identify four components of autobiographical reasoning: *temporal coherence*, which involves the sequencing of events in time; *causal coherence*, which serves to explain both life events and changes in the narrator's personality; *thematic coherence*, which involves an analysis of common themes among many different memories; and the *cultural concept of biography*, the cultural mores that dictate the events that are incorporated into a life story.

Given this review and the lack of a formal definition of narrative, what can we take as a working definition of narrative reasoning so that we can examine its loss with neural damage? This is important here because of the lack of a universal definition and because such loss is not an established field of study with its own name, as are the losses of visual or linguistic ability (i.e., agnosia or aphasia). Narrative reasoning is the ability to use structure above the level of the sentence, above the level at which most formal linguistic analysis and most studies of aphasia stop. It is the "mode of thought" (Bruner, 1986) used to describe particular incidents of goal-directed behavior in people and animate objects assumed to have humanlike motives. As a mode of thought it need not be expressed in language but can be expressed in forms such as pictures, cartoons, silent film, and mime and therefore could be tested using nonlinguistic means. Tests of narrative reasoning that have been used in the neuropsychological literature and that are therefore of use in our search include: (1) story comprehension as measured by recall or question answering, and, at a more difficult level, story comprehension when the goals or other structure have to be inferred; (2) showing understanding of a story by remembering or telling the same "important" parts as other people in your culture do; (3) showing appreciation of the goals, motives, and therefore mood or emotional tone of a story by analysis of recall protocols or by explicit questions; and (4) understanding nonliteral statements, jokes, or metaphors that require narrative-based leaps to understand, that is, leaps that you might explain to someone who did not "get it" with some form of a very short story. If the approach taken here is to be useful, we cannot define narrative reasoning, or any of the concepts used in this essay, in a fully satisfying way until we see which behaviors occur together and which behaviors are lost or remain intact together with neuropsychological insult (Rubin, 1992). The working definition and partial list of tests is our best attempt given the behavioral and neuropsychological data available and certainly will change if our understanding increases.

One final observation should be made in this section: People can have autobiographical memories and can recollect in ways that do not produce coherent narratives. One can have a vivid reliving of an isolated event or past sensory experience in the absence of any narrative structure. Brewer reviews the literature that shows that many philosophers of mind claim that a visual image is needed for recollection, but there is no consensus that a coherent narrative structure is. Therefore, it would not be surprising to find that a loss of narrative reasoning results in a loss of only some kinds of recollection and autobiographical memory.

Systems Needed for Recollection: Neuropsychological Data

Having outlined four component systems that are part of the set needed to have a recollection, we now ask what happens with loss to each. According to the consensus view of the neural mechanisms that support autobiographical

(or episodic) memory, the ability to consciously recollect past events is mediated by multiple systems spread throughout the brain (Damasio, 1989;
Mayes & Downes, 1997; Mishkin & Appenzeller, 1987, June; Moscovitch,
1995; Rubin, 1998; Schacter, Norman, & Koustaal, 1998; Squire & Knowlton,
1995; Wheeler et al., 1997). Encoding of new experiences for later recollection
is mediated by areas in the diencephalon and medial temporal lobes, especially
the hippocampus and surrounding areas (Squire, 1987, 1992; Squire & Knowlton, 1995), mammillary bodies, and medial thalamus, which are part of what
we have called the explicit memory system. The actual long-term storage of
information for conscious recall is not in these encoding centers but in sense-
specific locations in cortex as well as in cortical and subcortical areas that support emotion (Damasio, 1994). Retrieval of the stored information involves
the frontal lobes, especially the right frontal lobe, but like the diencephalon
and medial temporal lobes in encoding, the frontal lobes are not thought to
store most of the information but rather the retrieval strategies needed to access it (Moscovitch, 1995; Wheeler et al., 1997). That is, the explicit memory
system produces a memory that is localized in time and distributed in space.

When an autobiographical memory is recalled, information in widely separated areas of cortex are excited in time-locked, coactivated, or reverberating
circuits similar to those that were active at encoding. That is at recall, a temporally and spatially extended pattern of neural firing, which uses feedback,
results in a pattern of activation similar to that present during encoding. When
autobiographical memory fails in amnesia, it is usually due to structures in or
near the medial temporal cortex that prevent such coactivation from occurring
(Hirst, 1982). Areas of the frontal lobes are the most recent addition to the
explicit memory system probably because they are not the areas usually damaged in amnesia. Imaging studies have shown that areas in the right frontal
cortex, especially areas near Brodmann's area 10, are involved when episodic,
rather than semantic, memory searches are taking place (Buckner, 1996; Nyberg, Cabeza, & Tulving, 1996), whether or not the searches are successful.
Whether these areas in the frontal lobes should be considered part of the explicit memory system, the narrative reasoning system, or both is not clear from
the existing data.

Explicit Memory Loss

Given what is known about memory and amnesia, what should we expect
with damage to the central explicit memory system? When the nervous system
suffers damage, the loss of conscious explicit memory is different for events
encoded prior to the insult (i.e., retrograde amnesia) and those after the insult
(i.e., anterograde amnesia). In most cases the anterograde amnesia is more
severe. Events prior to the insult benefit from encoding with an intact nervous

system, and those after do not. However, events after the insult are encoded and retrieved by a similarly damaged nervous system and those prior are not. For almost all kinds of damage to the central explicit memory system, the retrograde loss is temporally graded, with the most severe loss near the time of insult. The same can be true of anterograde amnesia, as in closed head injury, or the loss can exist the remainder of the patient's life, as in Korsakoff's syndrome. The temporally graded nature of retrograde amnesia has been attributed to general processes such as consolidation, in which older memories become more resistant to damage through any number of (often unspecified) biological changes, or, in more specific terms, because the separately stored components of the memory develop interconnections that no longer involve the hippocampal circuits and so are left intact when these circuits are destroyed. The temporally graded nature of anterograde amnesia has been attributed to recovery in the nervous system or because new areas are recruited over time to compensate for those that are lost (see Rubin, 1998, for a more detailed description).

Loss in Other Systems

What would happen with damage to the neural systems outside the areas that subserve explicit memory? That depends on their function. If they are primarily areas that are assumed to store and process the different kinds of information that are retrieved when a recollection occurs, then with the loss of access to the store of information the memory could not be formed. If an area helps organize or communicate the stored information but stores little or no information itself, the loss may be more in the coherence of the memory than in its contents, though following our initial metaphor of putting "things" into "places," disruption of the organization that affects the search process would result in "things" not being found.

But the loss should not be equal for memories stored before and after the insult, and the pattern should not follow that of loss before and after an insult that occurs in the explicit memory system. For memories of events that occurred after the loss, no information would be stored in the damaged areas, but coherent patterns might be able to be stored in the intact areas of the brain. If we assume that the neural structures in the explicit memory system that encode information remain undamaged, such patients could compensate for their deficits, allowing nondamaged areas of the brain that store and process information to play a greater role. For example, with loss of the visual imagery system memories might still be stored and retrieved without a visual component. In contrast, for memories stored before the damage information that was part of the coherent memory would be lost, and if the information was interrelated and used to cue other information, without the missing information it might be impossible to "find" and reconstruct the remaining aspects of the memory into a coherent whole. This prediction is consistent with formal mathematical models of the nervous system (e.g., McClelland et al., 1995; Schmajuk & DiCarlo, 1992) as well as of neural models that stress coactivation of brain areas (e.g., Damasio, 1989, 1994), though with the exception of the research reviewed here, it is not explicitly stated or tested. Thus the retrograde amnesia would be more severe than the anterograde, with the actual severity of retrograde amnesia depending on how much information of a given kind is lost and how central it was to the memory (see Rubin, 1998; Rubin & Greenberg, 1998, for a more detailed description).

Imagery Loss

We know a great deal about the neural system that subserves vision. By assuming that at least the cortical areas of the visual system are included in the visual imagery system (Farah, 1988) we have a good idea about the neural location and functions of the visual imagery system. Moreover, these arguments can be extended to separate descriptive (or object) visual imagery from spatial imagery (Farah, Hammond, Levine, & Calvanio, 1988). Under this assumption, the neural substrate of imagery, like that of explicit memory and language, is not restricted to one small region of the brain but is spread over a large area with many identifiable subsystems.

What happens to people who make use of visual imagery throughout their lives, then suffer some trauma to the areas of posterior cortex that subserve it? Not all damage to visual cortex completely disrupts visual imagery. We therefore sought a subset of patients who could not access stored visual information. We were fortunate that this question had been addressed. Based on Kosslyn's (1980) detailed investigation of visual imagery, Farah (1984) developed a component model of visual imagery, which included a long-term visual memory for the store of visual information. To qualify as a case of *long-term visual memory loss*, the patient had to be able to (1) detect, draw, or describe the visual properties of an object that is present, demonstrating that their deficit did not stem from a motor or perceptual impairment, (2) demonstrate an inability to recognize an object on sight, by indicating either its name or its function; and (3) demonstrate an inability to draw an object from memory, although some stereotyped behaviors, like drawing simple shapes, were allowed. The first two criteria define associative visual agnosia; the last ensures that the problem is with the loss of memory of the visual information.

We tested our predictions by searching the literature for cases of long-term visual memory loss. We found 11 cases of long-term visual memory loss that met our three criteria (Rubin & Greenberg, 1998). Our results were striking. Of these 11 patients, all suffered from amnesia. That is, all suffered from a general loss in autobiographical memory that extended beyond visual memory to all areas of memory. Although medial-temporal damage (i.e., damage to the central explicit memory system) may have accounted for some of the memory loss in some of these cases, the reports of the location of neural insult and the pattern of behavioral deficits suggest otherwise; out of the 7 cases that described their patients' memory deficits in detail, 5 suffered from severe retrograde amnesia with more moderate anterograde deficits. Moreover, the temporal gradient was absent in the 4 cases in which it was described (see Rubin & Greenberg, 1998, for a fuller treatment of these cases). With damage to the explicit memory system, the normal pattern is of more severe anterograde amnesia with a sparing of childhood memories usually noted. These results are consistent with what would be expected from the loss of stored information severe enough to prevent the formation of a memory based on the information that remains. Thus to our great surprise (because the loss of visual information had not been summarized as a cause of a different kind or, for that matter, any kind of amnesia) but consistent with what would be expected in general from most models (e.g., McClelland et al., 1995; Schmajuk & DiCarlo, 1992) and from the analysis of specific cases (e.g., O'Connor, Butters, Miliotis, Eslinger, & Cermak, 1992; Ogden, 1993) a severe general amnesia occurred with visual memory loss.

From this reanalysis of existing cases we concluded that the visual imagery system, at least as measured by its loss with a visual memory deficit, is necessary for autobiographical memory and amnesia can occur in ways other than damage to the explicit memory system. It would be have been consistent with the behavioral data to find a loss in reliving without a complete loss in autobiographical memory with less severe visual memory loss, but we could not find such reports in the literature. Whether a loss of reliving could occur with less severe loss of visual imagery is an open question.

Language Loss

What would happen then with the loss of language? The classification of kinds of language loss, or aphasia, has been the subject of substantial debate. Among the many classifications of aphasia that can be made, the most important here makes the distinction between those aphasics who could produce language intelligible enough to have been tested and reported in the literature and those who could not. This exclusion is not for any logical or scientific reason but only because we could not find aphasics who were tested on autobiographical memory or on similar tasks using nonlinguistic means. The patients who could be tested were usually Broca's or nonfluent aphasics, who generally speak in short bursts of three or four words and who typically struggle to retrieve the proper word for a particular idea, or they were conduction aphasics, who suffer in part from a deficit of inner speech and lose the ability to "hear" words in their minds. The patients who could not be tested were usually severe cases of Wernicke's or fluent aphasia, who speak as fluidly and as easily as people without aphasia but pepper their speech with repetitions, neologisms, and irrelevant words.

The existing research indicates that aphasics manage to produce remarkably well formed autobiographical memories. We found two autobiographies written by aphasics (Luria, 1972; Wulf, 1979). Wulf's (1979) narrative begins with her memories of her stroke, then continues with her perspective on her impairment six years later; she repeatedly states that her speech impairment far outweighs any intellectual difficulties. Luria's patient Zasetsky produces thousands of pages of fluid, emotional narrative that describes his "shattered world" and his inability to use language in everyday life: "When a person has a serious head wound . . . he no longer understands or recognizes the meaning of words right away and cannot think of many words when he tries to speak or think" (Luria, 1972, p. 75). Even conduction aphasics do not typically manifest any major memory deficits; for example, E.B., a conduction aphasic, remembers his first day at the hospital and describes his sensations upon waking: "Began to see white and hear voices and hospital sounds and then could see nurse and young doctor above me, talking to me, asking me my name. Felt stunned, numb, and weak all over. Tried to move but nothing to move, tried to talk but could only make slurred sounds" (Levine, Calvanio, & Popovics, 1982, p. 394). Thus although aphasia can cause severe, obvious, and extensive changes to an affected patient's speech, if the patient is given a long time and a choice of modalities in which to record the memory aphasia does not necessarily prevent that patient from producing well-structured autobiographical memories. We therefore conclude that the loss of language in aphasia does not play a vital role in the encoding and retrieval of autobiographical memories. Aphasics who can find words and produce sentences slowly and with great effort produce coherent life stories with the same difficulty.

This broad statement comes with two caveats. First, we found no patients who suffered from a complete inability to use language in any modality. Therefore, none of the patients described earlier are analogous to the visual memory loss patients. If we could find such patients—and if we could find reliable, nonlinguistic ways of testing their autobiographical memories—we might uncover different results. Second is the rare form of aphasia known as semantic dementia, to which we can now turn.

One specific type of fluent aphasia presents an important exception to the generalization that aphasia causes only minor problems with autobiographical memory. A rare disorder known as semantic dementia, or progressive fluent aphasia (Hodges, 1992; Hodges, Patterson, Oxbury, & Funnell, 1992), often results in a severe impairment of autobiographical memory. Although perhaps better conceived as a disorder of semantic memory rather than of language, it is generally placed under the heading of a language disorder, as its most obvious effects are on the production and comprehension of language. Patients with this disorder suffer from a progressive anomia and loss of word comprehension, though their phonological and syntactical abilities are generally spared (Hodges, 1995); specifically, they suffer from a progressive loss of knowledge about the world (Graham, 1999). These patients manifest widespread damage to temporal neocortex, although the medial temporal structures of the explicit memory system generally appear intact, at least in the early stages of the disease (Graham & Hodges, 1997; Harasty, Halliday, Code, & Brooks, 1996). Here we follow the literature and assume most loss of memory is for the meaning of individual words.

Although early investigations suggested that the disorder spared episodic memory (Hodges et al., 1992), more recent work shows that semantic dementia may result in retrograde amnesia (Graham & Hodges, 1997; Hodges & Graham, 1998; Snowden, Griffiths, & Neary, 1996). Patients with semantic dementia performed near the level of controls when asked to retrieve recent memories but performed more poorly than even an Alzheimer's group when asked to retrieve early memories. A more detailed investigation of a single patient, who was given words and asked to produce a memory for each, yielded a similar result: the patient produced mainly superficial and impoverished memories, and most of the detailed, temporally located memories came from the two years prior to testing. Studies that attempt to separate a loss of autobiographical memory from a loss of recollection with a preservation of the facts of the autobiographical memory may be possible because semantic dementia does not produce a complete amnesia and is a progressive disease and so varies in severity.

On both a behavioral and neurobiological level, the deficits in semantic dementia patients parallel those with visual memory deficit amnesia. Patients with visual memory deficit amnesia can copy a drawing of an object, even if they cannot identify it; semantic dementia patients can repeat words, even if they no longer know what those words mean (Hodges et al., 1992). In semantic dementia, the presentation of a word no longer calls to mind its meaning; in visual memory deficit amnesia, the presentation of an object no longer calls to mind its meaning. Both disorders stem from neocortical pathology (of either the visual imagery or the language systems) in the absence of medial-temporal trauma to the explicit memory system; in both disorders, this damage results in the loss of information crucial to autobiographical memory; and in both disorders, the patients suffer retrograde amnesia with relatively mild anterograde deficits. The retrograde memory of semantic dementia patients is less severe, with a sparing of recent memories. This is opposite to the loss with damage to the central explicit memory system and may differ from the visual memory deficit loss only in degree. Overall, the contrast between minor loss in autobiographical memory functioning with most aphasia and major loss in autobiographical memory functioning with loss in the visual imagery system and with loss in semantic dementia is striking. Also striking is the parallel between loss in the visual imagery system and semantic dementia. Because semantic dementia does not affect primary sensory association cortices, our summary goes beyond the claims that such areas are necessary for recollection (Damasio, 1989) and offers a different interpretation. It appears that substantial amounts of stored information are necessary for recollection, whether or not they are sensory, because their loss removes information necessary to have the memory at all.

There exist two theoretical interpretations of the pattern of autobiographical memory deficits observed in semantic dementia. In the first interpretation the hippocampus is not involved in the recall of older memories (Graham, 1999; Graham & Hodges, 1997; Hodges & Graham, 1998), whereas in the second interpretation it is (Moscovitch & Nadel, 1999). In either case, both interpretations are consistent with the view presented here in that the loss that causes the retrograde amnesia is a loss in information stored in neocortex, that is, in information stored outside the explicit memory system. The extended consensus view presented here is neutral with respect to this debate in that either interpretation could be adopted as part of the consensus view of hippocampal function without affecting our discussion of what the rest of the brain is doing in autobiographical memory. One observation by Moscovitch and Nadel (1999) suggests another possible difference between semantic dementia and visual memory deficit amnesia and thus between the role of vision and semantic information. In visual memory deficit amnesia, the loss of visual information causes a loss of autobiographical memories that is often complete and thus does not depend on whether the stimulus used to cue the memory was visual or verbal. Moscovitch and Nadel mention a patient with semantic dementia who could not provide autobiographical memories to word cues but who could provide them to visual cues. Thus, for this patient, coactivation circuits could be maintained for at least some autobiographical memories when the initial cuing was not through the damaged system. It is not yet clear whether this difference is a matter of the severity of the damage or a fundamental difference between the role of language and the role of vision in autobiographical memory. Because Moscovitch and Nadel's patient could talk about the memories cued with pictures, however, it follows that nonlinguistic stimuli could activate stored semantic information.

The Sparing of Narrative Reasoning in Aphasia and Other Disorders

Before leaving the topic of aphasia, we need to emphasize the difference between a loss in language as defined by phonetics, syntax, and semantics and the loss of narrative reasoning. For this section we exclude semantic dementia because we could not find data on narrative reasoning for these patients. With few exceptions, aphasics' narrative reasoning abilities remain relatively intact. First, in spite of their clear difficulties with comprehension, aphasics frequently comprehend narratives at near-normal levels. When asked to retain narratives, aphasics frequently retain almost as much information as healthy controls (Hough, 1990; Wilcox, Davis, & Leonard, 1978); furthermore, both groups tend to remember the same elements, and properly identify themes and details (Stachowiak, Huber, Poeck, & Kerschensteiner, 1977). Context clues help aphasics overcome their comprehension deficits and allow them to understand and encode more information than they would if the data were presented in the form of distinct, individual sentences (Pierce & DeStefano, 1987; Wilcox et al., 1978). Aphasic patients performed at near-normal levels when the story text was combined with pictures (Huber & Gleber, 1982), a finding consistent with organization from imagery and narrative reasoning combining to compensate for losses in language. Consistent with these findings, standard tests of aphasia (which generally examine comprehension of phrases and sentences) do not reflect the patients' narrative abilities; for example, aphasics' paragraph comprehension scores do not correlate with their scores on the Boston Diagnostic Aphasia Examination and the Token Test, two standard tests of aphasia (Brookshire & Nicholas, 1984; Wegner, Brookshire, & Nicholas, 1984).

An analysis of aphasics' narrative production also reveals substantial preservation. On the surface, most aphasics' narratives again reflect their language impairments, manifesting severe problems with grammar and word retrieval (Freedman-Stern, Ulatowska, Baker, & DeLacoste, 1984). A closer examination, however, reveals that aphasics' narratives frequently preserve discourse structure. Aphasics retained an ability to judge relevance; like healthy subjects, they reported more relevant details than peripheral details (Ernest-Baron, Brookshire, & Nicholas, 1987). Fluent aphasics performed more poorly, manifesting a greater tendency to confabulate and embellish (Berko-Gleason et al., 1980; Glosser & Deser, 1990), though they still generally preserved narrative structure (Freedman-Stern et al., 1984). Thus, for one patient, M.A., "a detailed description of the language of this aphasic at a sentence and discourse level revealed preservation of discourse structure through proper use of cohesive devices despite severe disruption of linguistic structure at a sentence level" (Freedman-Stern et al., 1984, p. 181).

When aphasics do perform poorly on tasks that examine narrative structure, they tend to make errors of quantity, not quality (Freedman-Stern et al., 1984; Ulatowska, Freedman-Stern, Doyel, Macaluso-Haynes, & North, 1983). Aphasics typically manifest two deficits, both of which involve the loss of information: first, their stories are less complex than those of healthy subjects, and second, they include less information overall (Berko-Gleason et al., 1980; Ulatowska, North, & Macaluso-Haynes, 1981), though occasionally this effect is not significant (Ernest-Baron et al., 1987).

Fluent aphasics, that is, those who talk fairly easily in complete, seemingly syntactically correct sentences but include few content words, present the only exception to the quantity-versus-quality claim. On nearly every test of narrative ability, fluent aphasics perform more poorly than nonfluent aphasics do. Although some studies fail to separate their patients into these subcategories, those that do report that fluent aphasics generally confabulate more than either healthy subjects or nonfluent aphasics (Berko-Gleason et al., 1980). Thus our generalizations about narrative reasoning loss versus aphasia need to be tempered.

Not only is narrative reasoning not affected in most forms of aphasia; it is also difficult to disrupt in general. A wide range of populations, including those with affective disorder, Alzheimer's disease, closed head injury, developmental disabilities, Korsakoff's amnesia, language impairment, metabolic disorder, multi-infarct dementia, and schizophrenia, remember and forget the same parts of stories as do healthy controls. They may recall much less immediately after hearing a story and forget what they learned faster, but the parts of the story that are most and least likely to be remembered are the same (Bacon & Rubin, 1983; Rubin, 1985; Rubin, Olson, Richter, & Butters, 1981; Schultz, Schmitt, Logue, & Rubin, 1986). The robustness in the ability to appreciate narrative in the presence of other impairments helps isolate narrative reasoning from other aspects of behavior lost with these disorders.

Narrative Reasoning Loss

Narrative reasoning or, at least, the aspects of narrative reasoning that have been measured in the neuropsychological literature are exceedingly hard to disrupt. As just reviewed, they do not fail with most forms of localized brain damage, and this is one reason that it is hard to describe the effects of the loss of narrative reasoning. We searched in the neuropsychological literature for cases of patients who had lost narrative reasoning, or an aspect of it. We did not find studies of patients who were grouped together because their presenting behavioral symptom was a difficulty in narrative reasoning and then look for the location of the underlying damage, as we did with amnesia, agnosia, and aphasia. Rather, we found studies of patients who were grouped together because they had damage somewhere in large areas of the brain, studies that demonstrated that these patients tended to have deficits in aspects of what we are calling narrative reasoning. Another reason for the lack of studies of narrative reasoning loss rather than those of amnesia, agnosia, and aphasia appears when one considers what a severe, and therefore easy to measure, loss in narrative reasoning would imply. Consider a person who has difficulty in understanding complex stories, the nonliteral intent of a story, statement, or metaphor, and the likely emotional state of the protagonist. Such a person would be difficult to test. He or she might even be classified as demented, if we group narrative reasoning loss with other cognitive effects. Such a broadly described deficit is less likely to have a simple or localized cause, and thus it is less likely to lead to information about localization of function in the nervous system and less likely to be studied at all. Although there is a relative lack of studies, those that do exist are informative and point to some localization of function.

If narrative reasoning remains unimpaired in cases of aphasia and in many other clinical populations and so may be a function that can be lost in isolation, what is its neural basis? Both imaging studies (Bottini et al., 1994) and neuropsychological investigations (Goodglass, 1993) localize narrative abilities (at least in part) to the right hemisphere or the frontal lobes, although Wernicke's aphasics (who have left-hemisphere damage) do perform much like right-hemisphere patients (Freedman-Stern et al., 1984). Right-hemisphere patients manifest a series of deficits that reveal difficulty comprehending speech at the discourse level; though they retain the ability to speak "with appropriate phonology and syntax" (Goodglass, 1993, p. 147), they perform poorly on the sorts of judgments that narrative reasoning tasks require (but see Brookshire & Nicholas, 1984; Rehak et al., 1992, for conflicting views). Right-hemisphere patients frequently fail to judge the intent of nonliteral statements, and offer literal or nonsensical explanations (Brownell, Potter, & Bihrle, 1986; Wilcox et al., 1978). Along the same lines, right-hemisphere patients have substantial difficulty interpreting metaphors (Brownell, Simpson, Bihrle, Potter, & Gardner, 1990; Winner & Gardner, 1977) and drawing inferences from stories (Beeman, 1993), especially stories in which the utterances are literally false and require nonliteral interpretations (Kaplan, Brownell, Jacobs, & Gardner, 1990). Right-hemisphere patients also manifest a substantial impairment of their ability to organize and reorganize data. Hough (1990) showed that right-hemisphere patients had significant difficulty reproducing narratives when the theme was withheld to the end; left-hemisphere patients and healthy controls performed at ceiling levels, either because they were able to divine the theme or because they could hold the story information in memory and reorganize it after the theme was presented.

There may be one component of what we could consider narrative reasoning that might be separated behaviorally and neurally from the rest. The temporal order of autobiographical memory is a well-studied topic (Friedman, 1993; Larsen, Thompson, & Hansen, 1996). It appears that unlike many other aspects of autobiographical memory, the dating and sequencing of events is not an integrated property, like visual imagery or emotion, but rather is calculated using a variety of strategies (Brewer, 1996). Aspects of the relevant sequencing ability appear to be localized in the right parietal lobe (see Watson, 1994, for a review).

In short, right-hemisphere-damaged patients frequently lose their ability to appreciate context, presuppositions, affective tone, and the significance of the theme. Given the importance of these abilities to autobiographical memory, we might expect that their loss would induce at least some form of amnesia, but the studies of right-hemisphere patients do not report such deficits. The absence of such reports is significant in itself; if amnesia existed, it would almost certainly have been reported. However, these patients may often appear demented. Although the neural structures that subserve their memories might be intact, these patients might not be able to access those memories, and, if the memories are accessed, the patients might not be able to present them in a clear, coherent way. The difficulty in distinguishing between whether the memories can be retrieved but not communicated may contribute to the lack of reporting on autobiographical memory in the literature.

Frontal-lobe damage has clearer effects on autobiographical memory. Damage to the frontal lobes, particularly the right orbitofrontal regions, can lead to confabulations (Baddeley & Wilson, 1986; Moscovitch, 1995; Moscovitch & Melo, 1997; Schacter et al., 1998). Moscovitch (1989) has proposed a definition of confabulation that is adapted in part from Talland (1965); for our purposes, the following excerpt is most relevant:

> A confabulation is (a) typically, but not exclusively, an account, more or less coherent and internally consistent, concerning the patient. (b) This account is false in the context named and often false in details within its own context. (c) Its content is drawn fully or principally from the patient's recollection of his actual experiences, including his thoughts in the past. (d) Confabulation reconstructs this context, modifies and recombines its elements, employing the mechanisms of normal remembering. (e) This method is presented without awareness of its distortions or of its inappropriateness. (p. 134)

According to this definition, confabulations are (1) autobiographical; (2) inaccurate; (3) based upon actual memories, including memories of past thoughts (which may be inaccurately recalled as actual events); (4) cobbled together from data from disparate times; and (5) usually uttered without any awareness of their inaccuracy. Although confabulations do appear to be based on fragments of real experiences (Baddeley & Wilson, 1986; Moscovitch, 1989; Schnider, Gutbrod, Hess, & Schroth, 1996; Schnider & Ptak, 1999), some confabulations, occasionally called secondary confabulations, appear to be attempts to rationalize implausible statements that the patient has already made (Moscovitch, 1989).

Confabulating patients appear to be impaired on some but not all of Habermas and Bluck's (2000) four components of autobiographical reasoning. First, confabulators clearly have difficulty preserving the *temporal sequence* of their autobiographical memories, as they may combine statements from the past and the present when they are talking about their current lives; for example, they may state that they got married four months ago and then claim that they have four children over the age of 20 (Moscovitch, 1989). Because of this tendency, the confabulators' autobiographical memories may contain inaccurate or implausible *causal sequences*. They generally seem untroubled by the absence of causal coherence in their narratives; however, if their attention is called to their errors, they may engage in secondary confabulations in an attempt to restore this missing causal structure. Thus they may still be able to weave together a possible (if implausible and inaccurate) story from the discontinuous memories they have retrieved. It is unclear whether the *thematic coherence* of their narratives is affected; however, if confabulators generate inconsistent, erroneous, disorganized memories, it will likely be difficult for them to identify common themes among those elements.

We can now return to the question of the relation of narrative reasoning and language. Can narrative reasoning be seen as part of language? In the light of the information reviewed here, this seems to be a definitional problem. If you are a linguistic imperialist, all levels of structure used to produce coherent text can be seen as language. Under this view, however, phonetics, syntax, semantics, and narrative reasoning must be seen as partially separable components that can each be used for their own purposes without the others.

Discussion

There is much to be gained by integrating over levels of analysis and therefore over the disciplines that try to understand those levels. Such integration was a driving force in the formation of disciplines such as cognitive science in the 1960s and more recently of cognitive neuroscience. Here the goals have been more modest. We tried to take a particular problem, the role of narrative reasoning in recollection, and see what could be gained from an attempt at integrating the psychological and neuropsychological literatures. In doing this, we started with the view that recollection and even narrative reasoning might have widely distributed neural bases in the brain. Brain-imaging technologies tend to find the most active area or areas for each task and thus focus on a narrow localization. Here we tried to go against this trend and emphasize the distributed neural basis of cognitive functions, something that holds for integrated behaviors as "simple" as naming an object (Watson, Welsh-Bohmer, Hoffman, Lowe, & Rubin, 1999) and as global as the changes that accompany aging (Rubin, 1999).

Where does this view of recollection and narrative reasoning leave us? First, it makes sense in terms of behavior and underlying biology to view autobiographical memory as an integration of at least a handful of distinct skills, processes, or systems, of which narrative reasoning is just one. Second, if systems with a physical basis in the brain are taken as the main metaphor, then we gain a good deal of knowledge from neuroscience and especially from deficits in behavior that come with neural damage. Third, by reviewing published studies of neural damage in people in the context of what we already knew about behavior in people without such damage we found (1) that the loss of information, either visual or semantic, produces amnesia that extends beyond the modality of loss, (2) that the loss of language ability that results in the laborious production of speech results in the laborious production of autobiographical memories but little other loss, and (3) that narrative reasoning loss is separate from other kinds of language loss and its effects on autobiographical memory remain to be studied.

There are dangers and concerns with this approach. We do not want to replace the reification "autobiographical memory" with the reification of a handful of systems and do no more than this. In addition, our existing definitions of imagery, language, narrative, and memory must be renegotiated to integrate the information from all levels; the behavior alone, or the neuroscience alone, cannot define such terms if the approach used here is to be fruitful. Of most concern is the potential to lapse into a reductionist view of concepts such as imagery, language, and narrative, which are cultural or social products as well as neural ones. This concern holds for most concepts in psychology. But this is especially salient for the terms of interest here, which are central to the transmission of culture.

But what of the prospects of understanding narrative, a key concept that integrates this volume? Here we are in a much more primitive state than we are in other areas. We see two main reasons for this that have different implications for future work. First, it is not at all clear that what we are calling narrative reasoning is a unified function at the behavioral or neural level. We were unable to find studies that show that a loss in one of the measures that we are using as an indicator of narrative reasoning is accompanied by a loss in others. If we could describe which indicator tasks fail or are spared in the same patients, some basic classification could begin. A clear theory of narrative reasoning at the behavioral level would be a great aid in formulating such indicator tasks. The combination of having neither a behavioral nor neuropsychological theory or classification makes the investigation more difficult but does indicate what work could be done. We need a set of possible functions that we would consider to be part of narrative reasoning. Next we need to see if these functions or subsets of them fail or are spared in the same patients. To do this correctly requires that the tasks formulated to test the functions be graded in difficulty so that the difficulty of the task itself, independent of any narrative reasoning function, does not determine the results. Such work is common in many areas of psychology, but it is technically difficult.

Second, narrative reasoning may be more widely distributed in redundant ways in the brain than the other systems studied and so may just be less likely to be damaged unless there is diffuse and substantial brain damage, damage that would produce a host of symptoms unrelated to narrative. If different aspects of narrative reasoning evolved in different epochs and partially overlaid existing aspects that were in other brain structures (a common view in brain evolution), then this might occur. A way to study this would be to ask what behaviors in other species look like aspects of what would be considered narrative reasoning in people. If this is the state of nature, it will be more difficult for the approach tried in this chapter to produce knowledge about the localization of narrative reasoning, because the role of partially redundant subsystems will have to be understood.

But even with the paucity of findings on what aspects of narrative reasoning go together behaviorally and on the localization of its neural substrates, much has been learned by just asking the question of how narrative reasoning would fit into a behavioral and neural theory of recollection. We have noted gaps in our knowledge of the biological basis of autobiographical memory. We have made a distinction between and offered support for two kinds of systems. First are systems where damage causes a loss in autobiographical memory for events (and thus for recollection) that extends well beyond what would be expected by damage to the system itself (e.g., visual memory deficit amnesia and semantic dementia). Second are systems where damage causes a loss that does not extend beyond the system (e.g., most aphasias). The neuropsychological data do not exist to allow us to ask which kind of system best describes narrative reasoning, and neither the neuropsychological nor the behavioral data indicate whether narrative reasoning includes its own store of information.

We have provided evidence to support the usefulness of viewing memories as distributed across systems and retrieved by activating their component information at the same time. Under this view, narrative reasoning could just be another system or it could be central to the frontal lobe component of the explicit memory system as a guiding organization used in retrieval searches (but see Rubin, 1999, for some complications). The localization of narrative reasoning is ambiguous enough to allow either interpretation. Most important, we have tried to demonstrate that combing the neuropsychological and behavioral evidence on recollection reveals possibilities and limits speculation in ways that neither can do alone. With recent technological advances that allow localization of damage in patients to be known more accurately and that allow the localization of activation in various tasks in people without any known damage, more information about the neural basis of human behavior is becoming available. For research on autobiographical memory and recollection, the relative role of the brain as a metaphor is shrinking in relation to the role of the brain as physical entity about which a great deal is known. Sophisticated behavioral descriptions and analyses of complex behaviors such as narrative reasoning will be needed if information from these technologies is to be of use to questions like those raised in this chapter and in the rest of this volume.

References

Bacon, E., & Rubin, D. C. (1983). Story recall in mentally retarded children. *Psychological Reports, 53*, 791–796.

Baddeley, A. D. (1986). *Working memory*. Oxford: Oxford University Press.

Baddeley, A. D. (1992). What is autobiographical memory? In M. A. Conway, D. C. Rubin, H. Spinnler, & W. A. Wagenaar (Eds.), *Theoretical perspectives on autobiographical memory* (pp. 13–29). Dordrecht, The Netherlands: Kluwer Academic Publishers.

Baddeley, A. D., & Wilson, B. (1986). Amnesia, autobiographical memory, and confabulation. In D. C. Rubin (Ed.), *Autobiographical memory* (pp. 225–252). Cambridge: Cambridge University Press.

Bakker, E. J. (1988). *Linguistics and formulas in Homer*. Amsterdam: John Benjamins.

Bakker, E. J. (1993). Discourse and performance: Involvement, visualization and "presence" in Homeric poetry. *Classical Antiquity, 12*, 1–29.

Barclay, C. R. (1986). Schematization of autobiographical memory. In D. C. Rubin (Ed.), *Autobiographical memory* (pp. 82–99). Cambridge: Cambridge University Press.

Barclay, C. R. (1996). Autobiographical remembering: Narrative constraints on objectified selves. In D. C. Rubin (Ed.). *Remembering our past: Studies in autobiographical memory* (pp. 94–125). Cambridge: Cambridge University Press.

Barclay, C. R., & Smith, T. S. (1992). Autobiographical remembering: Creating personal culture. In M. A. Conway, D. C. Rubin, H. Spinnler, & W. A. Wagenaar (Eds.), *Theoretical perspectives on autobiographical memory* (pp. 75–97). Dordrecht, The Netherlands: Kluwer Academic Publishers.

Beeman, M. (1993). Semantic processing in the right hemisphere may contribute to drawing inferences from discourse. *Brain and Language, 44*, 80–120.

Bell, B. E., & Loftus, E. F. (1989). Trivial persuasion in the courtroom: The power of (a few) minor details. *Journal of Personality and Social Psychology, 56*, 669–679.

Berko-Gleason, J., Goodglass, H., Obler, L., Green, E., Hyde, M. R., & Weintraub, S. (1980). Narrative strategies of aphasic and normal-speaking subjects. *Journal of Speech and Hearing Research, 23*, 370–382.

Bluck, S., & Li, K. Z. H. (in press). Predicting memory completeness and accuracy: The role of emotion and exposure in repeated recall. *Applied Cognitive Psychology.*

Bottini, G., Corcoran, R., Sterzi, R., Paulesu, E., Schenone, P., Scarpa, P., Frackowiak, R., & Frith, C. (1994). The role of the right hemisphere in the interpretation of figurative aspects of language: A positron emission tomography activation study. *Brain, 117,* 1241–1253.

Brewer, W. F. (1980). Literary theory, rhetoric, stylistics: Implications for psychology. In R. J. Spiro, B. C. Bruce, & W. F. Brewer (Eds.), *Theoretical issues in reading comprehension* (pp. 221–239). Hillsdale, NJ: Erlbaum.

Brewer, W. F. (1996). What is recollective memory? In D. C. Rubin (Ed.), *Remembering our past: Studies in autobiographical memory* (pp. 19–66). Cambridge: Cambridge University Press.

Brookshire, R. H., & Nicholas, L. E. (1984). Comprehension of directly and indirectly stated main ideas and details in discourse by brain-damaged and non-brain-damaged listeners. *Brain and Language, 21,* 21–36.

Brown, R., & Kulik, J. (1977). Flashbulb memories. *Cognition, 5,* 73–99.

Brownell, H. H., Potter, H. H., & Bihrle, A. M. (1986). Inference deficits in right brain–damaged patients. *Brain and Language, 27,* 310–321.

Brownell, H. H., Simpson, T. L., Bihrle, A. M., Potter, H. H., & Gardner, H. (1990). Appreciation of metaphoric alternative word meanings by left and right brain–damaged patients. *Neuropsychologia, 28,* 375–383.

Bruner, J. (1986). *Actual minds, possible worlds.* Cambridge, MA: Harvard University Press.

Bruner, J., & Feldman, C. F. (1996). Group narrative as a cultural context of autobiography. In D. C. Rubin (Ed.), *Remembering our past: Studies in autobiographical memory* (pp. 291–317). Cambridge: Cambridge University Press.

Buckner, R. L. (1996). Beyond HERA: Contributions of specific prefrontal brain areas to long-term memory retrieval. *Psychonomic Bulletin & Review, 3,* 149–158.

Carruthers, P. (1996). *Language, thought, and consciousness: An essay in philosophical psychology.* Cambridge: Cambridge University Press.

Chafe, W. (1982). Integration and involvement in speaking, writing and oral literature. In D. Tannen (Ed.), *Spoken and written language: Exploring orality and literacy* (pp. 35–53). Norwood, NJ: Ablex.

Chafe, W. (1990). Some things that narratives tell us about the mind. In B. K. Britton & A. D. Pellegrini (Eds.), *Narrative thought and narrative language* (pp. 79–98). Hillsdale, NJ: Erlbaum.

Colegrove, F. W. (1899) Individual memories. *American Journal of Psychology, 10,* 228–255.

Conway, M. A. (1995). *Flashbulb memories.* Hillsdale, NJ: Erlbaum.

Conway, M. A. (1996). Autobiographical knowledge and autobiographical memories. In D. C. Rubin (Ed.), *Remembering our past: Studies in autobiographical memory* (pp. 67–93). Cambridge: Cambridge University Press.

Conway, M. A., & Pleydell-Pearce, C. W. (2000). The construction of autobiographical memories in the self-memory system. *Psychological Review, 107,* 261–288.

Conway, M. A., & Rubin, D. C. (1993). The structure of autobiographical memory. In A. E. Collins, S. E. Gathercole, M. A. Conway, & P. E. Morris (Eds.), *Theories of memory* (pp. 103–137). Hove, Sussex: Erlbaum.

Damasio, A. R. (1989). Time-locked multiregional retroactivation: A systems-levels proposal for the neural substrates of recall and recognition. *Cognition, 33,* 25–62.

Damasio, A. R. (1994). *Descartes' error: Emotion, reason, and the human brain.* New York: G. P. Putnam's Sons.

Ericsson, K. A., & Simon, H. A. (1993). *Protocol analysis: Verbal reports as data* (Rev. ed.). Cambridge, MA: MIT Press (Bradford Books).

Ernest-Baron, C. R., Brookshire, R. H., & Nicholas, L. E. (1987). Story structure and retelling of narratives by aphasic and non-brain-damaged adults. *Journal of Speech and Hearing Research, 30,* 44–49.

Farah, M. J. (1984). The neurological basis of mental imagery: A componential analysis. *Cognition, 18,* 245–272.

Farah, M. J. (1988). Is visual imagery really visual? Overlooked evidence from neuropsychology. *Psychological Review, 95,* 307–317.

Farah, M. J., Hammond, K. M., Levine, D. N., & Calvanio, R. (1988). Visual and spatial mental imagery: Dissociable systems of representation. *Cognitive Psychology, 20,* 439–462.

Fitzgerald, J. M. (1988). Vivid memories and the reminiscence phenomenon: The role of a self narrative. *Human Development, 31,* 261–273.

Fitzgerald, J. M. (1992). Autobiographical memory and conceptualizations of the self. In M. A. Conway, D. C. Rubin, H. Spinnler, & W. A. Wagenaar (Eds.), *Theoretical perspectives on autobiographical memory* (pp. 99–114). Dordrecht, The Netherlands: Kluwer Academic Publishers.

Fitzgerald, J. M. (1996). Intersecting meanings of reminiscence in adult development and aging. In D. C. Rubin (Ed.), *Remembering our past: Studies in autobiographical memory* (pp. 360–383). Cambridge: Cambridge University Press.

Fitzgerald, J. M., & Lawrence, R. (1984). Autobiographical memory across the lifespan. *Journal of Gerontology, 39,* 692–699.

Fivush, R., Haden, C., & Reese, E. (1996). Remembering, recounting, and reminiscing: The development of autobiographical memory in social context. In D. C. Rubin (Ed.), *Remembering our past: Studies in autobiographical memory* (pp. 341–359). Cambridge: Cambridge University Press.

Freedman-Stern, R., Ulatowska, H. K., Baker, T., & DeLacoste, C. (1984). Disruption of written language in aphasia: A case study. *Brain and Language, 23,* 181–205.

Freeman, M. (1993). *Rewriting the self: History, memory, and narrative.* London: Routledge.

Friedman, W. J. (1993). Memory for the time of past events. *Psychological Bulletin, 113,* 44–66.

Gergen, K. J., & Gergen, M. M. (1988). Narrative and the self as relationship. *Advances in Experimental Social Psychology, 21,* 17–56.

Glosser, G., & Deser, T. (1990). Patterns of discourse production among neurological patients with fluent language disorders. *Brain and Language, 40,* 67–88.

Goodglass, H. (1993). *Understanding aphasia.* New York: Academic Press.

Graham, K. S. (1999). Semantic dementia: A challenge to the multiple-trace theory? *Trends in Cognitive Sciences 3,* 85–87.

Graham, K. S., & Hodges, J. (1997). Differentiating the roles of the hippocampal complex and the neocortex in long-term memory storage: Evidence from the study of semantic dementia and Alzheimer's disease. *Neuropsychology 11,* 77–89.

Habermas, T., & Bluck, S. (2000). Getting a life: The emergence of the life story in adolescence. *Psychological Bulletin, 126,* 748–769.

Harasty, J. A., Halliday, G. M., Code, C., & Brooks, W. S. (1996). Quantification of cortical atrophy in a case of progressive fluent aphasia. *Brain, 119,* 181–190.

Hirst, W. (1982). The amnesic syndrome: Description and explanations. *Psychological Bulletin, 91,* 435–460.

Hirst, W., & Manier, D. (1996). Remembering as communication: A family recounts its past. In D. C. Rubin (Ed.), *Remembering our past: Studies in autobiographical memory* (pp. 271–290). Cambridge: Cambridge University Press.

Hodges, J. (1992). Exploring disorders of semantic memory. In L. C. Cermak (Ed.), *Neuropsychological explorations of memory and cognition: Essays in honor of Nelson Butters* (pp. 77–94). New York: Plenum.

Hodges, J. (1995). Retrograde amnesia. In A. D. Baddeley, B. A. Wilson, & F. N. Watts (Eds.), *Handbook of memory disorders* (pp. 81–107). Oxford, England: Wiley.

Hodges, J. R., & Graham, K. S. (1998). A reversal of the temporal gradient for famous person knowledge in semantic dementia: Implications for the neural organisation of long-term memory. *Neuropsychologia, 36,* 803–825.

Hodges, J. R., Patterson, K., Oxbury, S., & Funnell, E. (1992). Semantic dementia: Progressive fluent aphasia with temporal lobe atrophy. *Brain, 115,* 1783–1806.

Hough, M. S. (1990). Narrative comprehension in adults with right and left hemisphere brain-damage: Theme organization. *Brain and Language, 38,* 253–277.

Huber, W., & Gleber, J. (1982). Linguistic and nonlinguistic processing of narratives in aphasia. *Brain and Language, 16,* 1–18.

Johnson, M. K., Hashtroudi, S., & Lindsay, D. S. (1993). Source monitoring. *Psychological Bulletin, 114,* 3–28.

Johnson, M. K., & Raye, C. L. (1981). Reality monitoring. *Psychological Review, 88,* 67–85.

Kaplan, J. A., Brownell, H. H., Jacobs, J. R., & Gardner, H. (1990). The effects of right hemisphere damage on the pragmatic interpretation of conversational remarks. *Brain and Language, 38,* 315–333.

Kintsch, W., & Van Dijk, T. A. (1975). Recalling and summarizing stories. *Languages*, *40*, 98–116.

Kosslyn, S. M. (1980). *Image and mind*. Cambridge, MA: Harvard University Press.

Larsen, S. F. (1988) Remembering without experiencing: Memory for reported events. In U. Neisser & E. Winograd (Eds.), *Remembering reconsidered: Ecological and traditional approaches to the study of memory* (pp. 326–355). Cambridge: Cambridge University Press.

Larsen, S. F., Thompson, C. P., & Hansen, T. (1996). Time in autobiographical memory. In D. C. Rubin (Ed.), *Remembering our past: Studies in autobiographical memory* (pp. 129–156). Cambridge: Cambridge University Press.

Levine, D. N., Calvanio, R., & Popovics, A. (1982). Language in the absence of inner speech. *Neuropsychologia*, *20*, 391–409.

Lucy, J. A. (1992). *Language diversity and thought: A reformulation of the linguistic relativity hypothesis*. New York: Cambridge University Press.

Luria, A. R. (1972). *The man with a shattered world*. New York: Basic.

Marschark, M., Richman, C. L., Yuille, J. C., & Hunt, R. R. (1987). The role of imagery in memory: On shared and distinctive information. *Psychological Bulletin*, *102*, 28–41.

Mayes, A. R., & Downes, J. J. (1997). What do theories of the functional deficit(s) underlying amnesia have to explain? *Memory*, *5*, 3–36.

McClelland, J. L., McNaughton, B. L., & O'Reilly, R. C. (1995). Why there are complementary learning systems in the hippocampus and neocortex: Insights from the successes and failures of connectionist models of learning and memory. *Psychological Review*, *102*, 419–437.

Miller, P. J., & Sperry, L. L. (1988). Early talk about the past: The origins of conversational stories of personal experiences. *Journal of Child Language*, *15*, 293–315.

Mishkin, M., & Appenzeller, T. (1987, June). The anatomy of memory. *Scientific American*, *256*, 80–89.

Moscovitch, M. (1989). Confabulation and the frontal systems. In H. L. Roediger & F. I. M. Craik (Eds.), *Varieties of memory and consciousness: Essays in honour of Endel Tulving* (pp. 133–160). Hillsdale, NJ: Erlbaum.

Moscovitch, M. S. (1995). Models of consciousness and memory. In M. S. Gazzaniga (Ed.), *The cognitive neurosciences* (pp. 1341–1356). Cambridge, MA: MIT Press.

Moscovitch, M., & Melo, B. (1997). Strategic retrieval and the frontal lobes: Evidence from confabulation and amnesia. *Neuropsychologia*, *35*, 1017–1034.

Moscovitch, M., & Nadel, L. (1999). Multiple-trace theory and semantic dementia: Response to K. S. Graham. *Trends in Cognitive Sciences*, *3*, 87–89.

Neisser, U. (1967). *Cognitive psychology*. New York: Appleton-Century-Crofts.

Neisser, U. (1982). Snapshots or benchmarks? In U. Neisser (Ed.), *Memory observed*. (pp. 43–48). San Francisco: Freeman.

Nelson, K. (1993). The psychological and social origins of autobiographical memory. *Psychological Science*, *4*(1) 7–14.

Nyberg, L., Cabeza, R., & Tulving, E. (1996). PET studies of encoding and retrieval: The HERA model. *Psychonomic Bulletin & Review, 3,* 135–148.

O'Connor, M., Butters, N., Miliotis, P., Eslinger, P., & Cermak, L. (1992). The dissociation of anterograde and retrograde amnesia in a patient with herpes encephalitis. *Journal of Clinical and Experimental Neuropsychology, 14,* 159–178.

Ogden, J. A. (1993). Visual object agnosia, prosopagnosia, achromatopsia, loss of visual imagery, and autobiographical amnesia following recovery from cortical blindness: Case M.H. *Neuropsychologia, 31,* 571–589.

Paivio, A. (1971). *Imagery and verbal processes.* New York: Holt, Rinehart & Winston.

Paivio, A. (1986). *Mental representations: A dual coding approach.* New York: Oxford University Press.

Paivio, A. (1991). Dual coding theory: Retrospect and current status. *Canadian Journal of Psychology, 45,* 255–287.

Pierce, R. S., & DeStefano, C. C. (1987). The interactive nature of auditory comprehension in aphasia. *Journal of Communication Disorders, 20,* 15–24.

Pillemer, D. B. (1992). Remembering personal circumstances: A functional analysis. In E. Winograd & U. Neisser (Eds.), *Affect and accuracy in recall: Studies of "flashbulb" memories* (pp. 236–264). Cambridge: Cambridge University Press.

Pillemer, D. B. (1998). *Momentous events, vivid memories: How unforgettable moments help us understand the meaning of our lives.* Cambridge, MA: Harvard University Press.

Pillemer, D. B., Desrochers, A. B., & Eubanks, C. M. (1998). Remembering the past in the present: Verb tense shifts in autobiographical memory narratives. In C. P. Thompson, D. J. Herrmann, D. Bruce, J. D. Reed, D. G. Payne, & M. P. Toglia (Eds.), *Autobiographical memory: Theoretical and applied perspectives* (pp. 145–162). Mahwah, NJ: Erlbaum.

Pillemer, D. B., Picariello, M. L., Law, A. B., & Reichman, J. S. (1996). Memories of college: The importance of specific educational episodes. In D. C. Rubin (Ed.), *Remembering our past: Studies in autobiographical memory* (pp. 318–337). Cambridge: Cambridge University Press.

Popov, Y., & Rokhlin, L. (n.d.). *I. P. Pavlov, psychopathology and psychiatry: Selected works* (D. Myshne & S. Belsky, Trans.). Moscow: Foreign Languages Publishing House.

Rehak, A., Kaplan, J., Weylman, S., Kelly, B., Brownell, H., & Gardner, H. (1992). Story processing in right-hemisphere brain-damaged patients. *Brain and Language, 42,* 320–336.

Robinson, J. A. (1976). Sampling autobiographical memory. *Cognitive Psychology, 8,* 578–595.

Robinson, J. A. (1981). Personal narratives reconsidered. *Journal of American Folklore, 94,* 58–85.

Robinson, J. A. (1996). Perspective, meaning, and remembering. In D. C. Rubin

(Ed.), *Remembering our past: Studies in autobiographical memory* (pp. 199–217). Cambridge: Cambridge University Press.

Robinson, J. A., & Swanson, K. L. (1993). Field and observer modes of remembering. *Memory, 1,* 169–184.

Roediger, H. L., III. (1980). Memory metaphors in cognitive psychology. *Memory & Cognition, 8,* 231–252.

Rubin, D. C. (1980). 51 properties of 125 words: A unit analysis of verbal behavior. *Journal of Verbal Learning and Verbal Behavior, 19,* 736–755.

Rubin, D. C. (1985). Memorability as a measure of processing: A unit analysis of prose and list learning. *Journal of Experimental Psychology: General, 114,* 213–238.

Rubin, D. C. (1992). Definitions of autobiographical memory. In M. A. Conway, D. C. Rubin, H. Spinnler, & W. A. Wagenaar (Eds.), *Theoretical perspectives on autobiographical memory* (pp. 495–499). Dordrecht, The Netherlands: Kluwer Academic Publishers.

Rubin, D. C. (1995a). *Memory in oral traditions: The cognitive psychology of epic, ballads, and counting-out rhymes.* New York: Oxford University Press.

Rubin, D. C. (1995b). Stories about stories. In R. S. Wyer Jr. (Ed.), *Knowledge and memory: The real story* (pp. 153–164). Hillsdale, NJ: Erlbaum.

Rubin, D. C. (1998). Beginnings of a theory of autobiographical remembering. In C. P. Thompson, D. J. Herrmann, D. Bruce, J. D. Reed, D. G. Payne, & M. P. Toglia (Eds.), *Autobiographical memory: Theoretical and applied perspectives* (pp. 47–67). Mahwah, NJ: Erlbaum.

Rubin, D. C. (1999). Frontal-striatal circuits in cognitive aging: Evidence for the caudate. *Aging, Neuropsychology, and Cognition, 6,* 241–259.

Rubin, D. C., & Greenberg, D. L. (1998). Visual memory-deficit amnesia: A distinct amnesic presentation and etiology. *Proceedings of the National Academy of Sciences, 95,* 5413–5416.

Rubin, D. C., & Kozin, M. (1984). Vivid memories. *Cognition, 16,* 81–95.

Rubin, D. C., Olson, E. H., Richter, M., & Butters, N. (1981). Memory for prose in Korsakoff and schizophrenic populations. *International Journal of Neuroscience, 13,* 81–85.

Rubin, D. C., Schrauf, R. W., & Greenberg, D. L. (2000). *Remembering, reliving, and believing autobiographical memories: Inter- and intra-individual analyses.* Unpublished manuscript, Duke University, Durham, NC.

Rubin, D. C., & Schulkind, M. D. (1997). Distribution of important and word-cued autobiographical memories in 20-, 35-, and 70-year-old adults. *Psychology and Aging, 12,* 524–535.

Rumelhart, D. E., & Norman, D. A. (1986). Representation in memory. In R. C. Atkinson, R. J. Herrnstein, G. Lindzey, & R. D. Luce (Eds.), *Steven's handbook of experimental psychology: Vol. 2. Learning and cognition* (2d ed., pp. 511–587). New York: Wiley.

Schacter, D. L. (1996). *Searching for memory: The brain, the mind, and the past.* New York: Basic.

Schacter, D. L., Norman, K. A., & Koustaal, W. (1998). The cognitive neuroscience of constructive memory. *Annual Review of Psychology, 49,* 289–318.

Schafer, R. (1981). Narration in the psychoanalytic dialogue. In W. J. T. Mitchell (Ed.), *On narrative* (pp. 25–49). Chicago: University of Chicago Press.

Schank, R. C., & Abelson, R. P. (1995). Knowledge and memory: The real story. In R. S. Wyer Jr. (Ed.), *Knowledge and memory: The real story* (pp. 1–85). Hillsdale, NJ: Erlbaum.

Schmajuk, N. A., & DiCarlo, J. J. (1992). Stimulus configuration, classical conditioning, and hippocampal functioning. *Psychological Review, 99,* 268–305.

Schnider, A., Gutbrod, K., Hess, C., & Schroth, G. (1996). Memory without context: Amnesia with confabulations after infarction of the right capsular genu. *Journal of Neurology, Neurosurgery, and Psychiatry, 61,* 186–193.

Schnider, A., & Ptak, R. (1999). Spontaneous confabulators fail to suppress currently irrelevant memory traces. *Nature Neuroscience, 2,* 677–680.

Schrauf, R. W., & Rubin, D. C. (1998). Bilingual autobiographical memory in older adult immigrants: A test of cognitive explanations of the reminiscence bump and the linguistic encoding of memories. *Journal of Memory and Language, 39,* 437–457.

Schrauf, R. W. & Rubin, D. C. (2000). Identification of internal languages of retrieval: The bilingual encoding of memories for the personal past. *Memory & Cognition, 28,* 616–623.

Schultz, K. A., Schmitt, F. A., Logue, P. E., & Rubin, D. C. (1986). Unit analysis of prose memory in clinical and elderly populations. *Developmental Neuropsychology, 2,* 77–87.

Shepard, R. N. (1978). The mental image. *American Psychologist, 33,* 125–137.

Skinner, B. F. (1974). *About behaviorism.* New York: Knopf.

Snowden, J. S., Griffiths, H. L., & Neary, D. (1996). Semantic-episodic memory interactions in semantic dementia: Implications for retrograde memory function. *Cognitive Neuropsychology, 13,* 1101–1137.

Spence, D. P. (1982). *Narrative truth and historical truth: Meaning and interpretation in psychoanalysis.* New York: Norton.

Squire, L. R. (1987). *Memory and brain.* New York: Oxford University Press.

Squire, L. R. (1992). Memory and the hippocampus: A synthesis from findings with rats, monkeys, and humans. *Psychological Review, 99,* 195–231.

Squire, L. R., & Knowlton, B. (1995). Memory, hippocampus, and brain systems. In M. Gazzaniga (Ed.), *The cognitive neurosciences* (pp. 825–837). Cambridge, MA: MIT Press.

Stachowiak, F. J., Huber, W., Poeck, K., & Kerschensteiner, M. (1977). Text comprehension in aphasia. *Brain and Language, 4,* 177–195.

Talland, G. A. (1965). *Deranged memory.* New York: Academic Press.

Tulving, E. (1983). *Elements of episodic memory.* Oxford: Oxford University Press.

Ulatowska, H. K., Freedman-Stern, R., Doyel, A. W., Macaluso-Haynes, S., & North, A. J. (1983). Production of narrative discourse in aphasia. *Brain and Language, 19,* 317–334.

Ulatowska, H. K., North, A. J., & Macaluso-Haynes, S. (1981). Production of narrative and procedural discourse in aphasia. *Brain and Language, 13*, 345–371.

Watson, M. E. (1994). *Object and spatial subsystems in mental imagery: Behavioral investigations.* Unpublished doctoral dissertation, Duke University, Durham, NC.

Watson, M. E., Welsh-Bohmer, K. A., Hoffman, J. M., Lowe, V., & Rubin, D. C. (1999). The neural basis of naming impairments in Alzheimer's disease revealed through positron emission tomography. *Archive of Clinical Neuropsychology, 14*, 347–357.

Wegner, M. L., Brookshire, R. H., & Nicholas, L. E. (1984). Comprehension of main ideas and details in coherent and noncoherent discourse by aphasic and nonaphasic listeners. *Brain and Language, 21*, 37–51.

Wheeler, M. A., Stuss, D. T., & Tulving, E. (1997). Toward a theory of episodic memory: The frontal lobes and autonoetic consciousness. *Psychological Bulletin, 121*, 331–354.

Whorf, B. L. (1956) *Language, thought, and reality: Selected writings of Benjamin Lee Whorf.* Cambridge, MA: MIT Press.

Wilcox, M. J., Davis, G. A., & Leonard, L. B. (1978). Aphasics' comprehension of contextually conveyed meaning. *Brain and Language, 6*, 362–377.

Winner, E., & Gardner, H. (1977). The comprehension of metaphor in brain-damaged patients. *Brain, 100*, 717–729.

Winograd, E., & Neisser, U. (Eds.) (1992). *Affect and accuracy in recall: Studies of "flashbulb" memories.* New York: Cambridge University Press.

Wulf, H. H. (1979). *Aphasia, my world alone.* Detroit: Wayne State University Press.

Yates, F. A. (1966). *The art of memory.* Chicago: University of Chicago Press.

5 Material Selves: Bodies, Memory, and Autobiographical Narrating

Sidonie A. Smith

As my medical tests become more invasive, I am confronted with a material selfhood heretofore invisible to me. These continuous reminders of the materiality and interiority of my body challenge the ways that I have been used to thinking about my "self" as a fairly disembodied subject.
— Kay K. Cook, "Medical Identity: My DNA/Myself"

Not surprisingly, in the recall of such events, I referred to myself as "you." This was because "you" logically captured my relationship to myself. One develops an "I" in interaction with "the world." Donna didn't interact; the characters did. . . . I reverted to using "I" in a conforming effort to avoid [the therapist's] pedantic emphasis on the pronouns I was using. Her efforts to get me to refer to these incidents in a personal manner overlooked the fact that my use of "you" captured the impersonal way in which I had experienced the incidents at the time they happened. She probably felt that she had to help me to overcome my depersonalization, as though this were some recently developed defense reaction. I don't think she realized that I had actually experienced life this way since the creation of Willie and Carol, and my subsequent ability to communicate through them, thirteen years before.
— Donna Williams, *Nobody Nowhere: The Extraordinary Autobiography of an Autistic*

A self must have a past.
— Donna Williams, *Somebody Somewhere: Breaking Free from the World of Autism*

I begin with a simple point. Memory has a history, and so, too, the "knowledge" of memory. Historians, such as Frances A. Yates (1966) in *The Art of Memory*, have explored the conceptualization of memory at particular historical moments. As they've done so, they have considered what was understood to be in need of remembering as well as the practices of remembering within specific cultural contexts. Yates, for instance, looks at the role that mnemonics, the study of techniques of remembering, played from the classical era through to the early modern period in Europe. During this long period of mnemonic instruction, memory manuals offered guidance for remembering significant amounts of material, and, later, memory palaces provided visual metaphors for a veritable house of recall. Yet the radical expansion of the domain of knowledge during the early modern period brought with it anxiety about the possibility of remembering everything that needed to be remembered. Amnesia loomed, a threat to an ordered world and an ordered intelligence. The printed book came along just in time, providing a whole new mode of artificial remembering. Memory palaces collapsed. Mnemonics as a requisite for learning, authoritative leadership, and informed rule faded into the past.

As the philosopher Ian Hacking (1995) reminds us, however, mnemonics was a "knowing how." Always outer-directed and focused on the accumulation of data, it was not about the subject doing the remembering or invested in the remembering of one's own experiential history as a story of one's past and one's own person. In his provocative study of the history of the diagnosis of multiple personality, *Rewriting the Soul*, Hacking argues that with the medical diagnosis of double consciousness in the mid–nineteenth century the notion of some essential, biologically secured relationship between memory and personality emerged. This new field, the psychodynamics of memory, emerged alongside two other sciences of memory in the latter half of the nineteenth century. Neurological studies of the location of different types of memory—the Broca studies—mapped the brain as a spatial structure. Experimental studies of recall, associated with Ebbinghaus, pondered memory's temporally based how-to practices. It is the increasingly complex studies of subjectivity and memory that Hacking explores in detail, offering an extended historical narrative of the theory building of Janet on double consciousness and of Freud on repressed memories. Both pioneers in the study of embodied subjects take as their projects the production of knowledge about the relationship of remembering and a personal past understood as identity (selfhood) and psychodrama.

But why is it that these sciences of memory became such intense sites of scientific attention at this precise historical moment in the West? Granted each of the three sciences attempt to produce knowledge about the person (as material site, as set of behaviors, as marked by psychic trauma). But all this Hacking calls "surface knowledge" (p. 199). He's after the depth knowledge of the age, the underlying logic that supports this quest for surface knowledge. He concludes that the depth knowledge being pursued has to do with the cultural belief that "there is a body of facts about memory to be known" (p. 200), that there is something hidden that scientists must get to and reveal, and that the something hidden is the self or soul. The soul, wrested in the course of the nineteenth century from religion, gets turned over to science. "There could be no science of the soul," he writes: "So there came to be a science of memory" (p. 219).

Hacking calls this depth knowledge "memoro-politics," the politics of the human soul. "Memoro-politics," he writes, "is above all a politics of the secret, of the forgotten event that can be turned, if only by strange flashbacks, into something monumental. . . . We are concerned less with losing information than with hiding it. The background for memoro-politics is pathological forgetting" (p. 214). Against the threat of personal amnesia, the sciences of memory hurry to map, track, and heal the remembering subject. This is a third domain of politics that Hacking introduces to complicate and refine Michel Foucault's (1980) elaboration of two sites of politics in the nineteenth century—anatomo-politics (the politics of the human body) and bio-politics (the politics of the human population).

Material Selves

Memoro-politics continues to drive our journeys into the secret recesses of persons. Throughout the twentieth century, the sciences of memory took us deeper and deeper into the secret interior of the organism in order to discover/uncover the secret of the soul—even unto the subatomic level. As Hacking notes, two more sciences of memory emerged in the middle of the twentieth century: cell biology, the stuff of neuroscience; and computer modeling, the stuff of artificial intelligence. And each of these contemporary penetrations, each contemporary theory of the materiality of memory, projects a notion of material "selfhood."[1]

I am fascinated by the kinds of selves that can be extrapolated from current theories of the materiality of remembering. So I'd like to consider here, albeit only sketchily, the material selves of contemporary scientific theory.

Quantum Selves

Arguing that quantum physics must affect all of matter and thus the very materiality of the human organism, Danah Zohar (1990) elaborates a theory of the "self" as a quantum phenomenon (*The Quantum Self*). Through her analysis of the principal features of quantum physics—the wave/particle duality (that several possible realities coexist) and contextualism (that quantum reality shifts according to its surroundings)—Zohar stresses that indeterminacy is an inherent characteristic of quantum reality. Along with other physicists, among them Roger Penrose (*The Emperor's New Mind*, 1989), she argues that these indeterminate quantum structures constitute the brain; and she locates those quanta in bose-einstein condensates that activate neurons. Drawing parallels between the phenomena of quantum systems and the workings of the brain system leads her to find a material basis for the unity of consciousness that we understand as the self and our sense of free will. Speculating that the brain may embody three kinds of processing systems—serial processing or rational thinking, parallel processing that works by association, and quantum thinking— Zohar speculates that quantum structures create the sense of ourselves as holistic centers of perception. Of course there is much to critique in Zohar's discussion: her argument by analogy from quantum physics to quantum consciousness; her argument about the unity of consciousness and what she describes as the coherent person; the slippery links she asserts between fluid subjectivity and quantum material such as bose-einstein condensates. But there is also something intriguing in this attempt to think about the materiality of consciousness in new ways.

Genomic Selves

The culmination of the Genome Project and the circulation of discourses of genomics throughout the scientific and lay communities mean that we are forging new understandings of memory and destiny that now circulate through our bodies, as species and familial legacy. Braided in the material language of the genes, the self becomes a composite of genes and junk (as the scientists so inelegantly call the material that is not gene but necessary to the binding of genes in the chromosome). While scientists early on thought of the genetic material as a "blueprint" for the future of each human being, they are now redefining genetic material as a kind of "parts list" for the organism (with the realization that there are far fewer genes than originally projected—somewhere around thirty-one thousand rather than the fifty to one hundred thousand first estimated). As with the earlier metaphor of blueprint, the parts list functions as a set of future life scripts—material and narrative—encoded despite our awareness of them. They are histories that lie in material wait. And so the materiality of memory becomes a phenomenon of the future as well as a legacy of past materiality. Our genetic coding becomes a kind of intransigent memory, though with the experiments in genetic engineering this embodied memory will become increasingly open to reconstruction and rearrangement. New futures will become the effects of genetic dismembering, and selves will become malleable as surgeons of the interior's deepest recesses rearrange our futures away from our pasts. Perhaps the very processes of remembering will be remembered. In effect, as Kay K. Cook (1996) cautions in her exploration of "my DNA/myself," the self becomes material whose future needs will be "repair" (p. 64).

Neural Selves

Discourses of neural networks propose consciousness as the product of electrical ignitions across synapses. Here at the cellular level synaptic charges lay down tracks of memories for cueing to consciousness at a later time. Thus the neural system, distributed across the brain, forms a capacious and intricately interlocking holdall of possible memories. In his introduction to a special issue of *a/b: Auto/Biographical Studies* on autobiography and neuroscience, Thomas Smith (1998) notes that the new understanding of memory from neuroscience has produced three foundational premises: "Memories are distributed in many areas of the brain; these areas work together in varying ways to produce different kinds of memories; and memories are ever changing because they are reconstituted in different ways each time one remembers" (p. 2). Within neuroscience, however, there are distinct, sometimes radically divergent, sometimes overlapping, theorizings of the self as neural network, only one of which I take up here.

In his commitment to healing the mind–body split that is the legacy of the Enlightenment cogito by elaborating a neurobiology of rationality, Antonio R. Damasio has developed what he calls "the somatic marker hypothesis." Rethinking how rationality works, Damasio (1994) argues that rationality can only function effectively if it is accompanied by "an automated alarm signal" (based on processes of secondary emotions) that "drastically reduces the number of options" or outcomes of a decision (p. 173). In other words, emotions cannot be kept distinct from rational thinking; they must be understood as constitutive of rational thinking. Somatic markers, "feelings generated from secondary emotions," are linked through cognitive learning to representations of possible futures or outcomes, futures and outcomes that encode social conventions and modes of survival (p. 174). According to Damasio, somatic markers are aspects of the neural regulatory system evolved to ensure survival through which we understand ourselves as stable selves with subjective experience. This neural basis of the self depends upon two interlocking sets of representations: "representations of key events in an individual's autobiography, on the basis of which a notion of identity can be reconstructed repeatedly, by partial activation in topographically organized sensory maps," and "primordial representations of an individual's body . . . encompass[ing] background body states and emotional states" (p. 239). Here the self becomes a doubly mapped system of somatic markers ever in process.

Connectionist Selves

In a deconstructionist reading of cognitive theory that seeks to dislodge the hold of the computer model of cognition, Elizabeth A. Wilson (1998) argues for the connectionist understanding of remembering and knowing. PDP—parallel distributed processing—becomes for her a mode of understanding cognition that avoids the pitfalls of the politics of location in computer-based models of cognition. The problem Wilson identifies in various computer-modeling theories is the problem of a "where" to memory. Precisely where can it be found? For Wilson there is no where to the memory trace. "The trace," she suggests

> is no longer a preexisting and inert packet of information to be transformed by a universal cognitive machine. Consequently, the distinction between the connectionist trace and the connectionist architecture becomes incoherent, and the connectionist trace becomes breaching—both structure and trace, both the force that forges a track and the space that such a force discloses. (p. 195)

The trace and the architecture for remembering are mutually inextricable. The connectionist self becomes a kind of postmodern processing unit in which location and mobility are co-determinant.

The Multiply Material Subject

All of these theorists/scientists are after the secret of the organism, though they might not describe themselves as such. In their search for that secret they propose, implicitly or explicitly, theories of "self." Or, at the least, they tell stories about the self. Taken cumulatively, these multiple theories would give us a portrait of the self as multiply materialized. At the level of the subatomic particle there is the quantum self, constituted by the indeterminacy of the wave/particle function. At the level of the protein, there is the genomic self, a set of chemical prescriptors. At the systems level, there is the neural network self or the connectionist self. All of these selves are materially activated and materially enacted. All of these selves are in process, configuring and reconfiguring in constant mobility—of quanta, of genomic combinations, of neural nets and connections. Such theories suggest to us how malleable, how plastic, how responsive the material of our bodies might be to our lived experience in the world. Or to be more precise, they give us metaphors through which to understand the materiality of the self in new ways. As Paul John Eakin (1999) so provocatively explores in his recent book, *How Our Lives Become Stories: Making Selves,* they offer ways of understanding how it is that we have a sense of ourselves as bodies in space and a sense of ourselves as selves with identity stories in the world (p. 11).[2]

But how do we have an experience in the world that we understand as "ours" to narrate?

Selves to Narrate

Eakin explores in some detail recent work in neuroscience and cognitive and developmental science that suggests how it is that we become storied selves. He does so in order to think through the relationship between identity and stories, between healthy selves and healthy stories. Here I offer a far more truncated mapping of the relationship of material selves and stories, one designed to emphasize the cultural situatedness of the storied selves we become.[3]

In *White Gloves,* John Kotre (1996) offers a way of understanding the synchronous multitasking of remembering. Positing remembering as a process of meaning making and, as such, interactional, dialogic, and contextual, he proposes a hierarchy of memory, with singular events at the bottom and thematic trends in remembering higher up. As people remember (their own histories, their own past) they shift from level to level, from specific events to general statements about who they are. He goes on to explore how singular events get coded into the neurological system, in particular vivid memories. Vivid memories, he argues, have four features: they break a script, they are consequential, they often involve emotional charge, and they have symbolic value for the person remembering (pp. 93–94). The particular kind of symbolic value he is interested in here has to do with memories that are self-defining. Self-defining memories become so because they link the themes in a particular episode to already available themes of the self.

To clarify this synchronous process, Kotre proposes the figure of the self as "interpreter"—"the system of neuronal structure in the left hemisphere that monitors and synthesizes activity throughout the brain and tries to make sense of it" (p. 111). He suggests that we might understand this self as "the totalitarian ego" that remembers itself as at the center of things. Then he distinguishes two opposing elements in "the interpreter's" remembering: archival storage and self-mythmaking—the librarian element and the mythmaking element. "The remembering self, both as keeper of archives and as maker of myth," he concludes, "fashions a remembered self. *I* establishes *me*" (p. 118). With the notion of the fashioning of a self, of mythmaking, Kotre points to the absolute necessity of learning to tell stories of ourselves.

If Kotre offers ways of understanding how the brain system materializes as storytelling, cognitive and developmental psychologists explore how this narrating self comes into being. Katherine Nelson (1993), for instance, looks at the ways in which children learn to tell autobiographical narratives. Nelson adds "autobiographical" memory to the two common kinds of memory cognitive scientists talk about—generic event memory and episodic memory. She wants to understand "when and why an autobiographical system—in which some memories are retained for a lifetime—becomes differentiated from a general episodic system" (p. 7). Using a social interactionist model, Nelson claims that some memories "become valued in their own right—not because they predict the future and guide present action, but because they are shareable with others and thus serve a social solidarity function" (p. 12). Through social interaction with adults, children learn how to narrate their memories, what memories are valued, what stories of memories can be told. Nelson claims as well that these occasions of social interaction reinstate certain memories as significant. For her, children begin to "remember" in this way in the late preschool years. Thus autobiographical memory becomes possible with the achievement of certain linguistic skills—the familiarity with narrative. While Nelson doesn't pursue the ways in which this autobiographical memory system is socially constructed through interaction, her theory, based on a social interactionist model, enables this understanding of memory. We might say, then, that as autobiographical memory à la Nelson emerges, the child learns complex narrative forms—in terms of the agents of the narrative, the action in the narrative, the emotional valence of the narrative, the ideological context of the narrative, the mode of presentation, and the appropriate forms of address.

Nelson offers a way of understanding the temporally based origins of autobiographical storytelling. Roger C. Schank (1990) offers a way of understanding how our repertoire of stories becomes our sense of self. Resisting the distinction between semantic memory and episodic memory so commonly elaborated in the psychological literature, Schank argues instead for a distinction between event-based memory (storehouse or semantic memory) and story-based memory. Schank understands memories as a product of stories. "The stories we tell time and again," he concludes, "are identical to the memory we have of the events that the story relates" (p. 115). Particularly interested in the ways in which memories get disconnected over time and then reconnected, he suggests that "stories are a way of preserving the connectivity of events that would otherwise be disassociated over time" (p. 124). Our repertoire of stories thereby becomes "ourselves" to the extent that changing our stories changes our memories and our understanding of who we are, who we have been, who we will be.

If the materiality of our bodies makes it possible for us to tell stories about ourselves, to make selves in the telling, the very stories that we tell in turn

become the lives that we live and the material bodies that we are. In his influential essay, "Life as Narrative," Jerome Bruner (1987) claims that "we seem
to have no other way of describing 'lived time' save in the form of narrative"
and that "the mimesis between life so called and narrative is a two-way affair
. . . just as art imitates life . . . so life imitates art" (p. 12). Upon these two
theses he makes his central point about bodies, selves, and stories:

> Eventually the culturally shaped cognitive and linguistic processes that
> guide the self-telling of life narratives achieve the power to structure
> perceptual experience, to organize memory, to segment and purpose-
> build the very "events" of a life. In the end, we become the auto-
> biographical narratives by which we "tell about" our lives. And given
> the cultural shaping to which I referred, we also become variants of
> the culture's canonical forms. (p. 15)

Bruner probes beyond the simplistic formula that autobiographical memories
are turned into stories to argue that the relationship between autobiographical
memory and storytelling is mutually constitutive. The stories people use to
tell about their lives in turn shape the memories that are encoded as significant
(at both the individual and the generic levels that Kotre [1996] defines) and
thus the very materiality of our bodies. Thus narrative is identity is embodiment is narrative.

Autistic Embodiment and Autobiography

I want to bring together, in a reading of a particular narrative, the disparate
threads I've tried to weave through this all too sketchy meditation on materiality and narrative. I raised the complexity of the relation of materiality to
autobiographical storytelling in an essay I wrote (Smith, 1996) titled "Taking
It to a Limit One More Time: Autobiography and Autism." In that essay I
tried to tease out the implications of differently embodied subjectivity for narrative practices, specifically the limit of autobiography and autism.[4] Here I
want to return to that essay and elaborate on the intersectionality of materiality, memory, and narrative in Donna Williams's (1992) Nobody Nowhere:
The Extraordinary Autobiography of an Autistic.

Clinical psychologists have delineated a repertoire of physical and linguistic
behaviors they now gather together under the diagnosis of "autistic." Autistic
persons have difficulty with spoken language; they often echo the words of
others; they respond erratically to sensory stimuli; they display repetitive behaviors that can become obsessive; they fixate on objects for long periods of
time; they become emotionally and physically unsettled with unexpected
changes in environment; they retreat into a private "inner" world distant from

"the social world"; they have difficulty relating emotionally to other people.[5] These behaviors are symptoms, visible to the world, which in the gaze of the clinician are read off the body as signs of "abnormal" development. Behaviors thus become the descriptive and predictive script of an "autistic," who becomes the signified to which these signifiers point. "Autism" is a system of signs that point to a condition of difference. In a sense, then, the person diagnosed as autistic is assigned an autistic subjectivity and with it is provided an auto- or, more precisely a biographical script.

The gathering of this system of behavioral markers under the diagnostic sign "autism," rather than their dissipation in a larger field of heterogeneous markers termed *mental illness* or *mental retardation*, only took place in the mid–twentieth century when Leo Kanner (1943) coined the term *autism*. Since the identification of this specific condition and the consolidation of its discourse within clinical psychology, several generations of clinicians/experts have attempted to locate the "cause" or "origin" of these effects by probing further into the recesses of the autistic subject.[6] In the 1950s, clinicians proceeded to theorize the observational data on the basis of a "widespread belief in the psychogenic origin of childhood behavior disorders," a belief generated through a particular understanding of the relationship of the visible to the invisible (Rimland, 1965, p. 19). The behavioral, linguistic, and emotional differences of an autistic subject could only be accounted for in the unconscious nested deep within the subject. Thus the unintelligible condition of the autistic was explained (or rationalized) through a psychoanalytic frame of knowledge that traced dysfunctional conditions back to dysfunctional family relationships. But more particularly, the dysfunctional relationship was identified as the relationship of the child to an "unnatural" mother who refused to hold and nurture the infant adequately. The autistic subject was a subject of an inadequate pre-Oedipal relationship.

This explanation of origins, produced through the powerful cultural metaphor of psychoanalysis, has gradually been displaced by another explanatory model. Out of the research of neurophysiologists, a consensus has emerged in the clinical community that biochemical and neuroanatomical abnormalities in brain development cause persons diagnosed as autistic to be "oblivious to many of the social cues and to the constant stream of cause-and-effect sequences that give coherence and meaning to normal experience"; finding it difficult to process the information pressing upon them from the world, they experience life "as an incoherent series of unconnected events" (Bartak, 1992, p. xi). Neurons do not fire properly, and so the network does not transmit information in an effective form to an appropriate destination. Interruptions in internal processing units at the cellular level generate interruptions in the processing of exterior information at the level of consciousness. The brain, a complex processing unit, becomes dysfunctional. With this explanation researchers press even further into the recesses of the individual, now the cellular and subcellular recesses, and even further within the genetic coding of the double helix. The differences of the autistic person are the differences of genetic coding.[7]

This explanatory model constructs an everyday autistic subject along the following lines: The subjectivity of the autistic becomes a condition of surfeit, what we might call the surfeit of aporia: information-processing units cannot find the right way out for the transmission of messages. Everywhere there are excessive gaps in continuities and meanings. As a result the very materiality of the body, the materiality at the end of nerves and in the neurochemistry of the brain, the materiality that generates a processing system, interrupts an autistic person's efforts to assemble meaning through narratives. In effect the neurophysiological model consigns autistics to an unautobiographical life. Multiple gaps in message transmissions force a limit to/of everyday autobiography, frustrating efforts to get a narrative based on memory fragments together at all or to manipulate the story and its meanings in coherent and recitable narratives. Perhaps then autistics remain outside the linguistic, narrative, and communal circuits of autobiographical telling, unautobiographical subjects who cannot get the message into the narrative "life" in our everyday sense of the term. Biology/physiology would seem to outprocess or unprocess autobiography in a communication landscape traversed by processing units run amok.

"Narrowing in" on the microcellular causes of autism has been facilitated by the increasingly sophisticated processes through which researchers use computers to map localized response centers in the brain. (It has also been facilitated by the large amounts of funding provided by pharmaceutical companies with their own interests in supporting explanatory theories that lead to biologically based intervention strategies.) In this way, a new technology generates a new metaphor through which the unintelligibilities of an autistic subject can be comprehended, can be known in order to be treated, can be bio-graphed. The geneto-biography gets written in cellular and subcellular codings, and bioengineering becomes the strategy for intervention and cure.

However sophisticated the mappings of the brain as a composite of localized response centers might become, what exactly constitutes consciousness, in this case autistic consciousness, has thus far eluded the experts. The consciousness of the autistic subject remains a matter of speculation to clinicians. In this sense it is what some contemporary philosophers call secondness—"the materiality that persists *beyond* any attempt to conceptualize it" (Cornell, 1992, p. 1).[8] At this limit of the elusive and unknowable, the discourses of science can only invoke metaphor. An autistic subject can be conceived or known only through representations. So "autism" is itself a metaphor through which the differences of an unknowable subjectivity, in getting a (clinical) name, become culturally intelligible—and intelligible in historically precise ways within historically situated institutional settings. "Autism" becomes a metaphor through which experts can construct everyday "biographies" of different subjects with the hope and desire of making them over into "normal" subjects.

Persons diagnosed with severe autism often neither construct nor communicate an account of their experiential history. In this way they do not appear to get together an "I" and a "you" through which to develop a concept of a narrative subject and a narrative life. Autistics, then, in all their differences, throw out of kilter everyday expectations that all people assume themselves to be "I"s and situate themselves in various locations through their personal storytelling. They remain subjects for whom autobiographical narrating does not become an everyday practice. This silence that displaces personal storytelling disrupts the everyday activities through which people engage in the building of families and communities. And in this lack of speaking, as well as emotional bonding, lies so much of the profound pain and suffering experienced in real lives around them.

If autistics remain forever silent of speech or only become occasionally communicative through mimetic utterances, then they might in one sense be said to remain subjects outside discourse, subjects culturally uninscribed. From one point of view, an autistic subject seems to navigate through life in the midst of an acultural space, in which there is little to no subjection to/in language and discourse. Uninscribed by the subjectivities provided to persons through the everyday operations of power/knowledge, they seem to inhabit an elsewhere beyond the limit. But, of course, we cannot know them to be or not to be such subjects, because as such subjects they do not speak. We cannot know whether or not the scrambling of the means of perception of the world scrambles the technologies of selfhood that surround the autistic subject.

What we are told by high-functioning autistics who have been able to speak reflexively and to communicate with the world is that they in part imitate life through a kind of mechanical or rote mimesis of "scripts." "Mirroring, as with the matching of objects," reflects Donna Williams in *Nobody Nowhere* (1992), "was my way of saying: 'Look, I can relate. I can make that noise, too' " (p. 209). But the mimicry goes beyond words as autistics watch others for markers of appropriate performances of selfhood, developing scripts for everyday living through a personal glossary of appropriate responses. In an interview with Temple Grandin, whose narrative of autism she titles *Emergence, Labeled Autistic* (Grandin with Scarriano, 1996), Oliver Sacks (1995) reports that Grandin explained to him that

> she had built up a vast library of experiences over the years. . . . They were like a library of videotapes, which she could play in her mind and inspect at any time—"videos" of how people behaved in different

circumstances. She would play these over and over again and learn, by degrees, to correlate what she saw, so that she could then predict how people in similar circumstances might act. She had complemented her experience by constant reading . . . all of which enlarged her knowledge of the species. (p. 112)

High-functioning or recovering autistics apparently learn by rote the technologies of selfhood—the self-identifications, the narratives, the behaviors, the emotional scripts—through which people in their culture make sense of the world and themselves. They learn to program themselves to "perform" as "normal" human beings, the kind of human beings their culture expects them to be.

But if they perform as human beings what does that performance reveal about the dynamics of autistic consciousness? What must be performed since it is not felt or experienced? This slight misalignment of performance and experiential history both reveals and conceals a particular kind of difference. And it points to the gap between believing oneself to be a culturally intelligible subject and recognizing that identities are performative in a most dramatic sense. And to what extent and degree is this performance the same as or different from the performance of selfhood generated unconsciously in childhood? Are we not then brought to another limit, the technologies of technologies of selfhood?

A closer consideration of Donna Williams's *Nobody Nowhere: The Extraordinary Autobiography of an Autistic* (1992) gives us an opportunity to pursue these striking questions.

In this first of three memoirs, Williams struggles at the limits of narratability, since, as noted earlier, autistic consciousness might be understood as a site of un/memory. Williams tells her reader that autistics communicate through the compulsive ordering of things and through imitative and repetitive sound, a language indeed but a language at the limits of comprehensibility for those in the world. But there is little to no communication through narrative remembering, at least not of narrative in what she calls "the world's" wording.

I enter her narrative through a passage late in the text where she is describing her travels in Europe. She describes how, having suddenly decided to go see the ocean, she boards a train and sits alone in a compartment. A man sits across from her. And for three hours the two strangers "sat there, nervous, exposed, and embarrassed. . . . swapping trivia, talking via objects and events, and losing our self-awareness in the evasive jargon and complexity of the poetrylike speech that so often got our listeners lost" (p. 167). When the train comes into a particular station, the man tells Williams, "You can get off here if you want." She describes how "though afraid, I made a last-minute decision and jumped off the train as it ground to a halt" (p. 167). He invites her into his world, if obliquely; she gets off the train to enter into his world, if fearfully. In the time they spend together, Williams finds herself communicating with a stranger who understands her speech, her body language, her emotional reticence. The narrator specifies this moment as an initiatory moment of healing: she survives the "feeling" of this emotional connection and finds herself "beginning to win the battle" over her dissociated alternative personalities.

Williams has already presented "Carol" and "Willie" as "depersonalized, communicative, worldly versions of myself that were able to sound out people and environments for a self that could not cope with things of such complexity" (p. 134). These "alters" emerged as strategic means to survive everyday living, as strategic rhetorical addresses to the world. Carol enables her to engage with the world through scripts of normality. She is the sociable, voluble address to the world. Willie enables her to protect herself from the onslaught of antagonistic forces. He is the resilient, tough, combative address to the world. Isolated specialists, these versions of self take on the attributes of rigidly organized personalities, unified around a set of repetitive postures, behaviors, emotions. (In her second memoir, *Somebody Somewhere: Breaking Free from the World of Autism*, Williams describes her alters as "stored mirrored repertoires" [1994, p. 45].)

Here with this stranger from the train, "Donna"—the name the narrator assigns her "secret" self—"was not fighting to mirror someone else. She was fighting to come out to someone who was *her* mirror" (p. 170). "Donna" reads her "own language" in the discomfort, indirection, shyness, and physical withdrawal the stranger displays before her. Recognizing the repertoire of communicational affects she understands as her profound difference from others, "Donna" risks disclosing her "unaltered" self rather than retreating into a more functional version of herself such as "Carol," whose job it has been to perform as a normal person in the world. Glimpsing sameness in this mirror, Williams feels compelled to seek the source of this lingua franca of difference in the past. This search for the source of identity in difference requires an intentional act of remembering. For the narrator this moment in the railway compartment is epiphanic. In effect, this stranger (Shaun) becomes a virtual memory of Donna Williams, the embodied memory of the other inside her. This glimpse of something inside her that she reads off the body of the other requires that she remember this otherness inside, the otherness that comes to the present through the traces of the intrusive past.

Two strangers, Williams writes, "understood each other." It is her struggle to understand what it meant to understand Shaun, to understand what they "shared in common," that motivates Williams to enter the memory museum. I am using this metaphor purposefully here. A museum conjures up an archival space filled with objects that hold memories in disembodied place. And this is the system of memory Williams has described as her way of carrying the past with her. She carries objects, what she calls "treasures," with her in a trunk. It is to these treasures that she anchors memories. They become, she tells us, "the keys to myself" (p. 21). "For me, the people I liked *were* their things, and those things (or things like them) were my protection from the things I didn't like—other people" (p. 6). But this is a display case of memory objects, not a portmanteau of memory narratives. She can organize her relationships to her life by arranging and rearranging these objects of memory; but the effects of such ordering are limited in terms of connecting her to "the world" of people.

The remembering she would do at this point is narrative remembering, narrative remembering that in its very utterance is a sign of symbolic interaction with others. (Even in its limited utterance, that is, its address to herself, her narrative remembering signals a positing of an interlocutor.) "I began with the center of my world as far back as I could remember. The nights got longer as one page rolled into the next and I relived each moment, staring straight ahead and letting the words come from my fingers" (p. 187). There's a tremendous investment here in the sheer act of strenuous concentration on remembering—which she conjures up with the phrase "staring straight ahead." Staring ahead into space, the rememberer reconnects with the intrusive past in order to find the hidden (or secret) otherness of and in the past.

The second scene I take up focuses on one poignant and complicated moment of remembering in Williams's narrative, one that involves scene making inside of scene making. Williams describes how, several years before the time of narration, she sought out her aunt "who had been a regular visitor to the house during my early childhood" (p. 128) to find out what her aunt knew about her past. She thus solicits her aunt as a curator of and in her memory museum. She does so because she finds herself, after two years of therapy, "vulnerable to . . . ghostly reminders of a self that had been buried long ago but refused to die" (p. 128). In therapy Williams glimpses something that does not go away, which she identifies as her originary or "true" self. The "self" here is posited as a kind of subconscious origin, excessive to "Carol" and "Willie," the two faces of her address to the world.

The narrator tells us it is "Willie" who participates in the remembering her aunt shares with her: "Willie stood there remembering many of these, but did so without any feeling for the self who had experienced them." "Willie"'s remembering is without affect. It is memory outside emotional investment. It is, in effect, memory outside autobiographical subjectivity. But there is one memory that provokes a different response. The narrator recalls that "it triggered something, and my mind replayed it in all its vividness and horror." In the narrative past it is not "Willie" who is remembering at this point. The narrator assigns this remembering to the hidden or ghostly self, "Donna," whom she identifies as "I." This "I" finds herself in the midst of the vivid scene of being beaten with a cord while her mouth is stuffed with a dishcloth: "I was choking as I vomited up against it" (p. 130). This "I" remembers (visualizes) as well that all along her aunt has been present but silent in response to her mother's violent abuse. Here the narrating subject has remembered a remembering subject who feels an emotional, an embodied response to the past. Then the narrator continues: "There was a rising choke of vomit in my throat and a deafening scream inside my head that couldn't get out. Willie glared at my aunty, and the stifled tears had not even made it to his eyes. In a calm, hard, and stilted voice Willie had asked why she had done nothing" (p. 130). "Willie" reasserts public control by admonishing the aunt through his unemotional, antagonistic stance.

The narrator recalls this critical scene in which memory is simultaneously disembodied and embodied. Unable to make a social connection with others because of her estranged condition, Williams redirects memory into alters with their own styles of the body. "Carol" and "Willie" embody her generic memory scripts for dealing with the world, as sociable, as combative. They are part of her imitative system, her performativity in the world. In this way Williams has negotiated the world through objectifications of her alters as sites of memory. And memory itself has functioned as an otherness, encoded in the bodily affects of "Willie" and "Carol." This redirection of her exchanges with the world into "Willie" (and "Carol") also has the effect of dissociating Williams from the very body she inhabits.

In this scene the narrator reconstructs the dynamics of dissociation, the way in which Willie forestalls emotion and pain by assuming a combative stance to the world. Embodied emotional affects, which would inflect autobiographical memory with its potency, contextual valence, and meaning, are erased through the screen of "Willie" (see Damasio, 1994, p. 159). "Willie" takes her memories away from her in order to keep her invulnerable to the world. But the narrator also reveals the failure of "Willie" to control the context of exchange with the world. Something in excess of "Willie" feels the pain of the memory. The implication here is that Donna contains "Willie" in memory; but "Willie" does not contain Donna. In the act of pronouncing dissociation, the narrator locates the beginnings of recovery.

But this is not the end of this scene of remembering. Williams goes on to describe how she escapes from the room and her aunt and wanders "like an automaton" around the house until she comes to a room filled with her childhood furniture, since passed on to her cousin. Then she continues:

> Against the other wall was the wardrobe—the wardrobe in which
> Carol had left me behind. I held my breath in front of it. I ran my
> fingers along the pattern of the wardrobe door's handle. I was afraid
> and felt as though I was being swept up in a sort of magic. The magic

of childhood. I opened the door and got in. In the darkness, closing the door behind me, I sat down and curled up in a ball.

After awhile I got out of the cupboard and left the room in a hurry. I left my aunty's house like a cornered rat that had suddenly found a way out. I had begun to touch upon the answers to what was missing. I went home, curled up in a ball, and rocked for three days. (p. 131)

The way out, she implies, is the way back to the figure of the child withdrawn into the cupboard, to "Donna." Climbing back inside the cupboard of her childhood she enacts, through the commonly presented symptom of people diagnosed as autistic, the experience of having shut herself in, having tucked her secret self away, in order to participate through "Carol" and "Willie" in the world. Her search through memory for the past is the search for the secret self, the otherness inside, the "secret" feeling self she says she has kept hidden from the world. The cupboard, a material object in her past, functions here as an object in her memory museum. Through it she can take herself bodily back into the past, to the time when "Carol" "had left me behind" in order to enter "the world."

The narrator remembers this moment as a reentry into her body, a body she early on externalized as something "with a mind of its own." The reentry into the body is as critical to this narrator as the recovery of memory (of and through emotion), since material embodiment, memory, and subjectivity join in an autobiographical system. Remembering, and narrating those memories, enables Williams to claim an embodied "I" who does the remembering, an "I" who remembers "Donna" and "Carol" and "Willie" outside of the externalizations of "Carol" and "Willie." It becomes a means through which Williams can put virtual things, in this case memories, in their place and thereby order her world and order her relationship to "the world."

Now let me return to the passage where Williams refers to her writing project. After her last contact with Shaun she tells us she "bought a cheap plastic typewriter" and started to recall her past: "I was searching inside myself for a word for what I had shared in common with Shaun. As the pages mounted up, so did my visits to the library, where I buried my head in books on schizophrenia and searched desperately to find a sense of belonging within those pages that would give me a word to put to all of this" (p. 187). At various points in her narrative Willliams notes the way she took up particular discourses with which to put actions in her past under a new description, particularly the history of her antagonistic relationship with the world, her "them" versus "us" orientation. She develops a class analysis after taking a sociology class. At this stage, she recalls, "the idea of social class became my primary, more impersonal way of accounting for my feelings of 'them' and 'us' "

(p. 118). After studying psychology she uses the diagnosis of schizophrenia to give her an entrance into the memory museum. In part this diagnostic label seems promising because Williams has internalized the world's identification of her as crazy, mad, or retarded as the truth of her difference. If she acts, looks, and talks like she's crazy, according to the people of "the world," then she must be crazy.

But the word is not *schizophrenia*. It is the word *autism* that makes her "heart jump": "There upon the pages I felt both angered and found" (p. 187). Williams finds a place of belonging in the diagnostic category of autism (and more precisely of the high-functioning autistic). We can, following Steven Rose, talk of this clinical discourse on autism as a kind of "artificial memory" (1993, p. 326), the collective memory of contemporary culture's engagement with various "abnormalities" of the human being. The diagnostic label as artificial memory gathers to it what is remembered about the behaviors of a category of people. Williams comes to remember herself as a certain kind of subject with a certain kind of history as she self-diagnoses herself as autistic. The label offers her a paradigmatic scripting. That is, the diagnostic label offers her a metanarrative through which to credit and align the unruliness of recollective memories she assembles and to frame the analyses she attaches to memories. Autism opens the right door to the memory museum. As an aside, when she takes her narrative to a clinic to find someone to read it she chooses a particular doctor because, she says, she simply looked for a door with the right label on it (p. 188).

Describing how she completes a draft of her manuscript and takes it to a doctor, she writes: "By now I was developing a clear awareness of an 'I' and was becoming aware that I would have to lose my dependence upon the characters as something separate to myself" (p. 190). In becoming a narrator Williams claims a linguistic grasp of an embodied self in memory, a defining component of autobiographical consciousness (or a self-referencing consciousness). In a sense, then, the autistic self, the "I" of the narrative (who incorporates "Donna" and "Willie" and "Carol"), functions as a point of communication with the world.

In the process of narrative remembering Williams achieves a virtual recovery. The diagnosis establishes a limit of narratability that enables her to remember her way out of the limit of the diagnosis into a kind of virtual normality. She has, through the diagnosis of autism, achieved a certain knowledge of the past and an understanding of the self. She has become an autistic subject. But as I have suggested elsewhere, she has also unbecome an autistic in that she achieves an undoing of some of the limits of the diagnosis.

Her remembering exceeds the limits inscribed by the artificial memory of the diagnostic label of autism. Talking from within the diagnostic label, Williams draws upon her experiential history, her memory, to resist certain effects of the diagnostic label. And she positions herself as a tutor of the unnarrated, a tutor to the reader. Through recovery she turns the lens back upon normality and dis/credits conventional notions of the real. For instance, she argues that the responses of the autistic are designed to protect sanity, not signs of insanity. She argues that the autistic's desire to lose self needs to be redefined as a window onto another reality rather than a flight from the complexity of the world. She argues that the willingness to live in the "normal" world may be a form of "madness."

Throughout *Nobody Nowhere*, Donna Williams emphasizes that autistic persons are often identified and treated as crazy, loony, strange, unhinged; and they are often identified as the violent crazy since their frustrations often materialize in physically violent behavior. Since the experiential history of the autistic person troubles the limits of conventional understanding of autobiographical subjectivity, the strangeness of this difference is neutralized by reincorporation in conventional and reassuring identifications, identifications inflected with various discourses of otherness, of gendered madness, class-based madness, racialized madness among them. In other words, the differences of autistic behaviors are not "visible" to "normal" people except against the horizon of discourse that defines madness or mental retardation in their various guises. And that horizon, Williams acknowledges, can become an internalized landscape of autistic identity. "I am both insane and retarded," she announces. "I would add to this deaf, dumb, and blind; for, although the accuracy of this is being constantly disproved by what I am able to perceive or express, this was often the way I perceived myself to be, and behaved accordingly" (p. 199). She perceived herself to be mad because the people with whom she negotiated everyday life constructed her as mad, insane, or crazy and strange. Through her negotiations of a "world" that perceived her as mad, Williams learned to "be" a mad person.

Being diagnosed as autistic, learning that she is an autistic subject rather than a mad subject, provides Williams with a shape-shifting opportunity. Assembling her narrative life as the life of an autistic, she reframes the diverse and disconnected memories, assigning them a "place within the scheme of things" (p. 163), and reinterprets the patterns of her personal relationships, her experiences as a subject in/out of the world, and her relationship to her own body. As she becomes "somebody somewhere,"[9] she establishes an emotional and intersubjective basis for her conception of selfhood.

Williams understands her narrative project as a process through which she forges what she calls a "real self" out of her "alters"—"Carol" and "Willie." She works to understand how these alters function as specialized versions of herself, taking up bits and pieces of consciousness as if in isolation.[10] In this everyday fragmentation of identities, the "host" subject—"Donna"—cannot consciously take responsibility for herself in the world, cannot assemble an experiential history, even an experiential history that organizes itself around multiplicity. The versions cannot integrate into a coherent narrative the experiential history from which they are divided. She further understands her project as a process of reinhabiting a body from which she has disassociated: "I began to find some sort of a rhythm and permanence within my own body, and this has helped in my acceptance of my body as belonging to me rather than something with a mind of its own, constantly driving me crazy" (p. 202).

By bringing the disconnected and dissociated versions of herself that she turns to the world into alignment with a new definition of herself as a provisionally unified subject, separate from but mutually interdependent upon "the world," Williams, in fact, gets a life. As James M. Glass suggests about the struggle of persons with multiple personalities to integrate them, "the unity need not be monolithic, but it may be a unity representing a plurality of interests within the self, interests understood as emotions and moods" (1993, p. 268). "Carol" and "Willie" disappear: externalized and depersonalized multiplicities replaced by internalized multiplicities.

Through the very writing of her narrative Williams extracts herself from the subject position of the crazy child/young woman and claims for herself the subject position of the autistic. In turn this understanding of herself as an autistic subject enables her to change her perceptions and her experiences of her "madness." In reconstructing herself as an autistic, Williams begins to find a place in the world and "a clear awareness of an 'I' " (p. 190), that point of departure from which to engage the world. She becomes, that is, an autobiographical subject. But this description of the process does an injustice to the massive effort a concept of selfhood required. Just how profound a change in consciousness this represents is suggested by Williams's comment about herself at age 6: "Strangely, it took me four more years to realize that normal children refer to themselves as 'I' " (p. 23).

Williams attributes the shift from an undiagnosed crazy person to an autistic subject to several interrelated processes: diagnostic labeling, the confessional enunciation of an "I"; and the assemblage of a coherent narrative of her experiential history. Yet, in a spiraling action redolent of Michel Foucault's notion of the limit, Williams paradoxically becomes what she is not. In the very process of constituting herself as an autistic subject, she moves beyond its restricted otherness. That is, in the process of defining herself as autistic she exceeds the definition of an autistic subject and exceeds the definition through the very processes of confessional and assemblage. The autistic/recovering autistic subject becomes an autobiographical subject. In this way she situates herself both within and without the diagnostic label.

The very act of getting a life narrative thus generates an intriguing question. Is Williams still an autistic subject or is she a recovered/recovering autistic efficiently performing one or another version of a "life"? Bernard Rimland, a pioneering expert in the field of autism, calls Temple Grandin (whose *Emergence, Labeled Autistic,* co-written with Margaret M. Scarriano, offers another narrative of this limit) "a recovered autistic individual" in his introduction to her autobiographical narrative (1965, p. 7), thus implying that the ability to compose a life narrative signals the transformation of an autistic into a non-autistic, or "normal," person. From this point of view, getting a life narrative is tantamount to getting out of autistic subjectivity. Does this mean that a person cannot be an autistic and an autobiographical subject simultaneously? Or that the very framing of an autobiographical narrative does the cultural work of transforming the unknowable and different subject into a knowable subject? Perhaps, and perhaps because this is a certain metamorphosis, a change of the morphos of the structure of being itself, we can never know. The ground or subject of our knowing may be obliterated in the creation of an autobiographical subject.

In *Nobody Nowhere* the label of autistic functions as a mental construct through which Williams can remember and then claim an autobiographical "I." In *Somebody Somewhere* the diagnostic label becomes a limit of narratability that must be exceeded. In the latter text, Williams defines autism as "an invisible monster, a monster of self-denial" (1994, p. 34). If the diagnostic label gives her back a past through acts of remembering, it must be exceeded in order for her to go forward. "AUTISM IS NOT ME," she insists at the conclusion of *Somebody Somewhere* (p. 238).

Conclusion

In this limit case of autistic subjectivity we see an experiential site (the narrative acts and practices of Donna Williams) of Hacking's larger point about the historical moment of the sciences of memory. In her narratives, Williams is after the secret of her past. The discourse and diagnosis of autism gives her a vocabulary, a project, and a regime of remembering as an act of archeological uncovering. And the quest of the sciences of memory for the secret of the soul offers a cultural metaphor for her pursuit of that secret self or "soul" (a term she invokes in *Somebody Somewhere*). Williams presents "Donna" as that secret, that "true" self: "At home I would still spend hours in front of the mirror, staring into my own eyes and whispering my name over and over, sometimes trying to call myself back, at other times becoming frightened at losing my sense of myself" (1992, p. 56). "Donna" is hidden from her, and a secret from the world, overwritten as she is by her alters. And Williams represents the world as a secret from her, an impenetrable otherness negotiable

only through her alters "Willie" and "Carol." To write, for Williams, is to ex-
pose this "secret" and access the secret self she calls Donna. In composing her
life story, the narrator pieces together a narrative past through which she re-
covers "Donna" amid the psychic screens of "Carol" and "Willie."

Williams also writes to recover embodiment. Through the discourse of
autism she finds a way to represent how it is that she failed to experience her
body as her own and the way she failed to experience herself as an "I" in a
body. She presents her body as a space of habitation for the alters "Carol" and
"Willie." When in *Somebody Somewhere* she says that the first book had been
"more than a book, it had been an exorcism" (1994, p. 15), she invokes the
language of religion/the soul to represent the experience of being possessed
by "Carol" and "Willie," strangers in her strange body.

And finally, Williams writes to recover her memory. As noted earlier, Nelson proposes that the ability to understand narrative memory structures, which
are part of cultural and familial narrative practices, occurs in the late preschool
years. But Williams had by that time, according to her testimony, already
stored "Donna" in the cupboard of the subconscious and dissociated from her
body through "Willie" and "Carol." Williams had, as well, come to understand
her memory narratives as untrustworthy, since the people around her failed
to understand her form of running memory commentary. "With almost every
memory I had been told this was not my own life that I was remembering,"
she writes in *Somebody Somewhere* (p. 50). Twenty-five years later, she engages
in a practice of remembering through which she claims an "I" from which to
speak.

Theories of the material basis of consciousness, whether quantum, genomic, neural net, or connectionist, offer productive ways of understanding
the materiality of autobiographical subjectivity and the materiality of consciousness gone awry. Certainly these metaphors that enable the sciences of
memory give us etiologies and treatment options. Quantum theory, genomic
theory, neural net, and connectionist theories all offer us ways of understanding
the otherness of the condition of the autistic. And they underwrite certain
lines of research that eventuate in certain modes of intervention, most commonly now chemical. But people are, as Eakin emphasizes, "storied" selves.
And it is through their stories that we find other ways of understanding the
materiality of autobiographical subjectivity.

The body is a site of autobiographical knowledge. There is the embodied
materiality of memory and consciousness, whether quantum, genetic, neural,
or connectionist; there is the doubling of the body image, the materiality of
the body image as a mode of being a self in the world (see Eakin, 1999, p. 28)
and the sociality of body image as a mode of understanding the valence of
one's body in the social world; and there is the intersection of the materiality
of the body and cultural embodiment, in the sense that autobiographical nar-

ratives come from persons whose bodies are located historically and culturally and whose bodies are historical sites.

Mobilized to tell a story, memory is the intersection of material, experiential, and sociocultural forces. Producing situational meaning, acts of remembering and telling reform and rematerialize the embodied subject of narration. The materiality of our bodies, the sense we have of ourselves as centers of consciousness, and the stories through which we learn and choose to make our experiential history meaningful all conjoin, so that bodies, selves, memories, stories cannot be understood independently of one another.

But it is critical to remember that autobiographical subjects are embodied subjects of history and that in this historical moment in the West they are storied subjects of the sciences of memory. For me, the limit case of Williams's narrative provides a glimpse, at the remove of representation, into the conditions of the eccentrically embodied. Intriguingly, the secondness of the person diagnosed as autistic confuses the limits of the subject because it intimates another register of being, perhaps another register of embodied memory, to which the nonautistic person has no access except through these exceptional representations. Perhaps this representation of autistic personhood hints at a different subjectivity, only a portion of which is uneasily recuperable in culturally intelligible scripts even as those cultural scripts overwrite that representation.

Through narratives such as that of Williams, we can gain some access to the "experienced" difference of an embodiment seemingly gone awry. Through such narratives of everyday lives, we understand in different ways how the body acts as an active agent in the remembering of the world and in the knowing of the subjective world differently. But there are always more secrets of embodied remembering to be exposed. If the sciences of memory give us new metaphors for understanding, personal narrative, impossible without informing metaphors, offers interruptions in the adequate functioning of science's metaphors. The secret will out. The secret is safe. There is no secret without a theory of the secret.

Notes

1. In his recent book, *How Our Lives Become Stories*, Paul John Eakin (1999) suggests that despite the troubling of the term *self* by all kinds of postmodern theorists, including myself, *self* is still useful in its commonality of reference and preferable to alternatives such as *subject* because of its "indispensab[ility] to any treatment of autobiography" (p. 10).

2. Reflecting on the work of neuroscientists such as Gerald M. Edelman, Oliver Sacks, and Antonio R. Damasio and the work of the philosopher Elizabeth Grosz on embodiment, Eakin insists on putting the materiality of the body back in the self.

3. Narrative memory is not, of course, the only kind of memory. There is, as memory researchers elaborate, generic event memory (or habit memory or implicit memory), the kind of memory that comes into play in the "things happen this way" sense (how we negotiate a grocery store, for instance, or ride a bike). There is eidetic memory—the memory of images so prominent in childhood, the memory that seems to make of childhood memories a different order from adult memory. And there is episodic memory that involves, according to Katherine Nelson (1993, Jan.), "conscious recollection of previous experiences" (p. 7)—but previous experiences that are "remarkable." Such memories come to narrative through "mental constructs which people use to make sense out of experience" (Van der Kolk & Van der Hart, 1995, p. 160).

4. The general commentary on autism that follows is excerpted from Smith (1996). The reading of specific passages from Williams's (1992) *Nobody Nowhere* is new to this essay.

5. Of course, there is no one unified autistic subject but many persons diagnosed with varying degrees of autism. And so there are tremendous variations in the behavioral manifestations and differential capabilities of those persons diagnosed as autistic. There are those who remain permanently institutionalized; there are those identified as "idiots savants"—persons with remarkable powers in a specific area, such as the person upon whom Dustin Hoffman's character in *Rain Man* was modeled; and there are those identified with Asperger's syndrome who are high-functioning and are sometimes described as "recovered" or "recovering" autistics, persons who, having learned to adjust their behaviors, become active participants in society. The exact configuration of autistic behaviors/markers and their effects are individually specific.

6. For a discussion of the emergence of modern medicine and the modes through which it constituted the normal and the pathological subject, see Foucault (1973/1975).

7. There are, of course, many factors that affect the ways in which scientific and clinical research gets done, some of which are the sources of funding, the institutions in which research takes place and the forms of knowledge they promote, and the development of research technologies.

8. Cornell is reviewing Charles Peirce's formulation of secondness and relating it to Jacques Derrida's deconstructive practice.

9. *Somebody Somewhere* is the title of her second book. See Williams (1994).

10. For further discussions of multiple personalities and their relationship to the host subject, see Bliss (1986) and Glass (1993).

References

Bartak, L. (1992). Foreword. In Donna Williams, *Nobody nowhere: The extraordinary autobiography of an autistic* (pp. x–xi). New York: Times Books.

Bliss, E. L. (1986). *Multiple personality, allied disorders, and hypnosis.* New York: Oxford University Press.

Bruner, J. (1987). Life as narrative. *Social Research, 54,* 11–32.

Cook, K. K. (1996). Medical identity: My DNA/myself. In S. Smith & J. Watson (Eds.), *Getting a life: Everyday uses of autobiography* (pp. 63–85). Minneapolis: University of Minnesota Press.

Cornell, D. (1992). *The philosophy of the limit.* New York: Routledge.

Damasio, A. R. (1994). *Descartes' error: Emotion, reason, and the human brain.* New York: G. P. Putnam's Sons.

Eakin, P. J. (1999). *How our lives become stories: Making selves.* Ithaca, NY: Cornell University Press.

Foucault, M. (1975). *The birth of the clinic: An archaeology of medical perception* (A. M. Sheridan Smith, Trans.). New York: Vintage. (Original work published 1973)

Foucault, M. (1980). *A history of sexuality. Vol. 1. An introduction* (Robert Hurley, Trans.). New York: Vintage.

Glass, J. M. (1993). *Shattered selves: Multiple personality in a postmodern world.* Ithaca, NY: Cornell University Press.

Grandin, T., with Scarriano, M. M. (1996). *Emergence, labeled autistic.* Novato, CA: Arena Press.

Hacking, I. (1995). *Rewriting the soul: Multiple personality and the new sciences of memory.* Princeton, NJ: Princeton University Press.

Kanner, L. (1943). Autistic disturbance of affective contact. *Nervous Child, 2,* 217–250.

Kotre, J. (1996). *White gloves: How we create ourselves through memory.* New York: Norton.

Nelson, K. (1993). The psychological and social origins of autobiographical memory. *Psychological Science, 4*(1), 7–14.

Penrose, R. (1989). *The emperor's new mind: Concerning computers, minds, and the laws of physics.* Oxford: Oxford University Press.

Rimland, B. (1965). *Infantile autism: The syndrome and its implications for a neural theory of behavior.* London: Methuen.

Rose, S. (1993). *The making of memory.* New York: Anchor.

Sacks, O. (1995). *An anthropologist from Mars.* New York: Knopf.

Schank, R. C. (1990). *Tell me a story.* New York: Charles Scribner's Sons.

Smith, S. (1996). Taking it to a limit one more time: Autobiography and autism. In S. Smith & J. Watson (Eds.), *Getting a life: Everyday uses of autobiography* (pp. 226–246). Minneapolis: University of Minnesota Press.

Smith, T. (1998). Introduction: Autobiography in fresh contexts. *a/b: Auto/Biographical Studies, 13*(1), 1–5.

Van der Kolk, B. A., & Van der Hart, O. (1995). The intrusive past: The flexibility of memory and the engraving of trauma. In C. Caruth (Ed.), *Trauma: Explorations in memory* (pp. 158–182). Baltimore: Johns Hopkins University Press.

Williams, D. (1992). *Nobody nowhere: The extraordinary autobiography of an autistic.* New York: Times Books.

Williams, D. (1994). *Somebody somewhere: Breaking free from the world of autism.* New York: Times Books.

Wilson, E. A. (1998). *Neural geographies: Feminism and the microstructure of cognition*. New York: Routledge.

Yates, F. A. (1966). *The art of memory*. Chicago: University of Chicago Press.

Zohar, D., and in collaboration with I. N. Marshall. (1990). *The quantum self: Human nature and the consciousness defined by the new physics*. New York: Morrow.

PART III

*Autobiographical Narrative, Fiction,
and the Construction of Self*

6 Rethinking the Fictive, Reclaiming the Real: Autobiography, Narrative Time, and the Burden of Truth

Mark Freeman

Fiction and Reality

I shall begin this essay with three fairly strong assertions about the relationship between *fiction* and *reality* as these terms apply to autobiographical narratives. The first is that the notion of *fiction*, when used to refer to the processes that go into the fashioning of life narratives, is too often parasitic on an overly narrow—and very problematic—notion of what reality is and that, as a consequence, it ends up being degraded, given a lesser status.

The second assertion is that the conception of reality upon which this notion of fiction is parasitic is problematic for at least two basic reasons. The first is that it is equated with the allegedly raw and pristine, the uninterpreted and unconstructed, the "real stuff." The second and more complicated reason is that it is tied to a conception of time—basically, clock time, the time of lines, instants, sequences—that is better applied to the world of *things* than to the world of *people*. To put this a bit more simply, the conception of reality that usually surfaces when autobiographies are relegated to the status of fictions—or *mere* fictions, as they are often called—is one that is imagined to somehow be free of our own designs, a string of "stuff" that just happens, in time, and that we will inevitably falsify when we later look backward and try to impose some order. I am going to try to cast this conception of reality into question.

The third idea is as follows: By rethinking the notion of the fictive, there is the possibility not only of "reclaiming" the real—by which I mean restoring to it a fuller and more comprehensive range of meanings—but also of establishing a more adequate rendition of what *truth* might mean in the human realm.

The Dangers of Autobiography

"The fatal flaw of all biography, according to its enemies," writes Stephen Millhauser in the novel *Edwin Mulhouse* (1983), "is its helpless conformity to the laws of fiction. Each date, each incident, each casual remark contributes to an elaborate plot that slowly and cunningly builds to a foreknown climax: the hero's celebrated deed" (p. 100). For some, in fact, the entire genre can only be deemed "hopelessly fictional, since unlike real life, which presents us with question marks, censored passages, blank spaces, rows of asterisks, omitted paragraphs, and numberless sequences of three dots trailing into whiteness, biography provides an illusion of completeness, a vast pattern of details organized by an omniscient biographer" (p. 101). In the case of *auto*biography, of course, the situation becomes that much more problematic, for not only is there that sort of omniscient, synoptic, after-the-fact coherence of which Millhauser speaks, but there is also an additional psychic load bound up with the simple fact that the object of one's scrutiny here is oneself. In addition to the problem of false coherence, therefore, there are problems such as wishful thinking, defenses, illusions, delusions, and so on, all of which will likely find their way into one's story.

There is a whole host of other possible problems involved in the autobiographical project as well. "Slowly," Joanna Field has written in *A Life of One's Own* (1981), for instance, "I realized that the facts"—that is, the facts on which her own self-account was based—"were not separate things which were there for anyone to pick up, but an ever-changing pattern against a boundless background of the unknown, an immense kaleidoscope changing constantly according to the different ways you looked at it" (pp. 105–106).

There is also the problem of placing meanings onto the past that, in some sense, may not belong. "I reconstruct it here," Michel Leiris writes in *Manhood* (1984),

> according to my recollections, adding the observation of what I have subsequently become and comparing these later elements with those earlier ones my memory supplies. Such a method has its dangers, for who knows if I am not attributing to these recollections a meaning they never had, charging them after the fact with an affective value which the real events they refer to utterly lacked—in short, resuscitating this past in a misleading manner? (p. 22)

As for those autobiographers who ordinarily write fiction, these sorts of issues loom even larger. Philip Roth, for instance, writes of the need "to resist the impulse to dramatize untruthfully the insufficiently dramatic, to complicate the essentially simple, to charge with implication what implied very little—the temptation to abandon the facts when those facts were not so compelling as others I might imagine" (1988, p. 7). Similarly, Mary McCarthy in *Memories of a Catholic Girlhood* (1963) notes that "the temptation to invent has been very strong, particularly where recollection is hazy and I remember the substance of an event but not the details—the color of a dress, the pattern of a carpet, the placing of a picture" (p. 9). In point of fact, she confesses: "There are some semi-fictional touches here. . . . I arranged actual events so as to make a good story out of them. It is hard to overcome this temptation if you are in the habit of writing fiction; one does it almost automatically" (p. 153).

There are other problems of this sort at work in autobiographical writing as well: the fact that portions of our stories are hearsay, which comes from others; the fact that the autobiographer inevitably makes use of prevailing literary conventions; the fact that these conventions are themselves inseparable from prevailing cultural scripts, from the folk-psychological canon, as Jerome Bruner (1991) has put it, from which we draw in seeking to make sense of our lives. And then, of course, there are some significant existential issues that need to be thrown into the mix. Perhaps, some have suggested, autobiographical narratives are, in the end, defenses against our own dividedness and heterogeneity, consolations for our aimlessness, for the fact that, maybe, our lives have no meaning at all. And so on and so forth.

Hazel Barnes summarizes many of these issues nicely in her book, *The Story I Tell Myself* (1997):

> My efforts to write of my life have painfully confirmed my theoretical awareness of the degree to which an autobiography is perforce a novel. It is not only that . . . words distort even as they reveal, that what is lived can never be the same as what is told. Questions of sincerity, the reliability of memory, and concern for others' feelings turn out to be far more complex than I had imagined. The problem of selectivity, which in other contexts may be purely literary, becomes more urgent; to single out *these* factors as most important in shaping a self is to mold the self presented. The most I can claim, and this I do affirm, is that the fictional character portrayed here is, at least in my eyes, a true reflection of what I reflectively see. (p. xix)

For Barnes, "painful" though this entire process has been, there nevertheless remains talk of "true reflection." Somehow, she seems to say, the possibility of attaining a kind of truth still exists, even amid the inevitable fictionalization that is part and parcel of the process of writing about oneself. It is this very possibility, however, that a good deal of contemporary thinking has rejected.

The Problem of Truth

Let me shift gears for a moment and bring these ideas a bit closer to issues of narrative and consciousness. "We do know about the fiction of our lives— and we should want to know," writes Michael S. Gazzaniga in *The Mind's Past* (1998). "That's why I have written this book about how our mind and brain accomplish the amazing feat of constructing our past and, in so doing, create the illusion of self" (p. 1). Reconstruction of events," he continues,

> starts with perception and goes all the way up to human reasoning. The mind is the last to know things. After the brain computes an event, the illusory "we" (that is, the mind) becomes aware of it. The brain, particularly the left hemisphere, is built to interpret data the brain has already processed. Yes, there is a special device in the left brain, which I call the *interpreter*, that carries out one more activity upon completion of zillions of automatic brain processes. The interpreter, the last device in the information chain in our brain, reconstructs the brain events and in doing so makes telling errors of perception, memory, and judgment. The clue to how we are built is buried not just in our marvelously robust capacity for these functions, but also in the errors that are frequently made during reconstruction. Biography is fiction. Autobiography is hopelessly inventive. (p. 2)

The interpreter tries "to keep our personal story together," Gazzaniga goes on to explain. "To do that," he maintains, "we have to learn to lie to ourselves" (p. 26).

Notice the connection between the quite depersonalized vision of psychological functioning being presented here and the thesis of fictionalization, even lying. Notice, as well, that there would seem to be a paradox at work: in a distinct sense, it is consciousness itself, our very *awareness* of our existence and our attempt to make sense of it, that deludes us into presuming that "we," selves, are real.

Not that this is a problem, however. "Sure, life is a fiction," Gazzaniga proclaims, "but it's our fiction and it feels good and we are in charge of it. That is the sentiment we all feel as we listen to tales of the automatic brain. We don't feel like zombies; we feel like in-charge, conscious entities" (p. 172). But it isn't really so. "The interpreter constantly establishes a running narrative of our actions, emotions, thoughts, and dreams. It is the glue that unifies our story and creates our sense of being a whole, rational agent. It brings to our bag of individual instincts the illusion that we are something other than what we are" (p. 174).

From this point of view, in other words, *we*, conscious selves, seemingly in charge of at least a portion of our destiny, are not only fictitious, pejoratively understood; we are also entirely *other* than what we seem to be. Self-consciousness, such as it is, becomes a rather nasty trick and the search for meaning in our lives, which occurs at the behest of the interpreter, nothing more than a game, fun to play but bearing no relationship whatsoever to reality.

Gazzaniga's story line here is, admittedly, extreme. But the basic philosophical place from which he speaks is, in fact, a widely shared one. There is much more happening here than what Ian Hacking (1995) has called "the secularization of the soul" through the study of memory. What we are considering is the full-scale unmasking of the soul's innermost pretensions and, ultimately, its dissolution.

It should be noted here that some of these issues are very much continuous with current work on the failures of memory, the significance of distortion, and so on. As D. L. Schachter (1995), for instance, has put the matter, "The output of human memory often differs—sometimes rather substantially—from the input. Remembering can fail not only because information is forgotten over time, but also because it is changed and distorted" (p. 1). This doesn't mean, he hastens to add, that there isn't a good deal of accuracy in memory, for there often is. Nevertheless, the main question at hand for Schachter is: "Under what conditions is memory largely accurate, and under what conditions is distortion most likely to occur?" (p. 25). The leading terms here, therefore, once again, are *accuracy* and *distortion*, "true" memories, which correspond to reality, and "false" memories, which deform it. The implication is clear enough: to the degree that autobiographical recollection departs from what "really was," in the "past present" that it seeks, futilely, to recover, it must of necessity falsify experience.

In all fairness to Schachter, he does seem to question this stance in his book, *Searching for Memory* (1996). Drawing on David Rubin's work, among others', Schachter notes, for instance, that "what we experience as an autobiographical memory is constructed from knowledge of lifetime periods, general events, and specific episodes. When we put all this information together, we start to tell the stories of our lives" (p. 93). As such, there would seem to be not so much lying or falsification at work here as synthesis, the sort of synoptic seeing that is intrinsic to historical consciousness. He also goes on to suggest that "memories do not exist in one of two states—either true or false" (p. 277). Nevertheless, however, he quickly adds, "the important task," still, "is to examine how and in what ways memory corresponds with reality"

(p. 277). What, then, is reality, according to Schachter? It can only be that which exists in all of its fleshy immediacy before memory has its way. My aim here is not to condemn Schachter or, for that matter, Gazzaniga, either; the fact is, they are probably framing these issues as best they can given the available terms—*reality* and *fiction*, *truth* and *falsity*, *accuracy* and *distortion*. But these terms, as employed thus far at any rate, need to be rethought. I shall be giving it a try shortly.

For now, let me continue pursuing this set of issues by moving in a related direction. As Arnold Ludwig has noted in his book *How Do We Know Who We Are?* (1997),

> One of the major problems with any insight-oriented psychotherapy based on the uncovering of important, early-life experiences is that it is difficult if not impossible to establish the historical truth through the customary exploration of your memories, fantasies, and dreams, no matter how thorough the probing or how long the treatment. This is so for a lot of reasons. For one, your memories and perceptions are designed to support your biases. You selectively remember or repress certain information, and many of your experiences are indescribable or difficult to translate into words. Your memories tend to be shaped by the theoretical outlook of your therapist. And you tend not to include disconfirming experiences in your accounts. . . . For these reasons, what you come to regard as historical truth really represents plausibility. This plausibility involves how well your account embraces all the pertinent elements of your experiences and how cohesive it seems. (p. 155)

The basic situation Ludwig describes here, you will notice, is not unlike the one we considered via Gazzaniga and Schachter. For Ludwig, the historical truth is what exists prior to our biases, our selectivity and defenses. In addition, it is on some level "preinterpretive," prior to language and theorization, and therefore difficult, even impossible, to ever fully capture and contain. Similar to what Donald P. Spence (1982) had to say some years back in reference to psychoanalysis and its allegedly misguided pretensions to seek historical truth, there is really no choice here, Ludwig tells us, but to scrap it and to go instead with what he calls "plausibility," which, basically, is his version of Spence's idea of narrative truth. Drawing explicitly on Spence, in fact, Ludwig goes on to suggest that

> throughout psychotherapy, the patient deals with the conflict between what is true but hard to describe—that is, the pure memory—and what is describable but partly untrue—that is, the screen memory. The very attempt to translate the original memory destroys it because

the words, as they are chosen, likely misrepresent the image, and because the translation, no matter how good, replaces the original. (p. 156)

This is not to be lamented, however:

Even when the reconstruction of the past is entirely imaginary, it acquires the mantle of truth if it lets patients find coherence and meaning in their personal stories and make sense out of their chaotic experiences. And it becomes officially true and sometimes more real than actual historical truth when an authoritative figure, such as their analyst, gives the narrative the stamp of approval. (pp. 156–157)

The problem here is precisely the same as the one that characterizes Spence's work. There is a bifurcation, a split between historical truth and narrative truth and exactly that sort of parasitism I mentioned earlier: narrative truth is the domain of the fictitious, historical truth the domain of the real, untouched by all that analytic talk. It would be nice to be able to acquire the latter, he in effect says, but because we cannot we have to settle for the former, lesser though it may be. The best that can be hoped, therefore, is that the resultant narrative, despite its inevitable historical falsity, helps the person in question to carry on.

Narrative Time

I am going to pause for a moment now and shift gears again in a fairly substantial way. The portion of this essay that has led to this juncture was the portion I had completed prior to getting onto the van to the airport that would take me to the conference on which this volume is based. I had written some other things as well, but the part you just read was what I had committed to print thus far, my assumption being that I would continue on in much the same basic direction. That was the plan.

But things became more complicated—complicated enough, in fact, that on the ride into the airport I decided to write something rather different for the remainder. Just a couple of days before my departure for the conference, our 12-year-old daughter, Brenna, a really wonderful kid, had woken up and was barely able to talk. She seemed congested, her chest hurt, she was a little flushed, and so on. It turned out to be a case of pneumonia, viral supposedly.

I do not wish to get too sentimental here, but seeing one's child extremely ill can be very tough. Brenna is a bit frail and pale to begin with. And seeing her huddled under her blankets, her face peeking out, fixed on the TV, eyes glazed, murmuring a faint hello . . . it's hard not to have this kind of scene break your heart.

It's not as if I was a perpetual mess for the two days that followed the diagnosis. The doctor didn't seem too concerned and, by and large, it was life as usual—permeated by an extra load of worry (not to mention guilt over leaving my suffering family behind for the sake of "narrative," important though it is) but not radically different than most other days. The next night, however, my wife and I were watching the 10 o'clock news and we learned that a 10-year-old girl, from Boston (less than an hour away), had suddenly died. She had had flulike symptoms and been taken to the hospital just a day earlier—where nothing out of the ordinary had been diagnosed—and 24 hours later she was, mysteriously, especially given the speed with which her young body had been ravaged and destroyed, gone. Her beautiful smiling face was on a little box on the side of the TV screen as the newscaster reviewed her fate. It was probably one of those photos they take of kids in school, where they wear their Sunday dresses or their clip-on ties. . . .

She had apparently contracted a very virulent form of *bacterial* pneumonia. In another child's body, the TV doctor had explained, there might hardly have been a problem. And it was extremely rare for anything like this to occur. Sometimes this sort of catastrophe is just a matter of sheer bad luck, the doctor went on to say: a receptive body meets up with a dreadful bacterium and, in a matter of hours, a little girl, thoroughly alive just a day before, is dead. But it was extremely, extremely rare, the doctor reiterated. And it was bacterial, not viral.

Not a good piece of news to watch the night before leaving for the dry plains of Lubbock, Texas. How exactly did our doctor know that what Brenna had was viral and not bacterial? And how did we know—*did* we know—that she didn't have one of those terrible rare bodies, which might serve as an all too willing host to an unspeakably hostile germ? And so on and so forth.

The next morning she looked a little better (or so I told myself). At least she didn't seem to have taken a turn for the worse. It wasn't that intense a morning, in fact, and I have no interest in making it any more dramatic than it was. Things changed, though, for a few moments, as I looked at my wife and Brenna standing in the doorway, looking at me presumably—though I actually didn't know if they could see me behind the smoky glass of the limo van. When I waved, they didn't wave back. There they were, the two of them, one taller and ruddy, the other shorter and pasty, soon to recede from view.

What would be the meaning of that morning, that picture, etched in my mind's eye? The fact is, I did not know. I *could* not know—not, that is, until further experiences came along and gave it a more definite meaning. This was a kind of protonarrative, as Philip Lewin (1999) has put it, a not-yet story, waiting to be told. When I left, things were wide open and I could only hope that the story I would eventually tell had a happy ending—unexciting though it would have to be. The story was contingent on the future, on what would happen over the next couple of days.

"Consider what happens," Gabriel Marcel (1950) has written,

> when we tell our friends the very simplest story, the story, say, of some journey we have made. The story of a journey is told by someone who has made the journey, from beginning to end, and who inevitably sees his earlier experiences during the journey as coloured by his later experiences. For our final impression of what the journey turned out to be like cannot but react on our memories of our first impression of what the journey *was going to be like*. But when we were actually making the journey, or rather beginning to make it, these first impressions were, on the contrary, held quivering like a compass needle by our anxious expectations of everything that was still to come. (p. 192)

Marcel does not mean to suggest, and nor do I, that the present—present experience—is completely indeterminate or meaningless. It is not. What he is suggesting here instead is that the present must await the future in order for its meaning and significance to be discerned. Or, to put the matter a bit differently, the meaning and significance of experience often emerge or are transformed in retrospect, when that experience assumes its place as an episode in an evolving narrative.

Occasionally our memories can, in fact, lead us back to something like, or something that *feels* like, the past, that is, a previously present experience, a reliving. More often, however, particularly when we are trying to make sense not just of an event but also of some significant period of the personal past— some chapter, as it were—we do not seek to "recapture" what was, in its openness and indeterminacy. Rather, we *interpret* the past from the standpoint of the present, seeking to determine how it might have contributed to this very moment. And this is a determination that cannot possibly be made *until* this moment has arrived.

Does this mean that we are distorting our past or falsifying it or foisting meanings onto it that don't belong there by virtue of the fact that we are not retrieving it accurately? No, not necessarily. What we are doing is remembering and narrating, which means situating the experiences of the past—rewriting them—in accordance with and in relation to what has happened since, as understood and reunderstood from now, the moment of narration. As David Carr (1986) has succinctly put the matter, "Narrative requires narration. . . . What is essential to the story-teller's position is the advantage of . . . hindsight, a . . . freedom from the constraint of the present assured by occupying a position after, above, or outside the events narrated" (p. 60).

Now, to the extent that one equates "reality" with immediate experience, autobiographical recollections are bound to be seen as *distortions* of reality, as falsifications. And if truth is understood to be that which imitates this reality, then autobiographical narratives, in turn, are bound to be seen as fictions. Finally, if both reality and truth are predicated in terms of linear time, or clock time—this happened, this happened, this happened, our experiences simply ticking away, one after the other—then, once again, the entire autobiographical enterprise becomes condemned to the status of being "hopelessly inventive," as Gazzaniga had put it: because there is no possibility of ever returning to those ticking moments and telling it like it really was, autobiography—and, by extension, the process of self-reflection itself—can lead to nothing but illusions. Evolutionarily speaking, it would seem that we are born liars; and again, it is the very existence of self-consciousness that seems to be at fault. The situation is a paradoxical one.

But there is a conflation at work: *narrativity*, by virtue of its constructiveness, is being linked with *fictionality*, such that the constructed, or the poetic, becomes the *untrue*. What's more, the very process of *interpretation* itself becomes, from this perspective, suspect as a vehicle of understanding.

What I would like to do is try to think beyond this perspective. And the key to doing this, I believe, lies in moving beyond clock time and seeing in *narrative time* (see especially Ricoeur, 1981; also Freeman, 1998) a possible inroad into rethinking the problem of truth.

Memory and Poiesis

Let me turn once more to Marcel's notion of a journey to try to concretize all this. This time I shall refer to a quite real journey I took some time ago and that I have recently had to occasion to write about (Freeman, 2002). You will pardon another brief autobiographical digression. (I am well aware that this is risky territory.)

For a number of years during adolescence, my father and I had an okay, but somewhat strained, relationship. He could be stern and a bit impatient, I was basically a hairy wayward hippie into rejecting authority, and at times it just didn't make for that happy a mix. My brothers, I might note, were older and very successful, and so by contrast I am sure that I seemed rather less than an ideal specimen. In any case, at the end of my sophomore year at college, by which time I had just begun to be a bit more serious about my studies and about the world, my father helped me pack up all my belongings for the summer and drove me home. And for the first time in a long, long while—maybe even ever—we talked, about lots and lots of different things. It was good; I have come to think of it as a moment of contact and redemption.

It's not like it was incredible. We didn't embrace or apologize for past sins or anything like that, but in his own measured way he basically ratified my existence and told me I was okay. I did the same. And when we got home, I probably went out to run around with my friends.

When I went away a month later to work at a camp a few hours away from home, it was the last time I saw him. He was 55.

Had my father continued to live beyond that fateful summer, this ride home that we took together might have been seen as eventful but also might not have. There might have been other rides home, other points of contact, other points of no contact, and, perhaps, much more. It might therefore have simply been "a nice ride." But as things turned out, it was a highly significant event—far more significant, in fact, than I could have possibly known. Indeed, it has become something of a monument in my past.

There is nothing at all illusory about this. Memory is not about returning to an earlier immediacy. Nor is it a matter of constructing a story in such a way as to place significance on the event. It is about drawing out meanings and about explicating a significance that could only emerge as a function of what came after—and, of course, what did not. The point, in any case, is that we do not live only in the time of clocks. We also live in the time of stories, and through this time it is sometimes possible to see things and to feel things that could not be seen or felt earlier on.

A qualification is in order: There is unquestionably a constructive aspect to my framing of this episode and its significance, an aspect of *imagining*. One could call it, following Valerie Gray Hardcastle (this volume) and Katherine Nelson (this volume), a process of meaning making, in the sense of poiesis. Now, if the notion of fiction is simply taken to refer to construction or to meaning making, there is not much to take issue with. Sometimes this is, in fact, the meaning that is given to the term. The problem, again, is when the idea of the fictive, when applied to *nonfictional* texts, becomes seen in terms of illusions or deformations of the real.

Hacking's (1995) work may be helpful here. Not unlike Marcel, he reflects on the indeterminacy of the past—not the indeterminacy of *memory*, he emphasizes, "but the indeterminacy of what people actually did" (p. 235). The issue isn't that we simply find out more about the past (though, clearly, that sometimes happens); it is that "we present actions under new descriptions" (p. 243). As Hacking goes on to note, "What matters to us may not have been quite so definite as it now seems. When we remember what we did, or what other people did, we may also rethink, redescribe, and refeel the past. These redescriptions," he writes, "may be perfectly true of the past. That is, they are truths that we now assert about the past. And yet, paradoxically, they may not have been true in the past" (p. 249).

Notice in this context that although these truths emerge in and through narrative time, the time of looking backward over the landscape of the past, Hacking speaks not of *narrative truth*, à la Spence and Ludwig and others. He is speaking about *truth* and is thereby encouraging us to expand our sense of what truth might be by taking it beyond that which represents the discrete events of the past. What is being considered here is a truth that is *made available* by narrative and by the poetic processes that go into the telling of the past.

The Challenge of Narrative

One more very brief autobiographical excursion, before closing, may serve to clarify some of this just a bit more. As I thought more about the episode with my daughter and about the ride home with my father during the few days that preceded my own conference presentation, I had something like an insight, that is, a possible understanding of an aspect of my own past. It could very well be, I realized, that there was some connection, that there *is* some connection—psychical in nature—between how I had responded to her as I drove away in the van and what had happened that summer after my sophomore year: it could be, it can always be, the last time. Perhaps that earlier wound is fresher and more powerful than I sometimes assume and has created, on the fringes of consciousness, a certain fragility and uncertainty in how I think and feel about people I care for.

I have framed this in terms of "what led to what," almost in a causal way. But the narrative dimension is key. Only in virtue of the later event was it possible to think anew about the earlier one and about the possible relation between the two.

What happened during the course of those days is something I would be inclined to call not only an insight but also a possible truth, a possible entry into autobiographical self-understanding—provisional and revisable though it may be. This sort of interpretation, which is actually quite common in autobiographical narratives, has nothing to do with accuracy or with faithful representation; a correspondence view simply doesn't make sense in this context. Neither, however, is the idea of coherence of much help. As self-deceived people show, often loudly and clearly, autobiographical narratives can be perfectly coherent and utterly delusional. Nevertheless, it does seem that, occasionally, insight and self-understanding are possible. And *if* these are possible, the burden of truth, or a "region" of truth, remains. As for what self-understanding and the kind of truth to which it sometimes leads might be about, I find myself turning again to the idea of the poetic, to poems and to fiction, which often seek to make sense of the world, to give form to it, to say something that is not just interesting or coherent but also worth hearing. Somehow, good poems and novels—and autobiographies—seem to be able to speak truth. Lawrence Langer refers in his chapter (this volume) to the power of both fiction and nonfiction alike, particularly in the hands of great writers. The more imagination and artistry, he seems to suggest, the greater the possibility of speaking the truth. How all this happens is difficult to say.

Someone had asked a question during the conference in response to Bob Neimeyer's presentation, which Bob then paraphrased by asking: Just how serious are we about all this narrative stuff? He was inclined to answer this question in terms of a "playful" approach to the issues, to see how far one could go with them. I am sympathetic to this point of view. But my own response would be a bit different. It's not stretching things to say that, in a distinct sense, *the narrated life is the examined life*, where one steps out from the flow of things and seeks to become more conscious of one's existence. Along these lines, autobiographical narratives are not only about what happened when, how these happenings might be emplotted, and so forth, but also about how to live and whether the life is a good one.

The burden of truth, as I have called it, is therefore partly cognitive and partly ethical. The classical notion of recollection, or anamnesis, is itself very much about this dual burden. On the one hand, there is reference to recounting and understanding. But on the other hand, there is a reference to gathering together, to remembering what is most significant and worthwhile in a sometimes forgetful life. This is the kind of truth one sometimes experiences pulling away in a limo van, seeing people who, too often, stay unseen, taken up into routines and preoccupations. As it turned out, Brenna's illness wasn't too bad. Thankfully, there wasn't much of a story after all.

In autobiographical narrative, then, the category of truth becomes very complicated, far more complicated than the fiction/reality opposition tends to convey. I hope some of what has been discussed here shows why this is so and why it might be important to think beyond it.

References

Barnes, H. (1997). *The story I tell myself.* Chicago: University of Chicago Press.

Bruner, J. (1991). Self-making and world-making. *Journal of Aesthetic Education, 25*(1), 67–78.

Carr, D. (1986). *Time, narrative, and history.* Bloomington: Indiana University Press.

Field, J. (1981). *A life of one's own.* Los Angeles: Tarcher.

Freeman, M. (1998). Mythical time, historical time, and the narrative fabric of the self. *Narrative Inquiry, 8*(1), 1–24.

Freeman, M. (2002). The presence of what is missing: Memory, poetry, and the ride home. In R. J. Pellegrini & T. R. Sarbin (Eds.), *Between fathers and sons.* New York: Haworth Clinical Practice Press.

Gazzaniga, M. S. (1998). *The mind's past.* Berkeley: University of California Press.

Hacking, I. (1995). *Rewriting the soul: Multiple personality and the new sciences of memory*. Princeton, NJ: Princeton University Press.

Leiris, M. (1984). *Manhood*. Chicago: University of Chicago Press.

Lewin, P. (1999). *Protonarrativity and the fragmentation of consciousness*. Unpublished manuscript.

Ludwig, A. (1997). *How do we know who we are? A biography of the self*. Oxford: Oxford University Press.

Marcel, G. (1950). *The mystery of being: Vol. 1. Reflection and mystery*. Chicago: Regnery.

McCarthy, M. (1963). *Memories of a Catholic girlhood*. New York: Berkley.

Millhauser, S. (1983). *Edwin Mulhouse*. New York: Penguin.

Ricoeur, P. (1981). Narrative time. In W. J. T. Mitchell (Ed.), *On narrative* (pp. 165–186). Chicago: University of Chicago Press.

Roth, P. (1988). *The facts*. New York: Farrar, Straus, & Giroux.

Schachter, D. L. (1995). Memory distortion: History and current status. In D. L. Schachter (Ed.), *Memory distortion: How minds, brains, and societies reconstruct the past* (pp. 1–43). Cambridge, MA: Harvard University Press.

Schacter, D. L. (1996). *Searching for memory: The brain, the mind, and the past*. New York: Basic.

Spence, D. P. (1982). *Narrative truth and historical truth: Meaning and interpretation in psychoanalysis*. New York: Norton.

7   Dual Focalization, Retrospective Fictional Autobiography, and the Ethics of *Lolita*

James Phelan

One of the most startling narrative sequences in Vladimir Nabokov's *Lolita* occurs toward the end of part 1, when Humbert Humbert follows his account of his first sexual intercourse with Dolores Haze[1] with a description of the murals that he imagines painting on the wall of, The Enchanted Hunters Hotel. Here is the final portion of his narration of the intercourse; it ends chapter 29:

> My life was handled by little Lo in an energetic matter-of-fact manner as if it were an insensate gadget unconnected with me. While eager to impress me with the world of tough kids, she was not quite prepared for certain discrepancies between a kid's life and mine. Pride alone prevented her from giving up; for, in my strange predicament, I feigned supreme stupidity and had her have her way—at least while I could bear it. But really these are irrelevant matters. I am not concerned with so-called "sex" at all. Anybody can imagine those elements of animality. A greater endeavor lures me on: to fix once for all the perilous magic of nymphets. (1955/1991, p. 134)

Here is the description of the murals, which takes up almost the whole of chapter 30:

> Had I been a painter, had the management of The Enchanted Hunters lost its mind one summer day and commissioned me to redecorate their dining room with murals of my own making, this is what I might have thought up, let me list some fragments:
>   There would have been a lake. There would have been an arbor

in flame-flower. There would have been nature studies—a tiger pursuing a bird of paradise, a choking snake sheathing whole the flayed
trunk of a shoat. There would have been a sultan, his face expressing
great agony (belied, as it were, by his molding caress), helping a callypygean slave child to climb a column of onyx. There would have
been those luminous globules of gonadal glow that travel up the opalescent sides of juke boxes. There would have been all kinds of camp
activities on the part of the intermediate group, Canoeing, Coranting,
Combing Curls in the lakeside sun. There would have been poplars,
apples, a suburban Sunday. There would have been a fire opal dissolving within a ripple-ringed pool, a last throb, a last dab of color,
stinging red, smarting pink, a sigh, a wincing child.[2] (pp. 134–135)

The sequence is startling because Humbert's narration in chapter 30 contradicts
his statements of purpose at the end of chapter 29. He says nothing about
"the perilous magic of nymphets," opting instead to invite us to reflect on the
"animality" of the scene through the images of one animal preying upon another and, most remarkable of all, offering his audience a glimpse of Dolores's
pain: "stinging red, smarting pink, . . . a wincing child."

This essay will attempt to uncover the narrative logic behind this sequence
and to explore its ethical consequences. I will seek to explain how Humbert's
act of autobiographical narration leads to the kind of contradiction evident in
this sequence, and I will explore what such a contradiction means for the
ethical dimension of our response to Humbert as fictional narrator and to Nabokov as author. In analyzing the narrative logic of Humbert's autobiography,
I will focus on three interrelated elements of his narration: unreliability, self-
consciousness, and focalization. In exploring the ethical consequences of contradiction in the narrative, I will attempt to illustrate the connection between
technique and ethics. Thus, before I turn to a detailed analysis of the passages
quoted earlier, I would like to locate that analysis in a broader context of
debates about the novel.

Although the controversy can be found in the criticism of the novel, I will
highlight its major features by reporting on two of my experiences in teaching
it, once in a graduate seminar, once in an NEH Summer Seminar for College
Teachers.[3] People in both groups, especially those who were encountering the
book for the first time, had very strong but very different reactions. Some
thrilled to Humbert Humbert's cleverness, fancy prose style, and ability, in
the prefatory words of John Ray, Jr., to use his "singing violin to conjure up
a tendresse" (p. 5). Others found the experience of reading the book to be
painful and resented being asked to be exposed to the perspective of a pedophile, regardless of his stylistic brilliance. These readers pointed out that
what we know about the incidence of sexual abuse makes it likely that one

or more members of any class would have experienced such abuse and that it was, therefore, irresponsible to make the book required reading. Others would respond that the book's focus on illicit sexual desire raised important questions about desire in general and that part of its value was to make us uncomfortable. Although neither group split neatly along gender lines, the arguments sometimes linked gender to response, with a few women saying, "It's mostly you men who like the book, and although you talk in class about its aesthetic qualities, what you really like is the way Humbert acts out male sexual fantasies." And a few men said, "It's mostly you feminists who don't like the book because it's definitely not PC and your politics prohibit you from getting past the surface story and appreciating Nabokov's transformation of his offensive subject matter into articulate art."

Those on the different sides of the debate took the same elements of the novel as evidence for their positions. Those who defended the book would point to the shift in the purpose of Humbert's narration (from defending himself to condemning himself), to his heartfelt protestations of love for the adult Dolores, and to his wish to have his confession give her immortality. Those who attacked the book countered that the shift in purpose was another effort on Humbert's part to manipulate his audience into sympathizing with him, that his love was impoverished because he still had no idea who she was, and that his confession is another way of objectifying her.

This debate is ultimately about the ethics of reading as they apply to *Lolita*. Readers and critics who defend the book are making two key ethical assumptions: (1) a literary work's specific treatment of its topic is more important than the topic itself, and (2) we ought to remain open to the possibility of reform—and even a modicum of redemption—in others, including those as reprehensible as Humbert Humbert. Those readers and critics who find the book offensive are making two different ethical assumptions: (1) the very act of representing some subjects from some perspectives—which include pedophilia from the perspective of the pedophile—is ethically suspect and not capable of being defended on aesthetic grounds, and (2) giving credence to Humbert's questionable claims about his new understanding of feelings for Dolores puts the ethical emphasis in the wrong place: on Humbert the narrator rather than on Dolores and what Humbert the character has done to her. The difficulty in adjudicating this debate—and of course there are positions between total defense and all-out attack—is the difficulty of finding a set of ethical assumptions that all parties will agree to and find relevant to *Lolita*. Rather than proposing such a set of assumptions directly, I would like to propose a way for exploring the ethics of reading and then see what kind of light it will shed on the debate.

I regard the ethical dimension of reading as an inextricable part of the experience of narrative. I've been trying to theorize the experience of narrative by conceiving of narrative as rhetoric. In making this move, I mean to emphasize narrative's existence as a rhetorical act: somebody telling somebody else on some occasion and for some purpose that something happened. In fictional narrative such as *Lolita*, the rhetorical situation is doubled: Humbert tells his story to his narratee for his purposes, while Nabokov's telling of Humbert's telling to us accomplishes other purposes. This doubled rhetorical act, not surprisingly, involves a multilevel communication from author to audience, one that involves the audiences's intellect, emotions, psyche, and values. Furthermore, these levels interact with one another. Our values and those set forth by the narrator and the implied author affect our judgments of characters (and sometimes narrators), and our judgments affect our emotions. The trajectory of our feelings is itself linked to the psychological and thematic effects of the narrative. At the same time, the doubled communicative situation of fictional narrative—somebody telling us that somebody is telling somebody else that something happened—is itself a layered ethical situation. The narrator's treatment of the events will inevitably convey certain attitudes toward the subject matter and the audience, attitudes that, among other things, indicate his or her sense of responsibility to and regard for the audience. Similarly, the author's treatment of the narrator and of the authorial audience will indicate something of his or her ethical commitments. At the same time, the very act of reading has an ethical dimension: reading involves doing things such as judging, desiring, emoting, actions that are linked to our values. More generally, the audience's response to the narrative will indicate their commitments to and attitudes toward the author, the narrator, the narrative situation, and the values expressed in the narrative.[4]

Among the many approaches to ethics now being developed, this one is most closely related to those of Wayne C. Booth (1988) and Adam Zachary Newton (1995). Each of them, like me, wants to root narrative ethics in narrative itself rather than in some abstract ethical system. Indeed, Booth emphasizes the pervasiveness of ethics in critical responses to literature and Newton says that he wants to conceive of "narrative *as* ethics." Each of them moves, in his own way, from narrative, to theoretical treatments of narrative, and then back to narrative. In Booth's case, those theoretical treatments can be found in his own earlier work on the rhetoric of literature. His title, *The Company We Keep*, and his main metaphor, books as friends, grow out of his earlier exploration of the way that writing and reading make possible a meeting of minds between author and reader. *The Company We Keep* moves beyond Booth's earlier major emphasis on how such meetings occur to the contemplation of how our values are engaged as we read, especially the ethical consequences of desiring as the text invites us to desire. *The Company We Keep* also gives greater emphasis to the communal nature of ethical response, sug-

gesting that the activity of discussing the values of texts, what Booth calls co-
ducing, is ethically more important than getting the text "right."

Newton investigates the "ethical consequences of narrating story and fictionalizing person, and the reciprocal claims binding teller, listener, witness,
and reader in that process" (p. 11), an investigation that leads him to describe
three kinds of ethical structure in narrative: the narrational, the representational, and the hermeneutic. Narrational ethics are those associated with the
telling; they occur along the line of narrative transmission from author, to
narrator, to narratee, to reader. Representational ethics are those associated
with "fictionalizing person" or creating character. Hermeneutic ethics are those
associated with reading and interpreting, the obligations readers and critics have
to the text. Newton synthesizes work of Mikhail Bakhtin, Stanley Cavell, and
Emmanuel Levinas as he does his analyses, borrowing especially Bakhtin's concept of *vhzivanie* or live-entering (empathy with the other without loss of self),
Cavell's concept of acknowledging (being in a position of having to respond),
and Levinas's concepts of Saying (performing a telling) and Facing (looking at
or looking away).

While I share much with Booth and with Newton, I do not want to adopt
Booth's overarching metaphor of books as friends, because it seems too lim-
iting, or Newton's idea that narrative is equivalent to ethics, because that seems
not to recognize all the other things narrative is as well. Furthermore, although
I find Bakhtin, Cavell, and Levinas all to be strong theorists, I am less inclined
than Newton to look to theory for recurrent ethical concerns and more inclined
to let individual narratives develop their own sets of ethical issues.

From this perspective, then, the very act of reading entails ethical engagement and response, but those entailments arise in conjunction with the
narrative's technique, our cognitive understanding, and our emotional response. I refer to these entailments as our ethical positioning. Indeed, the central construct in my approach to the ethics of reading is *position*, a concept
that combines being placed in and acting from an ethical location. At any given
point in a narrative, our ethical position results from the dynamic interaction
of four ethical situations:

1) that of the characters within the story world;
2) that of the narrator in relation to the telling, the told, and the
    audience (unreliable narration, for example, constitutes a differ-
    ent ethical position from reliable narration; different kinds of fo-
    calization also position the audience differently);
3) that of the implied author in relation to the authorial audience
    (the implied author's choices to adopt one narrative strategy
    rather than another will affect the audience's ethical response to

the characters; each choice will also convey the author's attitudes toward the audience); and

4) that of the flesh-and-blood reader in relation to the set of values, beliefs, and locations.

Given the controversy about *Lolita*, I want to start with the first three ethical situations; I will address the fourth in the final pages of this essay. Consider, then, the novel's famous davenport scene, in which Humbert contrives to bring himself to orgasm, without Dolores's knowledge, from the contact between his body and hers. The scene runs for almost five pages in the printed version; I will focus here on its conclusion as a representative sample:

> There was, I swear, a yellowish-violet bruise on her lovely nymphet thigh which my huge hairy hand massaged and slowly enveloped— and because of her very perfunctory underthings, there seemed to be nothing to prevent my muscular thumb from reaching the hot hollow of her groin—just as you might tickle and caress a giggling child— just that—and: "Oh it's nothing at all," she cried with a sudden shrill note in her voice, and she wiggled, and squirmed, and threw her head back, and her teeth rested on her glistening underlip as she half-turned away, and my moaning mouth, gentlemen of the jury, almost reached her bare neck, while I crushed out against her left buttock the last throb of the longest ecstasy man or monster had ever known. (pp. 60– 61)

Our ethical positioning in this passage—and throughout the scene—is both complicated and uncomfortable, as we can see by tracing the relations among the first three ethical situations. That between the characters is easy to apprehend: Humbert treats the young and innocent Dolores as a sex object and uses her for his sexual gratification, transforming her from a child into a sexual toy. Earlier in the scene, he suggests that because she is unaware of what he is doing, his pleasure is innocent. Indeed, he seems to take great pride in his ability to manipulate the situation, to have Dolores be "safely solipsized" (p. 60). The second and third ethical situations—Humbert's relation to his subject matter and audience and Nabokov's relation to *his* audience and to that same subject matter (plus Humbert)—exist in a very complicated relation to each other, one that makes the scene very discomfiting to read. It is notable, first, that Nabokov has Humbert describe the action from the perspective of the experiencing I: Humbert the narrator does not interject his present-tense thoughts except to reinforce the perspective of Humbert the character. And that perspective is one of pride in his cleverness, eager anticipation of his success, and finally satisfaction: "the last throb of the longest ecstasy man or monster had ever known." Simply to read the scene is to take on Humbert's perspective, and to take on his perspective means to see his perverse desire from the inside. Furthermore, because Humbert's effort in the scene is not merely to deny that he is doing anything wrong but also to communicate his pride and satisfaction, he is also attempting to seduce his audience into accepting his perspective as the appropriate one. In other words, Humbert implicitly asks his audience not only to take on his perspective but also to approve it. Because Nabokov gives Humbert such formidable verbal skills and rhetorical power, we can't help but feel the force of his appeal.

At the same time, Nabokov provides numerous signals that we ought to resist Humbert's appeal, to recognize that the line between solipsizing and molesting is paper-thin, and, above all, to regard Humbert's use of Dolores for his pleasure as an ab-use of her. Nevertheless, some of these signals themselves increase our discomfort. For example, Nabokov uses Humbert's acute awareness of what he might do with his "muscular thumb" both to underline the physical disparity between Humbert and Dolores and to suggest how close Humbert is to molesting her. While Humbert compares the possible motion of his thumb with caressing and tickling a giggling child, his references to her "perfunctory underthings" and "the hot hollow of her groin" actually conjure up a more explicit sexual act, one that is painful to contemplate. In the final sentence in the passage I've quoted, Nabokov invites us to see Humbert as vampire: "*my moaning mouth* . . . almost reached *her bare neck*, while I [en-joyed] the longest ecstasy man *or monster* had ever known" (emphasis added).

Through these signals, Nabokov clearly communicates his ethical disapproval of Humbert and invites the authorial audience to share in it. Yet Nabokov's technique also means that before we can stand with Nabokov and away from his character, we have to stand with Humbert and share his perspective. It's a very uncomfortable ethical position because it allows Nabokov to have his cake and eat it, too: to indulge in pedophilic fantasies through his creation and then to say, "But of course we right-thinking people condemn such fantasies." Indeed, if Nabokov always restricted the perspective to that of Humbert at the time of the action, I would, as a flesh-and-blood reader, be inclined to join with those who would not teach the book. But it is precisely because Nabokov shows, in sequences such as the one between chapter 29 and chapter 30 of part 1, a complex interplay between Humbert's perspective at the time of the action and his apparently changing perspective at the time of the narration that I find the narrative to be so ethically challenging. Before I discuss the fourth ethical situation further, that between Nabokov and flesh-and-blood readers, I want to consider that apparently changing perspective, especially as it gets revealed at the end of part 1. In order to appreciate what Nabokov is doing with Humbert's perspective in that sequence, we need to consider how self-consciousness and unreliability in first-person (or what Genette [1980] calls homodiegetic) narration may function.

By self-consciousness I mean the narrator's awareness of him- or herself as the teller of the story. When a narrator is self-conscious, we attribute to him or to her such global things as the design of the narrative and such local things as the choice of diction. As M. Elizabeth Preston (1997) has argued, however, self-consciousness is not the same thing as aesthetic control, that is, control over the effects of a narrative. Humbert Humbert rates very high on the scale of self-consciousness: he says on the first page: "You can always count on a murderer for a fancy prose style" (Nabokov, p. 9); he says, after Dolores reveals the name of the man she escaped with: "Quietly the fusion took place, and everything fell into order, into the pattern of branches that I have woven throughout this memoir with the express purpose of having the ripe fruit fall at the right moment" (p. 272). And most of the word play and the allusions, detailed so extensively by Alfred Appel, Jr., in *The Annotated Lolita* (Nabokov, 1955/1991), also point to Humbert's conscious crafting of the narrative.

Yet for all the artistry and cleverness of Humbert's telling, his control over the effects of his narration has significant limits, the most important of them involving his unreliable ethical judgments. As my analysis of the passage from the davenport scene indicates, Nabokov uses Humbert's narration to send us signals that Humbert is not fully aware of. Other examples abound throughout the narrative, especially in part 1, and I will cite just a few of them here. Humbert is totally oblivious to the way his narration of his marriage to Valeria makes her look like a long-suffering saint and him like a cruel egoist. He also seems unaware, despite the lesson of Charlotte's reading, of the effect that the diary of the first weeks in the Haze household is likely to have on his audience. He introduces it, after all, as "exhibit number two" (p. 40), part of his defense, something that he apparently believes will work toward his exoneration at least as much as exhibit number one, the story of his abortive love for Annabel Leigh, will. But what the diary details, of course, is the Portrait of a Pedophile as a Lusting but Cautious Boarder. In short, Humbert is an unreliable self-conscious narrator.

Let us return now to the end of chapter 29:

> My life was handled by little Lo in an energetic matter-of-fact manner as if it were an insensate gadget unconnected with me. While eager to impress me with the world of tough kids, she was not quite pre-pared for certain discrepancies between a kid's life and mine. Pride alone prevented her from giving up; for, in my strange predicament, I feigned supreme stupidity and had her have her way—at least while I could still bear it. But really these are irrelevant matters. I am not concerned with so-called "sex" at all. Anybody can imagine those el-ements of animality. A greater endeavor lures me on: to fix once for all the perilous magic of nymphets. (p. 134)

With Mary Patricia Martin, I have argued elsewhere (Phelan & Martin, 1999) that unreliability can occur along three axes: the axis of facts/events, the axis of knowledge/perception, and the axis of values, and that there can be two kinds of unreliability along each axis—an account that is erroneous and an account that does not go far enough. In other words, there are six types of unreliability: underreporting and misreporting, underreading and misreading, and underregarding and misregarding. Humbert's narration here exhibits underreporting, misreporting, and misregarding. The underreporting is evident in the swerve the narration takes after his admission that he let her have her way "at least while I could still bear it." Prior to this move, Humbert has given many details about how Dolores suggested that he and she play the game Charlie Holmes taught her at camp and has begun his account of their game, complete with an acknowledgment of "certain discrepancies" between Dolores's expectations and his adult male body. Once Humbert becomes the main actor—after his lust conquers his patience—he stops reporting the behavioral details and goes so far as to claim that they are "irrelevant." He is misreporting because he is absolutely concerned with sex, and he is misregarding when he resorts to the Nymphet Defense—a subtle but ultimately transparent way of blaming the victim.

The interaction of the unreliability with the self-consciousness is consistent with Humbert's main motive for telling during part 1. He wants to defend himself not only against a charge of murder but even more against the condemnation he knows his pedophilia would normally receive. In narrating the event of the first intercourse, he deliberately underreports his own actions so that he can maximize Dolores's role as the initiator and he deliberately resorts to the Nymphet Defense to make himself seem more eccentric than perverse. Indeed, if his fancy prose style and attention to the magic of nymphets take in credulous ladies and gentlemen of the jury so much the better. What, then, is the narrative logic that underlies his shift to the description of the murals he imagines himself painting?

> Had I been a painter, had the management of The Enchanted Hunters lost its mind one summer day and commissioned me to redecorate their dining room with murals of my own making, this is what I might have thought up, let me list some fragments:
>
> There would have been a lake. There would have been an arbor in flame-flower. There would have been nature studies—a tiger pursuing a bird of paradise, a choking snake sheathing whole the flayed trunk of a shoat. There would have been a sultan, his face expressing great agony (belied, as it were, by his molding caress), helping a callypygean slave child to climb a column of onyx. There would have been those luminous globules of gonadal glow that travel up the opal-

escent sides of jukeboxes. There would have been all kinds of camp
activities on the part of the intermediate group, Canoeing, Coranting,
Combing Curls in the lakeside sun. There would have been poplars,
apples, a suburban Sunday. There would have been a fire opal dissolving within a ripple-ringed pool, a last throb, a last dab of color,
stinging red, smarting pink, a sigh, a wincing child. (pp. 134–135)

The differences from chapter 29 are remarkable: Where chapter 29 is riddled
with unreliability, chapter 30 is utterly reliable. Where chapter 29 is dominated
by Humbert's concern for how he comes across and is very much a part of
self-conscious strategic defense, chapter 30 progresses toward the spontaneous
overflow of powerful feeling. Furthermore, this powerful feeling belongs to
Humbert the narrator, and it is so powerful as to be a major factor in mo-
tivating Humbert to change the purpose of his narrative. These claims will
become clearer after I analyze the focalization, the way in which Nabokov
controls the "vision" or "perception" of Humbert's narration.

In an essay titled "Why Narrators Can Be Focalizers and Why It Matters"
(Phelan, 2001), I contest the position, advanced by such narratologists as Seymour Chatman (1990) and Gerald Prince (2001), that narrators cannot be
focalizers. Chatman and Prince want to preserve the distinction between story
and discourse as an absolute dichotomy, and so they contend that only characters can be focalizers because only characters are part of the story world and
thus only characters can be said to "perceive" events in that world. According
to this position, heterodiegetic (or third-person) narrators report and homodiegetic (or first-person) narrators remember, but no narrators perceive events
or characters because, by definition, they are part of the discourse and so do
not occupy the same ontological space as the characters. In my view, by contrast, the story/discourse distinction has heuristic, not absolute, value and narrators ought to be understood as focalizers because their reports simultaneously
provide an angle of vision or perception that provides readers one path rather
than another through the story world. I argue further that first-person narration
can display dual focalization, a technique that shows a narrator at the time of
the telling perceiving his former self's perceptions at the time of the action.
My chief example is the last sentence of chapter 3, part 2 of *Lolita*, a sentence
that, I submit, Humbert would not have written if he had not already written
chapter 30 of part 1.

And so we rolled East, I more devastated than braced with the satisfaction of my passion, and she glowing with health, her bi-iliac gar-
land still as brief as a lad's, although she had added to inches to her
stature and eight pounds to her weight. We had been everywhere.
We had really seen nothing. And I catch myself thinking today that
our long journey had only defiled with a sinuous trail of slime the

lovely, trustful, dreamy, enormous country that by then, in retrospect, was no more to us than a collection of dog-eared maps, ruined tour books, old tires, and her sobs in the night—every night, every night— the moment I feigned sleep. (pp. 175–176)

The first part of the last sentence is focalized through Humbert the narrator ("I catch myself thinking today . . ."). However, when Humbert the character's focalization enters in the second half of the sentence ("by then, in retrospect, [the country] was no more to us than a collection of dog-eared maps, ruined tour books, old tires, and her sobs in the night—every night, every night—the moment I feigned sleep"), Humbert the narrator's focalization does not drop away. Instead, the narrator's focalization contains the character's. The source of this effect here can be found in the syntax, which clearly indicates that everything in the sentence is included in what Humbert catches himself "thinking today." The syntax is sufficient to produce the effect, but it is reinforced by the temporal ambiguity of the phrase "in retrospect," which can refer to either a retrospect from the narrator's present moment or a retrospect from the character's. Thus, although it is only the narrating I who draws the conclusion that their journey had defiled the country, it is both the narrating I and the experiencing I who envision Dolores sobbing "every night, every night." Moreover, the narrating I is also perceiving his former self's awareness of that sobbing.

In chapter 30 of part 1, the movement between focalization through the narrator and focalization through the character goes in the other direction. The present tense ("this is what I might have thought up") signals that Humbert the narrator is the focalizer. And for much of his catalog of the fragments he would have painted he remains the sole focalizer. The catalog is notable for the contrast it forms with Humbert's unreliable claims at the end of chapter 29 about not being "concerned with so-called 'sex.' " As noted earlier, the catalog includes metaphors of Humbert's predatory behavior toward Dolores that suggest something of the "animality" of that behavior: the "nature studies" are of "a tiger pursuing a bird of paradise, a choking snake sheathing whole the flayed trunk of a shoat." But then the next fragment reverts to Humbert's focus on his own desire even as its miniallegory again underlines the difference in power and size between himself and Dolores: "a sultan, his face expressing great agony (belied, as it were, by his molding caress), helping a callypygean slave child to climb a column of onyx." The focus on Humbert's own pleasure continues in the next fragment: "those luminous globules of gonadal glow that travel up the opalescent sides of jukeboxes." Furthermore, the catalog contains references to previous scenes of sex that involved each of them: "all kinds of camp activities," an allusion to the game she played with Charlie Holmes, "apples, a suburban Sunday," an allusion to the davenport scene. Then a more dramatic shift occurs in the last sentence: "a fire opal dissolving within a ripple-ringed pool, a last throb, a last dab of color, stinging red, smarting pink, a sigh, a wincing child." First, Humbert abandons the pretense of listing only paintable images as the catalog expands to include "a last throb" and "a sigh." Second, Humbert's narration shifts to dual focalization. Humbert the narrator is perceiving (once again) what Humbert the character perceived and felt at the end of his intercourse with Dolores: his last throb (the phrase itself echoes the davenport scene and in so doing highlights the weakness of his claim for the innocence of his actions then) and his sigh intermingled with her "stinging," "smarting," "wincing" child's body. The rethinking of the event by Humbert the narrator as he develops his catalog of fragments has brought him to the point of reseeing it. Consequently, Humbert obliquely rewrites the scene of the first intercourse, and in this revision his selfish violence and Dolores's pain are foregrounded.[5]

In terms of ethical positioning, then, the dual focalization indicates significant changes in the first two situations. Humbert, through the very act of telling his story, the effort of perceiving and reperceiving himself and Dolores, is changing his relation to the story as well as to himself, to Dolores, and to his audience. That the focalization is dual is crucial: during the first intercourse he has seen her wincing, stinging, and smarting and during his two years with her he has seen the kind of suffering that led to her sobs in the night, but he refused to let those sights affect his behavior. During the act of telling, however, Humbert allows himself to look upon what he had previously turned away from. Since the more he allows himself to see, the less he can pursue his exoneration, the motive for his telling shifts.

It is significant, however, that chapter 30 does not mark a total break with Humbert's original motive or his unreliability. In chapter 31, he seems to shift back to the sensibility that governs the end of chapter 29 as his narration returns to the nature of "nymphet love": "I am trying to describe these things not to relive them in my present boundless misery, but to sort out the portion of hell and the portion of heaven in that strange, awful, maddening world—nymphet love. The beastly and the beautiful merged at one point, and it is that borderline I would like to fix, and I feel I fail to do so utterly" (p. 135). Yet even here Humbert's emphasis on the "portion of hell" and "the beastly" imply, however indirectly, a new willingness to admit the horror of his behavior. Yet the next paragraph reverts to the kind of rationalization that Humbert has engaged in before, as he cites legal precedents for adult–child sexual relations ("the stipulation of the Roman law, according to which a girl may marry at twelve, was adopted by the Church, and is still preserved, rather tacitly, in some of the United States") and claims: "I have but followed nature. I am nature's faithful hound" (p. 135). But the next sentence suggests that even he is no longer completely convinced by such protestations: "Why then this horror that I cannot shake off?" The end of chapter 30 has provided an answer, but Humbert the narrator is not yet ready to deal with its consequences and so he moves back toward exoneration: "Did I deprive her of her flower? Sensitive gentlewomen of the jury, I was not even her first lover" (p. 134).

In terms of the third ethical position, then—Nabokov's relation to his authorial audience—this sequence and especially the technique of dual focalization indicate, first, that Nabokov is using Humbert's act of telling as itself part of the represented action of the novel. Part of what we need to attend to, in other words, is how the autobiographical act affects Humbert the narrator's development. More specifically, Nabokov uses this sequence and the dual focalization to add a significant layer to the narrative: the ethical struggle of Humbert the narrator. The struggle, at the most general level, is about whether he will continue to justify and exonerate himself or shift to admitting his guilt and accepting his punishment. More specifically, the struggle is one about vision: whether he will continue to look away from Dolores and focus only on himself or allow himself, as he does at the end of chapter 30, to look upon what he has done to Dolores. One important effect of this layer of the narrative—and Humbert's move toward seeing more—is to make Humbert both more sympathetic and more hateful. It makes him more sympathetic because it shows him taking responsibility for what he's done, but it makes him more hateful because it more clearly reveals the horror of his actions: he was aware of Dolores's pain at the time of the action but refused to attend to it. Similarly, in the authorial audience we find Nabokov's communication both more remarkable and more difficult to take in: Humbert's struggle becomes a significant part of our interest, even as it becomes increasingly painful to see what he sees about his past behavior.

This sequence has implications for the larger debates about the novel. It provides evidence that Humbert's shift to condemning himself is not a self-conscious manipulation of his audience but an unplanned shift that develops as he writes. He does not, in other words, calculatedly follow his unreliable narration at the end of chapter 29 with the reliable dual focalization of chapter 30 and then the vacillations of chapter 31. Not even Humbert is devious enough to say, "I know, I'll be amazingly inconsistent in my attitudes toward the crucial event in the first half of the narrative giving my audience a glimpse of a clearer-visioned self and thus generating sympathy." Instead, the very effort of telling the story in the span of 53 days between his arrest and his death leads him to represent himself in inconsistent ways. Or to put it another way, it is Nabokov who calculatedly makes Humbert inconsistent at the end of part 1 in order to show that he is not completely depraved.

Following out this logic, we can see that Humbert's protestations of his love for Dolores and his self-condemnation are sincere. This sincerity is not enough to erase what he has done to Dolores or to redeem him, and as Michael

Wood (1995) points out, there are still real limits on Humbert's vision of himself, Dolores, and his behavior. Nevertheless, the sincerity of his declarations of love provides the final piece for our understanding of the dual focalization. Why does Humbert allow himself to see Dolores at the time of the narration in a way that he refused to allow himself at the time of the action? Because he is now looking with love—or at least his flawed version of it—rather than with lust. Furthermore, his allowing himself to see Dolores in this way makes his situation more poignant. The act of telling intensifies not just his love and loss but also his awareness of how deeply and irrevocably he has injured her. And so by the end of the narrative, his dominant emotion is not self-pity but regret for what he has done to Dolores. And he does deliberately save for almost the very end, in yet another instance of dual focalization, the revelation of "a last mirage of wonder and hopelessness," the scene that leads him to admit how much of Dolores's life he had stolen from her: "I stood listening to that musical vibration [of children at play] from my lofty slope, to those flashes of separate cries with a kind of demure murmur for background, and then I knew that the hopelessly poignant thing was not Lolita's absence from my side, but the absence of her voice from that concord" (p. 308).

More generally, then, this analysis has tried to demonstrate the ethical complexity of Humbert's narration. He is, indeed, a horrible pedophile who uses his stylistic virtuosity and his theory of nymphets both to induce his audience to participate in his lust and as someone who realizes, albeit imperfectly, how much pain and suffering he has caused. And in telling the story, as Kauffman (1992) makes clear, Humbert never really allows his audience to see Dolores except as he sees her, either as character or as narrator, and he never sees her as Dolores—only as Lolita, a creature of his invention. As a result, his story evokes both our sympathy and our reproach—and so I would say that the extreme reactions in praise of and in condemnation of the book are each well justified but each partial.

Finally, however, I want to return to Nabokov's role in this ethical drama and to my flesh-and-blood response: what are the ethics of asking us to participate in Humbert's story, to watch the trajectory of his life and of his changing motives for telling about his life? The author who created this book is someone to be admired but also someone to be wary of. Nabokov's narrative project is enormously difficult—showing us the horror of Humbert in word, deed, and consequence and then asking us to find him worthy of sympathy—and executed with stunning skill. At the same time, this success does not obliterate my distaste either for Humbert the character or for the experience of participating in his worst moments—and in order for me to participate, Nabokov has to fully enter into Humbert's imagination. Like Dolores, he enters umber and black Humberland, but unlike her, he does not survey it with a shrug of amused distaste but rather lives there with a kind of perverse relish. That, to my vision, is the ethical dark side of this book.[6]

A final word: As this last paragraph shows in making the link between the analysis of technique and the ethics of fiction, the individual critic's own values and value judgments will inevitably come into play. Consequently, I realize that my way of moving from technique to ethics may not be one my readers find compelling or persuasive. But that does not mean—at least it does not necessarily mean—that either I or my readers are ethically deficient. Instead, it means that we could have a lot to talk about.

Notes

1. In order to differentiate my own perspective from that of Humbert Humbert I shall refer to the girl whom he calls Lolita by her given name.

2. There is one short intervening stretch of narration between the end of chapter 29 and the passage I have just quoted from chapter 30, an address by Humbert to possible narratees:

> I have to tread carefully. I have to speak in a whisper. Oh you, veteran crime reporter, you grave old usher, you once popular policeman, now in solitary confinement after gracing that school crossing for years, you wretched emeritus read to by a boy! It would never do, would it, to have you fellows fall madly in love with my Lolita! (p. 134)

This passage clearly locates Humbert's perspective in the time of the narration, and it reveals, in the wake of the narration of the intercourse, his lingering desire to possess Dolores himself and his belief that other men harbor similar desires. The passage makes psychological sense, given Humbert the narrator's awareness that Quilty was present at The Enchanted Hunters Hotel on the night of the first intercourse. All of these effects make the shift in Humbert's narration that occurs in the rest of the chapter all the more striking.

3. The history of criticism of *Lolita* itself makes an interesting narrative, with most of the early responses focusing on the novel's aesthetics (perhaps to counter the charge that it was pornographic) and, in Lionel Trilling's (1958, Oct. 11) case, its status as a love story. Alfred Appel, Jr.'s appreciative work has contributed not only the very helpful *The Annotated Lolita* (Nabokov, 1955/1991) but also considerable understanding of Nabokov's allusions and parodic techniques. The turn to an ethical criticism that finds significant fault with the novel is relatively recent, spurred primarily by Kauffman (1992). For important later contributions see especially Wood (1995) and Patnoe (1995). I should add that in my chapter on *Lolita* in a 1981 book on style I, too, focus on the book's aesthetics, arguing, among other things, that during the davenport scene readers simultaneously condemn

Humbert's actions and admire his—and Nabokov's—virtuoso style (Phelan, 1981).
For a good sample of essays see Bloom's (1993) collection, and for a fuller sense
of the critical history from 1977 to 1995 see Jones (1997).

4. For further discussion of this approach see my *Narrative as Rhetoric* (Phelan, 1996), especially the introduction.

5. Patnoe (1995) argues that Humbert's narration is so unreliable and ambiguous in chapter 29 that we have reason to doubt that Dolores makes the first
move. Although I don't see the ambiguity in Humbert's account of Dolores's suggestion, I have been influenced by Patnoe's argument that even if we regard Dolores
as the initiator, she does not really know what sex with an adult male means and
so Humbert cruelly and selfishly inflicts himself upon her.

6. For an intriguing case that Nabokov's creation of Humbert comes out of
more than a fertile imagination, see Centerwall (1990).

References

Bloom, H. (Ed.) (1993). *Lolita*. New York: Chelsea House.
Booth, W. C. (1988). *The company we keep: An ethics of fiction*. Berkeley: University of California Press.
Centerwall, B. (1990). Hiding in plain sight: Nabokov and pedophilia. *Texas Studies in Language and Literature, 32*, 468–484.
Chatman, S. (1990). *Coming to terms: The rhetoric of narrative in fiction and film*. Ithaca, NY: Cornell University Press.
Genette, G. (1980). *Narrative discourse: An essay in method* (J. E. Lewin, Trans.). Ithaca, NY: Cornell University Press.
Jones, N. J. (1997). Vladimir Nabokov's *Lolita*: A survey of scholarship and criticism in English, 1977–95. *Bonner Beitrage, 54*(2), 129–147.
Kauffman, L. (1992). *Special delivery: Epistolary modes in modern fiction*. Chicago: University of Chicago Press.
Nabokov, V. (1991). *The annotated Lolita*. (A. Appel, Jr., Ed.). New York: McGraw Hill. (Original work published 1955)
Newton, A. Z. (1995). *Narrative ethics*. Cambridge, MA: Harvard University Press.
Patnoe, E. (1995). *Lolita* misrepresented, *Lolita* reclaimed: Disclosing the doubles. *College Literature, 22*, 81–104.
Phelan, J. (1981). *Worlds from words: A theory of language in fiction*. Chicago: University of Chicago Press.
Phelan, J. (1996). *Narrative as rhetoric: Technique, audiences, ethics, ideology*. Columbus: Ohio State University Press.
Phelan, J. (2001). Why narrators can be focalizers and why it matters. In W. van Peer & S. Chatman (Eds.), *New perspectives on narrative perspective* (pp. 51–66). Albany: SUNY Press.
Phelan, J., & Martin, M. P. (1999). The lessons of "Weymouth": Homodiegesis, unreliability, ethics, and *The Remains of the Day*. In D. Herman (Ed.), *Nar-*

ratologies: New perspectives on narrative analysis (pp. 88–109). Columbus: Ohio State University Press.

Preston, M. E. (1997). *Homodiegetic narration: Reliability, selfconsciousness, ideology, and ethics.* Unpublished doctoral dissertation, Ohio State University, Columbus.

Prince, G. (2001). A point of view on point of view or refocusing focalization. In W. van Peer & S. Chatman (Eds.), *New perspectives on narrative perspective* (pp. 43–50). Albany: SUNY Press.

Trilling, L. (1958, Oct. 11). The last lover—Vladimir Nabokov's *Lolita. Encounter, 11*, 9–19.

Wood, M. (1995). *Lolita* revisited. *New England Review: Middlebury Series, 17(3),* 15–43.

PART IV

Narrative Disruptions in the Construction of Self

8 The Pursuit of Death in Holocaust Narrative

Lawrence L. Langer

Autobiographical narrative by its very nature explores a journey that has not yet reached its end. A recent study of the genre is called *Memory and Narrative: The Weave of Life-Writing* (Olney, 1998). It occurs to me that a study of Holocaust memory and narrative might justifiably be subtitled *The Weave of Death-Writing*. Although Holocaust testimonies and memoirs are of course concerned with how one went on living in the midst of German atrocities, their subtexts offer us a theme that is more difficult to express or understand: how, under those minimal conditions, slowly but inexorably, one went on dying—every day, every hour, every minute of one's agonizing existence. We are forced to redefine the meaning of survival, as the positive idea of staying alive is usurped by the negative one of fending off death. The impact on consciousness of this dilemma is a neglected but important legacy of the experience we call the Holocaust.

The Holocaust survivors I am speaking of do not merely recover their lives in their narratives. Through complex associations with their murdered comrades, family members, and communities they also recover what I call their missed destiny of death. Because the logic of existence in places such as Auschwitz dictated that you should die, witnesses often feel that survival was an *abnormal* result of their ordeal in the camps, a violation of the expected outcome of their detention. They were not meant to return. Charlotte Delbo calls the first volume of her Auschwitz memoir, *Auschwitz and After, None of Us Will Return* (1965/1995). This has nothing to do with guilt or what some label a death wish but with a stubborn intuition that unlike the others, through accident or luck, those who held out somehow mistakenly eluded their intended end. In many instances the sensation of being dead while alive reflects a dual thrust of their present being: in chronological time they seek their future, while in durational time, those isolated moments of dreadful memories that do not dissipate but congeal into dense claws of tenacious consciousness, a lethal past relentlessly pursues them.

According to Auschwitz survivor Jean Améry (1966/1986), mass murder in the form of genocide forced its victims to live not next door to but in the same room as death. Distinguishing between the violence of war and the rigid milieu of the camps, Améry observed: "The soldier was driven into the fire, and it is true his life was not worth much. Still, the state did not order him to die, but to survive. The final duty of the prisoner, however, was death" (p. 15). In other words, the *necessity* of dying replaced the possibility of dying, even as many inmates struggled to stay alive—which is different from resolving to survive. Their surroundings, rather than some internal system of values inherited from their normal life, infiltrated the mental content of their days. What this meant can be illustrated by two brief excerpts from witness testimonies. Renee H., who was little more than 10 years old at the time, recalls a scene from Bergen-Belsen:

> Right across from us was a charnel house filled with corpses, not just inside but overflowing all over. There were corpses all over. I lived, walked beside dead people. After a while it just got to be so that no one noticed, and one had to say to oneself, "I am not going to see who it is. I am not going to recognize anyone in this person who is lying there." It got to a point where I realized that I had to close my eyes to a number of things. Otherwise I would not have survived even at that time, because I saw people around me going mad. I was not only having to live with all things, but with madness. (Greene & Kumar, 2000, pp. 173–174)

We need to imagine how such imagery imprints itself on consciousness, despite efforts to avoid the unavoidable, but even more, we need to acknowledge the impact of such imagery on the unfolding of Holocaust narrative as memory stumbles repeatedly over death while it seeks to recount episodes of life in the camps under conditions of atrocity.

The second example is both more vivid and more graphic. It documents with uncanny, if unintended, precision a moment of failed purgation, as if the *body* were seeking to expel what memory could not cast out from consciousness:

> I got a job carrying people's waste out from the barrack at night. . . .
> I was very sick. I got diarrhea. That was already recuperating a little
> bit from the malaria. I walked out with two pails of human waste

and I was going toward the dump. I walked out, and between the barracks was a mountain of people as high as myself.

The people died at night, they were just taken out on the dump— you know, a big pile of people. And I said to myself, "O God. Must I walk by?" But in the meanwhile, I couldn't hold back, and I just put down the two pails and I sit down because I had a sick stomach. And the rats were standing and eating the people's faces—eating, you know, they were having a . . . [*long silence*]. Anyway, I had to do my job. I was just looking, what's happening to a human being. That could have been my mother. That could have been my father. That could have been my sister or my brother. (Greene & Kumar, 2000, pp. 174–175)

The sheer physicality of the description would dampen the ardor of those who insist on the triumph of the spirit even in Auschwitz, which is the locale of this remembered episode. The fusion of excrement, corpses, and predatory rats creates a cluster of images that forces us to redefine our notion of dying. At that moment the witness seemed to be trapped by a cycle of decay from which there was no escape. The cherished idea of the family as an intimate unit succumbed momentarily to the horrible alternative of the family as prey for hungry rodents. It leaves us numbed by the challenge of absorbing into our hopes for a human future this grim heritage of unnatural death.

I said that the witness, Hanna F., succumbed *momentarily* to a new and unprecedented vision of her family's fate, but this was more a charitable concession than a discovered truth. Such images may lurk in consciousness undeciphered, but they inspire insight only after being filtered through a mind determined to wrestle with the implications of the harsh burden that the Germans imposed on their victims. Jean Améry spent his postcamp life, which ended in suicide, unsuccessfully trying to placate the ghost of unnatural death that plagued him after his survival. In a now classic work called *At the Mind's Limits* (1966/1986) he reported:

There was once a conversation in the camp about an SS man who had slit open a prisoner's belly and filled it with sand. It is obvious that in view of such possibilities one was hardly concerned with whether, or *that*, one had to die, but with *how* it would happen. Inmates carried on conversations about how long it probably takes for the gas in the gas chambers to do its job. One speculated on the painfulness of death by phenol injections. Were you to wish yourself a blow to the skull or a slow death through exhaustion in the infirmary? It was characteristic for the situation of the prisoner in regard to death that only a few decided to "run to the wire," as one said, that is, to commit suicide through contact with the highly electrified barbed wire. The wire was after all a good and rather certain thing, but it was possible that in the attempt to approach it one would be caught first and thrown into the bunker, and that led to a more difficult and more painful dying. Dying was omnipresent, death vanished from sight. (p. 17)

Améry's variations on a theme of dying in Auschwitz leave little space for consolation. "These were the conditions under which the intellectual collided with death," he concluded. "Death lay before him, and in him the spirit was still stirring; the latter confronted the former and tried—in vain, to say it straight off—to exemplify its dignity" (p. 16).

Dying among the living, even when it is abrupt and painful, is a termination, and for those left behind society provides rituals of closure, which include grief for the departed—we even have an appropriate vocabulary of solace—to ease the separation. But dying among the dying leaves us with no analogy to help us imagine the ordeal and find a suitable place in consciousness to lodge it. We have few narratives that portray such dying and its effect on traditional versions of the self. Améry's prisoners who discuss their possible doom bear no agency for their fate. They are left with a permanent uncertainty about the responsibility for their anguish, unable to blame a gas chamber or a hypodermic needle or the crushing force of a club. The absence of an identifiable human killer that allows one to trace a clear path from cause to effect is joined by another important hiatus that afflicts the memory of survivors, and that is the missing ritual of mourning. This is complicated by the foreknowledge that their own dying, when it occurs, will preclude a similar ritual for themselves. Permanently barred from details of how members of their families died, witnesses often seem less distressed by the illogic of those early deaths than by the "illogic" of their own continued lives. The psychic discontinuity implicit in such experience prevents the deaths of others—really, the murders of others—from being integrated into the natural rhythms of existence and leaves the survivor vainly groping for some tie between consequential living and inconsequential dying. The former is the text, the latter the subtext of numerous Holocaust narratives, oral and written, which leads to a constant tension between pursuit and escape as divided consciousness seeks to integrate what cannot be reconciled—except perhaps in the ambiguous landscape of art.

The rift in time and memory that separates the unnatural deaths of others from one's own staying alive cries out for a bridge, but continuity is not its name. The vision of decay that reminds Hanna F. of her family's wretched end spreads its sway over the surrounding narrative terrain, contaminating efforts to soothe the transition from past to present or to free one to enter tranquilly into the future. The view that Holocaust survivors should be able to generalize their anguish in order to leave behind them the aura of death derives from unfamiliarity with how durational time assails the memory of so many witnesses. On the deepest level, their life stories are also death stories, which include the partial death of the self in ways that still need to be interpreted. The quest for a rebirth of that part of the self is as futile as would be any effort to transform Hanna F.'s pile of corpses into a sacred community of the dead. This may be a dark view, but there is overwhelming evidence from Holocaust narratives that it is a realistic one, from which we have much to learn. The effect of atrocity, and not only Holocaust atrocity, on the modern sensibility is a virgin territory into which few analysts have yet ventured.

One of the many victims of these narratives is the very notion that we can expel from consciousness, and hence from being, zones of memory that threaten our intact spirits. Unnatural death creates an inversion of normality that we cannot easily dismiss. In her Auschwitz trilogy Charlotte Delbo (1965, 1970, 1971/1995) reproduces a monologue by a fellow survivor named Mado that because of its stylized intensity approaches the level of art but nonetheless conveys the despair of a woman who is denied the remission of amnesia. She begins:

> It seems to me I'm not alive. Since all are dead, it seems impossible that I shouldn't be also. All dead. . . . All the others, all the others. How could those stronger and more determined than I be dead, and I remain alive? Can one come out of there alive? No, it wasn't possible. . . . I'm not alive. I see myself from outside this self pretending to be alive. I'm not alive. I know this with an intimate, solitary knowledge. (1971/1995, p. 257)

Mado's paradoxical refrain—"I'm not alive"—accents the need for a narrative form to capture the postwar effects of the daily rule during her imprisonment that to be alive was to be a candidate for death. Delbo has taken the liberty of discarding the chronological text of her friend's testimony, forcing us to face the full unblemished impact of Auschwitz time.

The thrust of Mado's existence is backward, as if loyalty to her dead and sometimes murdered friends requires her to embrace a rupture between then and now that infiltrates and finally pollutes the purity of her aspirations toward the future. When her son is born she tries to feel happy. But memory will not allow her to. "The silky water of my joy," she says, "changed to sticky mud, sooty snow, fetid marshes. I saw again this woman—you remember this peasant woman, lying in the snow, dead, with her dead newborn frozen between her thighs. My son was also that newborn" (pp. 261–262). Thus even her current family is shrouded by the subtext of dying in the camps. The challenge of learning how to live while continuing to participate in the unnatural deaths of others haunts Mado as a persistent melancholy legacy from that time.

As the habit of "holding out" *then* nurtures in Mado the practice of "making do" *now*, a psychology of endurance breeds in her a new sense of who she is, of what she has become. She recalls her companions arguing in the camps that if they returned home after the war, everything would be different. But they were wrong. "Everything is the same," Mado discovers. "It is within us that nothing is the same" (p. 263). This is not a loss of identity but a *shift* in identity, a painfully honest confession that the self has been split not by some psychotic condition but by the twin realities that inhabit her spirit. Mado admits that to forget the durational subtext in order to return to the chronological narrative of her life would be atrocious, then adds that it would be impossible, too. "People believe memories grow vague," she ends her monologue, "are erased by time, since nothing endures against the passage of time. That's the difference: time does not pass over me, over us. It doesn't erase anything, doesn't undo it. I'm not alive. I died in Auschwitz but no one knows it" (p. 267).

Of course, Mado is right. No one but she and Delbo and the handful of other Frenchwomen who returned from their transport to Auschwitz can hope to enter the dark inner realm where the theme of being dead while alive enacts its paradoxical drama. Yet perhaps Mado is mistaken, too. Her words allow us to see feelingly, then to imagine the contours of that alien world and the missed destiny of death that assaults it. An alliance with atrocity is part of the burden of modernity, though it is both simpler and less troublesome to pretend that it is not. Atrocity narrative requires us to abandon the conviction that the gift of life is antithetical to the menace of unnatural death. Writers such as Delbo entreat us to discard this consoling template of reality as a remnant of an ancient nostalgia, rather than retaining it as a still useful blueprint for designing the future after Auschwitz.

Sometimes episodes surface in Holocaust testimonies that seem to transgress our sense of the possible, to reveal a reality so beyond our imaginings that we rush to consign them to the realm of fantasy. But anyone immersed in this world of atrocity will be forced to concede that few powers of invention could conjure up some of the most gruesome moments of the camp experience. From an eyewitness in the Natzweiler concentration camp comes the following account to confirm the intricate bond that links living and dying for the victimized in the Holocaust universe:

> On July 8, 1942, I was witness to a terrifying event that will never fade from my memory. In the corridor of the infirmary stood six coffins in a stack. They were crates hammered together of rough boards, out of which blood seeped through the joints. Suddenly a knocking

could be heard from the bottom coffin. A weak voice quavered, "Open up! Open up! I am still alive!" The greens [deported criminals] pulled out the bottom coffin and opened it. A Polish prisoner with an injured head and broken legs stared out at us from the coffin, in which he was lying with a dead man. I wanted to intervene, to free him from his terrifying situation, but I was immediately pushed aside by one of the professional criminals. A few dull thuds, then the coffin was nailed -shut again and sent to the crematorium. (Hackett, 1995, p. 372)

Edgar Allan Poe's literary fascination with similar imagery seems an amateurish harbinger of this grisly historical version of a troika that joined the living, the dying, and the dead. It introduces into the discourse of atrocity a fresh concept for defining consciousness after the Holocaust, the idea of a coffined self to share with more vital contents of identity the numbing legacy that the un-natural deaths of others have bequeathed us.

The visible distance that separates life from death was at times narrowed to a fine line in the Holocaust universe; at others, it seemed to disappear entirely. As the reverence for life vanishes, the customary reverence for the dead and the dying fades, too. For students of this era, some space must be found for an intellectual response to reports such as the following from Buchenwald, which violate our sense of reason and logic, to say nothing of humanity, but which nevertheless form part of the memory of those open to their impact:

In my service as a mason during the building of the new crematorium, I could observe things that probably are still not known.

As long as the new ovens were not yet finished, the old one was still used. Between the old and the new ovens was a wall of boards. After the first new oven was ready, the wall was moved between it and the second new oven under construction.

At this time many Russian prisoners of war were murdered by shots to the base of the skull. When the murderers arrived with a truckload of victims, the bodies were delivered directly into the basement through a built-in shute. Every time the Nazis let bodies slide down into the cellar, howling and groaning arose—proof that many of the victims were not yet completely dead, since they returned to consciousness when they struck the cement floor of the cellar. Whether these still-living, unfortunate victims of the murderous beasts were then beaten to death or were sent into the ovens while still alive, I don't know.

When we built the chimneys of the crematorium, I once saw three and another time two Russian soldiers standing alive, in the courtyard. They were led into the crematorium—and then I saw nothing of them again. (Hackett, 1995, pp. 239–240)

To familiar tales of the living dead we must now add sinister hints of the dying living, drawn not from the annals of superstition but from an authentic record of witnessed incidents.

Straight narrative cannot begin to help us absorb the shock of this brutal transition from life to death without any clear sign of the cessation of one before the advent of the other. As the conditions of being and nonbeing merge and blur, we are left groping for a way to extend the range of implication that assaults us from the region of that crematorium. "For those who were in Auschwitz," Charlotte Delbo wrote in *Useless Knowledge* (1970/1995), the second volume of her Auschwitz trilogy, "waiting meant racing ahead of death" (p. 168). For those who returned from Auschwitz, she might have added, memory became a path that led to and through death; she sought to capture this twisted journey of consciousness in a concise poem that entwines both worlds in a knot of intimacy that not even reading can disentangle:

> I've come back from another world
> To this world
> I had not left
> And I know not
> Which one is real
> Tell me did I really come back
> From the other world?
> As far as I'm concerned
> I'm still there
> Dying there
> A little more each day
> Dying over again
> The death of those who died
> and I no longer know which is the real one
> this world, right here,
> or the world over there
> now
> I no longer know
> when I am dreaming
> and when
> I do not dream. (p. 204)

If lines such as "Dying over again / the death of those who died" express not merely a memory of the past but also an abiding presence, then we are left dwelling in a middle realm where living and dying mix and re-form and for which few narrative strategies help us to understand how they might blend in contemporary consciousness.

Fortunately, at least one writer has made this issue the focus of his artistic career, and his extensive reflections on the theme allow us to enter the anteroom of the creative imagination as it struggles to nurture its vision with the residue of unnatural death. Born in Spain in 1924, raised and educated in France after the defeat of the Spanish republican forces, Jorge Semprun joined the French resistance movement as a teenager and in 1943 was arrested by the Gestapo. In January 1944 he was deported to the Buchenwald concentration camp, near Weimar, where he remained until his liberation in April of 1945. Among his translated works, the novels *The Long Voyage* (1963/1964) and *What a Beautiful Sunday!* (1980/1982) and the memoir *Literature or Life* (1994/1997) explore the fictional and nonfictional narrative possibilities of his Buchenwald experience, whose corrosive influence, as with Primo Levi, remained imprinted on Semprun's imagination long after the time of the ordeal itself.

In *Literature or Life*, originally published in 1994 as *L'ecriture ou la vie* (*Writing or life*), Semprun addresses the question of which obstacles the writer must overcome in order to evoke the reality of Holocaust atrocity. Semprun is blunt in dismissing the common charge that the event is indescribable. "The 'ineffable' you hear so much about," he alleges, "is only an alibi. Or a sign of laziness" (p. 13). The problem was not with the "form of a possible account" (p. 13) but with the *content* that, though describable, might be unbearable. How to tell what is too painful to be told, how to turn an experience, grotesque and agonizing as it may have been, into narrative? The French title, *Writing or Life*, implies that whatever model Semprun devises for a narrative frame, it will sanction an alternative to rather than an expression of his existence after Buchenwald. The details of his camp experience were like unwieldy clay, stubbornly resisting efforts to mold or shape them into a form that an audience not used to such dense matter might recognize and accept.

Semprun left Buchenwald still bathed in the odor and memories of the death that had consumed so many of his underground companions, to say nothing of the thousands of others, especially Jews, who had perished in other parts of the camp. Indeed, as we learn from the text, he initially planned to call his memoir *L'ecriture ou la mort* (Writing or death), here suggesting an equivalency rather than an opposition, but subsequently changed his mind, leaving to his readers the chore of deciphering the subtle meaning of the shift. What Semprun had discovered was that the joys of writing could not dispel the sorrows of memory. Having learned to identify the many smells of death in Buchenwald, Semprun was left with the dilemma of luring readers committed to life into the perimeters of this lethal regime, the domain of what he called "despairing memory." This was no easy task. One who outlived the catastrophe wrote about it with a ghost mentality, struggling to connect to the living while mired in the reminiscence of a doom that changed the identity of virtually all victims into effigies of future corpses.

Despairing memory is a prime source of narrative consciousness, as Semprun searches for the precise brew that will combine the sense experience of unnatural death with its verbal expression. "And suddenly," he writes, "borne on the breeze, the curious odor: sweetish, cloying, with a bitter and truly nauseating edge to it. The peculiar odor that would later prove to be from the crematory ovens" (1994/1997, p. 6). The transition is swift: "The strange smell would immediately invade the reality of memory. I would be reborn there; I would die if returned to life there. I would embrace and inhale the muddy, heady odor of that estuary of death" (p. 7). He has only to close his eyes, and in an instant he is sucked from what he calls "the shimmering opacity of life's offerings" (p. 6) back into the maw of death at Buchenwald. There is memory as recall and memory as affliction, and Semprun nurses both until they swell into a deluge that submerges him without offering warning or refuge.

Semprun is left with two problems: finding a style to depict how the reign of death in Buchenwald has afflicted him and making this feeling accessible to his audience without shocking them into disbelief or flight. Death is a constant companion of the survivor: "I'm struck by the idea," he writes, "if one can call it an idea . . . struck by the sudden overwhelming feeling, in any case, that I have not escaped death, but passed through it. Rather: that it has passed through me. That I have, in a way, lived through it. That I have come back from it the way you return from a voyage that has transformed and—perhaps—transfigured you" (1994/1997, pp. 14–15). It was as if Buchenwald were surrounded by a river Styx: souls ferried across it into the realm of death left some of their lives behind, while those who violated its rule by returning in the other direction—we call them survivors—had left some of their *deaths* behind but brought back with them the memory of their own premature and partial demise.

The result in Semprun's language would be a transfigured ghost, though I think a more accurate name would be a "disfigured" one. If the impact of a journey through the otherworld of Buchenwald is to be properly characterized, then we might do well to avoid terms such as *transfigured*, which echo a spiritual reality far from Semprun's intentions. Indeed, Semprun seems aware of this danger when he ironically introduces a vocabulary of redemption to subvert its relevance to his ordeal: "Perhaps I have not simply survived death, but been resurrected from it. Perhaps from this moment on, I am immortal" (1994/1997, p. 14). He invites his readers to distinguish between a near-death and a "post-death" experience, knowing that the only language available to them is the language of immortality that he has just used himself. The main thrust of his discourse is to sabotage the value of such words in the context of Buchenwald memory. For most of us, the idea of a postdeath experience is a logical impossibility when it is beyond the pale of debate about eternal life. Semprun invites us to consider an unprecedented passage from life through death back to life, not as a voyage into a mythical underworld, such as the ones undertaken by Odysseus and Aeneas, but as a human journey on earth. The ensuing paradox is not easy to absorb, to say nothing of translating it into the art of narrative. But Semprun is ready for the challenge: "On this April morning [the day of his liberation from Buchenwald], it is exciting to imagine that thenceforward, growing old will not bring me closer to death, but quite the contrary, carry me away from it" (p. 15).

In his novels one of Semprun's greatest innovations was to break the hold of chronological time and find a narrative technique to sustain a new disjointed relationship among past, present, and future. He struggled in his memoir to outline the mortal injury that death in Buchenwald had inflicted on chronology:

> The essential thing about this experience of Evil is that it will turn out to have been lived as the experience of death. . . . And I do mean "experience". . . . Because death is not something that we brushed up against, came close to, only just escaped, as though it were an accident we survived unscathed. We lived it. . . . Because it's not believable, it can't be shared, it's barely comprehensible—since death is, for rational thought, the only event that we can never experience individually. . . . That cannot be grasped except in the form of anguish, of foreboding or fatal longing. . . . In the future perfect tense, therefore. (1994/1997, pp. 88–89)

As the past continued to overtake and displace the future, society had to consider a new phenomenon, the deathlife of the self that the Holocaust had introduced into current dialogue about the possible effects of atrocity on modern consciousness. Semprun expressed more lucidly than any of his literary confederates the philosophical and artistic idea that was invading Holocaust thinking and marked the difference, as he saw it, between traditional and post-camp sensibilities. He drew a distinction between living life and living death, arguing that rational deliberation had no category for the reality introduced by the camp ordeal. Semprun boldly redefined brotherhood as the relationship between those who had lived the experience of death as a collective and even fraternal experience. It took time for him to understand what this meant. He described the impasse that led him, some months after his release from Buchenwald, to suspend writing for more than a decade the novel that would become *The Long Voyage*: "The two things I had thought would bind me to life—writing, pleasure—were instead what estranged me from it, day after day, constantly returning me to the memory of death, forcing me back into the suffocation of memory" (pp. 108–109). Semprun's meditations on this finding provide a dramatic instance of the literary imagination at work trying to shape what I call a narrative of atrocity. "Fundamentally," he concluded, "I was nothing other than a conscious residue of all that death" (p. 120). As he elaborates, savoring his words as if they were items on a gourmet menu, we overhear the voice of the artist in search of an imagery to join ordinary present consciousness to extraordinary past experience: "An individual patch in the impalpable material of that shroud. A dust mote in the ashy cloud of that agony. A still-flickering light from the extinguished star of our dead years" (p. 120). Surviving the unnatural death of others, at least *this* death of *those* others, shrinks (without effacing entirely) the life impulse. Slowly, Semprun drafted the terms for turning this insight into narrative:

> I possess nothing more than my death, my experience of death, to recount my life, to express it, to carry it on. I must make life with all that death. And the best way to do this is through writing. Yet that brings me back to death, to the suffocating embrace of death. That's where I am: I can live only by assuming that death through writing, but writing literally prohibits me from living. (p. 163)

Originally, as we have heard, he called his memoir *Writing or Death*, only to discover that his presumed antonyms had become synonyms; hence the change to *Writing or Life*, stressing the hard-won reversal that had emerged from his discovery of the price one must pay for an art of atrocity.

These are alien intellectual aromas for those of us who have not breathed the toxic air of German concentration and death camps until it became a natural form of inhalation, leaving a residue in the lungs of memory that a return to normal living could not purge. Semprun called it a wisdom of the body, a physical knowledge that would last forever in the secular eternity where his mental intelligence dwelt. Buchenwald time was durational rather than fleeting, and throughout his career Semprun strove to fashion a literary voice for this notion. That voice, he came to believe, must be artistic, not historical, since only the art and artifice of fiction could beguile the imagination into embracing what was being said. Writing, he insisted, revived and sharpened the sorrow of memory, whose barbs were a constant reminder of the interlocking truth that what he had lived through was also and at the same time what he had died through. For all their other merits, he felt, historians could not convey the ambiguity of this essential truth of the Holocaust universe with the vigor and conviction of the literary craftsman.

To have as an artistic goal "to make life with all that death" through writing is to specify the main hazard of Holocaust narrative, and like George Steiner (1967) and others, Semprun is wary of the limits of language that hinder this labor. In his memoir he struggled with various translations of Wittgenstein's seemingly obvious statement that "Der Tod ist kein Ereignis des Lebens. Den Tod erlebt man nicht"—"Death is not an event in life. Death cannot be lived" (pp. 170–171), because he knew that Buchenwald had vandalized its accuracy. Semprun varied the translation, striving for more precise meaning. For "Death cannot be lived" he substituted the more active "One cannot live death," and, later, "Death is not a lived experience." Finally, he decided that "Wittgenstein's pronouncement ought to be phrased like this: . . . *my* death is not an event in *my* life. I will not live *my* death" (p. 171). For Semprun and his fellow survivors death *was* an event in life, and they *had* "lived" death, the death of others, though no available explanations helped make the magnitude of that insight more credible. *Erleben* meant to live through an event, but there was no word to signify an event that one had died through (*ersterben* means to die away or become extinct). Yet Semprun knew a Holocaust literature that lacked this concept could not be totally authentic, faithful to the incidents it tried to imagine.

The imagination was the crucial faculty that had to be addressed and transformed, injected with a literary serum to enable it to add to its capacity a wholly new power of representation. Semprun's search for a narrative "I" to re-create for his readers "death experienced right up to its blinding limit" (p. 181) took him far beyond the aspirations of a Tolstoy in *The Death of Ivan Ilych*. For Tolstoy, suffering, even the extreme physical agony of the dying Ivan Ilych, could be a redemptive occasion because Tolstoy and most of his readers shared belief in the model of a compassionate Redeemer. Writing Ivan Ilych's story was an act of spiritual liberation. Contrast this with Semprun's account of the impact on him of writing his Buchenwald novel, *The Long Voyage*:

> It thrust me back into death, drowning me in it. I choked in the unbreathable air of my manuscript: every line I wrote pushed my head underwater as though I were once again in the bathtub of the Gestapo's villa in Auxerre [where Semprun had been tortured to make him reveal the names of other underground members]. I struggled to survive. I failed in my attempt to speak of death in order to reduce it to silence: if I had continued, it would have been death, in all probability, that would have silenced me. (1963/1964, p. 250)

Only after he absorbed into his own consciousness the recognition that life and death were no longer a sequence but an unsettling alliance, a fusion of forces that constantly operated on each other, could he finish his novel. He pacified death's pursuit of him in memory by allowing his pursuit of death in narrative to dominate the world of his imagination. Narrative form displaced the chaos of remembering.

Watching a familiar newsreel after the war, of bulldozers shoveling dead bodies into mass graves, Semprun intuitively grasped why such images of atrocity seemed so inadequate. "They were silent above all," he writes, "because they said nothing precise about the reality they showed, because they delivered only confused scraps of meaning" (1994/1997, pp. 200–201). For him, the process of witnessing was not enough. Images had to be situated "not only in a historical context but within a continuity of emotions" (p. 201). The impulse that steered Semprun to the vocation of Holocaust writer was enshrined in controversial assertions such as the following, which are still subject to dispute among Holocaust commentators: "One would have had to treat the documentary reality, in short, like the material of fiction" (p. 201). The revelation freed him to invent the imagined universe of *The Long Voyage*, a novel whose roots reach deep into his Buchenwald experience but which achieves its narrative form by rearranging in its narrator's mind the details of the deathlife he has survived.

Concepts like "deathlife" and "the coffined self" are not to be found in histories of the Holocaust. Tracing the course of Germany's mass murders through documentary records is an essential scholarly task for our understanding of those events, but their psychological and emotional milieus constitute equally compelling themes whose expression requires utterly different narrative strategies. The first-person narrator of Semprun's *The Long Voyage* is in a boxcar on its way to Buchenwald throughout the novel, but his journey is internal as well as external. Even as he undergoes the ordeal of the trip in the present, he remembers and "foremembers," since the experience has fragmented him into a splintered self: he is simultaneously a partisan in the French underground, a deported prisoner of the Germans, and a survivor of Buchenwald. Details of his life in past, present, and future flow through his memory like multiple currents in an unimpeded stream. Death spreads its tentacles in both directions, tainting recollections of innocent prewar friendships because he learns later that many of his friends have been killed and poisoning his postwar life through his discovery that being alive after Buchenwald is not the same as having survived it intact. By re-creating consciousness as an intersection of three time zones, Semprun is able to duplicate for the reader the fluid timeless ordeal of the camp inmate who has lost his sense of life as a chronological passage from yesterday through today into tomorrow. He also converts the idea of death as a single, natural fate into a mutation that plots death as a common, unnatural doom.

Semprun's narrator begins to learn about this unnatural doom on the journey itself, which lasts for five days and four nights. He is jammed up against another deportee whom he calls "the guy from Semur" (a village in France), and during the voyage they exchange reminiscences about their earlier lives and speculations about their destination. They appear to be bonded in life, whatever the future holds for them, but as they arrive at Buchenwald death anticipates them, as the exhausted guy from Semur slumps against the narrator's shoulder and dies. Earlier the guy from Semur had complained that he felt as though his heart were dead, and when the narrator asks him what that

means, he replies, "I wouldn't know how to tell you. . . . You don't feel anything in your heart, like a hole, or else like a very heavy stone" (1963/1964,
p. 93). It is a workable definition of the condition I call deathlife, although it
will be some time before the narrator grasps its meaning. The act of "fore-
membering" gives us a glimpse into how that process will work.

The narrator has a vivid impression of the impact of deathlife on memory
while dining at a friend's house after the war, when his hostess announces that
she has planned a Russian dinner. This triggers a time warp in consciousness
for the narrator, who explains:

> And so it was that suddenly I had a piece of black bread in my hand,
> and mechanically I bit into it, meanwhile continuing the conversation.
> Then, the slightly acid taste of the black bread, the slow mastication
> of this gritty black bread, brought back, with shocking suddenness,
> the marvelous moments when, at camp, we used to eat our ration of
> bread. . . . I was sitting there motionless, my arm raised, with my
> slightly acid, buttered slice of good black bread in my hand, and my
> heart was pounding like a triphammer. (p. 126)

His hostess asks him if anything is the matter, and his reverie continues. "Nothing was the matter. A random thought of no consequence. Obviously I couldn't
tell her that I was in the throes of dying, dying of hunger, far far from them,
far from the wood fire and the words they were saying" (p. 126).

As someone who had fended off death in Buchenwald, Semprun belongs
to a generation of survivors—their numbers continue to grow today—who enact in a portion of consciousness "the throes of dying" even as they move on
with their lives. As unnatural dying, mass murder or some other form of atrocity spreads across the landscape of modernity, Semprun's struggle to find for
it an artistic voice seems an early recognition of its complex and disconcerting
force. Elie Wiesel (1968/1970) once remarked of his father's miserable end
in Buchenwald that the Germans deprived him not only of his life but also
of his death, and this is the very paradox from which Semprun seeks to wrest
some significance in his narrative. But the first step is to find a way of expressing
the idea that the meaning of one's life can no longer be separated from the
meaningless death of others, and to do this he literally transmutes consciousness into a physical substance and plunges the reader directly into its wounded
core:

> In the spongy mass that sits behind my forehead, between my painful
> neck and burning temples, where all the throbbing pains in my body,
> which is breaking into a thousand pieces of sharp glass, in that spongy
> mass from which I would like to be able to draw with both hands
> (or rather with delicate tongs, once the bony plate which covers it

has been lifted) the cotton-like filaments, streaked perhaps with blood, which must fill all the cavities and keep me from thinking clearly, which becloud the whole interior, what they call consciousness, into that spongy mass there works its way the idea that perhaps my death will not even manage to be something real, that is, something that belongs to someone else's life, at least one person's. Perhaps the idea of my death as something real, perhaps even that possibility will be denied me, and I cast about desperately to see who might miss me, whose life I might affect, might haunt by my absence and at that precise moment, I find no one, my life hasn't any real possibility, I wouldn't even be able to die, all I can do is efface myself, quietly eliminate myself from this existence, Hans would have to be alive, Michel would have to be alive for me to have a real death, a death somehow linked to reality, for me not to vanish completely into the stench-filled darkness of this boxcar. (Semprum, 1963/1964, p. 197)

Hans and Michel are two of his murdered comrades, and if memory and consciousness cannot resurrect them, at least through the anguish of Semprun's art they may be made to seem less dead. This must be what Semprun had meant when he wrote in his memoir: "I possess nothing more than my death, my experience of death, to recount my life, to express it, to carry it on. I must make life with all that death" (p. 163). To make life with all that death: it may be that the anxiety nurtured by this issue in *The Long Voyage* and in much other Holocaust testimony and narrative will prove to be nothing more than a prelude to a fundamental and persistent challenge that is destined to afflict modern consciousness well into the future.

References

Améry, J. (1986). *At the mind's limits: Contemplations by a survivor on Auschwitz and its realities* (S. Rosenfeld & S. P. Rosenfeld, Trans.). New York: Schocken. (Original work published 1966)

Delbo, C. (1995). *Auschwitz and after [None of us will return, Useless knowledge, The measure of our days]* (R. C. Lamont, Trans.). New Haven: Yale University Press. (Original works published 1965, 1970, 1971)

Greene, J. M., & Kumar, S. (Ed.) (2000). *Witness: Voices from the Holocaust.* New York: Free Press.

Hackett, D. A. (Ed.) (1995). *The Buchenwald report* (D. A. Hackett, Trans.). Boulder, CO: Westview.

Olney, J. (1998) *Memory and narrative: The weave of life-writing.* Chicago: University of Chicago Press.

Semprun, J. (1964). *The long voyage* (R. Seaver, Trans.). New York: Grove Press. (Original work published 1963)

Semprun, J. (1982). *What a beautiful Sunday!* (Alan Sheridan, Trans.). New York: Harcourt Brace Jovanovich. (Original work published 1980)

Semprun, J. (1997). *Literature or life* (L. Coverdale, Trans.). New York: Viking. (Original work published 1994)

Steiner, G. (1967). *Language and silence: Essays on language, literature and the inhuman.* New York: Atheneum.

Wiesel, E. (1970). "The death of my father." In *Legends of our time* (pp. 13–21). New York: Avon. (Original work published 1968)

9 Community and Coherence: Narrative Contributions to the Psychology of Conflict and Loss

Robert A. Neimeyer
Finn Tschudi

The process of writing this chapter constitutes a story in itself. One of us (RAN) initially accepted the invitation to participate in this project in a flush of enthusiasm, one born of his own keen interest in the rich implications of narrative theory for the practice of psychotherapy (Neimeyer, 1995; Neimeyer & Levitt, 2001; Neimeyer & Stewart, 2000). Certainly narrative concepts and methods had long informed his clinical practice and grafted seamlessly onto the roots of his interest in a constructivist, meaning-making approach to studying and facilitating human change (Kelly, 1955/1991; Neimeyer & Mahoney, 1995). The postulate that human beings attempt to order their experience largely (though not exclusively) through use of the architecture of narrative form had proven immensely illuminating, particularly in his work with clients whose profound losses undermined the very foundations of their constructions of self and world (Kaufman, 2001; Neimeyer, 2001c). But as he turned again and again to the task of writing this chapter, the muse abandoned him. Somehow, the increasingly familiar presentation of narrative psychology from a broadly cognitive perspective seemed to have lost some of the novelty and boldness that originally accompanied the importation of narrative concepts into the clinical domain. As a result, he could not work up excitement over recounting the familiar story of psychological distress as a form of breakdown in personal capacities to form a coherent narrative of troubling experiences and of psychotherapy as a form of narrative repair. Like a hackneyed story with a predictable plot structure, the "metanarrative" of narrative therapy seemed in need of new material to make possible a fresh telling.

This sense of frustration eventually found expression in late-night conversations between the two authors. FT's abiding interests in constructivism, human emotion, and peace psychology had grown in recent years to include a passionate concern with conflict and its transformation both within local human communities and at broader cultural levels. Both of us had been drawn to situate individual attempts at meaning making within a broader, socially constructed context (Galtung & Tschudi, 2000; Neimeyer, 1998),[1] one whose relevance to human problems and their solution was incontestable. What ensued was a lively dialogue about the relevance of narrative concepts and methods for understanding *inter*personal as well as *intra*personal conflict, a dialogue that effectively bridged the individualistic interventions of many narrative therapists with the collective concerns of people working toward the repair and transformation of conflictual communities. Our goal in this chapter is to further cultivate the cross-fertilization of these two fields, in the hope that narrative principles might be more actively extended to the conceptualization of human distress at molar as well as molecular levels. We will begin with a brief exposition of narrative principles as applied to individual distress and its treatment and then seek to elaborate these as a fruitful model for interpreting conflict at broadly communal levels when the fabric of human connection is torn and in need of repair.

Narration and the Quest for Coherence

As human beings, we live our lives in stories. We relate accounts of our day to our loved ones when we return home from work, exchange family and personal narratives in annual holiday letters and at reunions, and tell bedtime stories to our children. Likewise, we assimilate the stories of our place and time—and other places and times—through immersion in countless narratives offered to us on television, in films, on stage, or in print. Sometimes, when troubled, we sort through stories of our current struggles and childhood conflicts with those we trust, including helping professionals. Even dreams and spontaneous fantasies often take on a storied form. Indeed, we are so thoroughly "marinated" in narrative activity that engagement in non-narrative processing of experience might be more the exception than the norm (Neimeyer & Levitt, 2001).[2] So pervasive is the human tendency to integrate experience through the (co)construction of stories that we as a species might appropriately be named *Homo narrans* rather than *Homo sapiens* (Hermans 2002).

If narration is such a prototypical form of human activity, what function might it serve? In some sense, the answers to the question might be as diverse as the stories told and the audiences to which they are directed. Surely we construct stories to entertain, to impress, to persuade, to accuse, to educate, and to consult, and sometimes the same story will represent a distillation of several of these goals. But on an intrapersonal level, many of these intentions could be viewed as serving a master motive; namely, they represent ways of seeking continuity of meaning in our lived experience (Neimeyer, 1995). That is, by punctuating the "booming, buzzing confusion" (to borrow a phrase from William James) of daily life into discrete segments and by organizing these according to meaningful sequences, we seek to discern the implicit order in events and give them thematic significance (Kelly, 1955/1991). Viewed in this perspective, the narrative organization of our lives reflects our basic quest for coherence, the pursuit of an account of important life events that literally "makes sense" of the story-world and ourselves as protagonists.

At another, more interpersonal level, narration also serves vital social functions, helping us consolidate relational and familial identities by revisiting shared stories of our lives together—whether these are configured as histories, romances, comedies, or tragedies. In this latter, more social constructionist view, we not only tell stories, but we also enact them before relevant audiences (Goffman, 1959; Wortham, 1999). In so doing, we implicitly assign moral positions to ourselves and others, often in a self-serving fashion (Edwards & Potter, 1992), as when we display our martyrdom at the kitchen sink by loudly washing dishes as other family members idle before the TV. Importantly, however, our performed narratives are not limited to enactments of fixed cultural or personal scripts but can represent ways to "act beyond ourselves" or "perform a head taller than oneself" (Holzman, 2000; Newman & Holzman, 1993) in a way that promotes our development, as in the spontaneous role-plays of children.[3] Indeed, every self-narrative we relate or enact "(temporarily) asserts the primacy of a particular version of the self of the storyteller; it constructs an 'as if' frame within which not only one's life, but also one's identity achieves fictional coherence" (Neimeyer, 2000, p. 216).

From a clinical perspective, how might we understand the breakdown of this meaning-making activity and its consequences for our relationship to our own biography, as well as our lives with others? One answer would be to discriminate between two forms of narrative disruption: narrative disintegration on one hand and narrative dominance on the other (Neimeyer, 2000). Disintegration of a once-adequate self-narrative occurs when an individual confronts traumatic events that shatter the coherence of his or her assumptive world, undermining taken-for-granted beliefs in life's predictability, fairness, and essential benevolence (Janoff-Bulman & Berg, 1998). One concomitant of the encounter with such events is the disruption of one's sense of autobiographical continuity, as the person one becomes seems radically incoherent with the person one used to be (Arciero & Guidano, 2000). Constructivist research has documented the impact of traumatic losses of various kinds, which ranged from the death of a child (Milo, 1997) to participation in military combat (Sewell et al., 1996) and exposure to mass murder (Sewell, 1996). In each case, the potential for devastation of one's pretraumatic construction of self and life is profound, precipitating a painful and ongoing search for a revised narrative adequate to the new and darker world in which one must now find orientation (Davis, Nolen-Hoeksema, & Larson, 1998; Neimeyer & Stewart, 1996). Although it is sometimes possible to assimilate even tragic losses into a still viable system of meaning (e.g., understanding the sudden death of a child as God's will), more often such traumatic life transitions challenge us to accommodate our belief systems to make sense of the new reality (Viney, 1991). When successful, such accommodation can promote not merely post-traumatic stress but also post-traumatic growth (Tedeschi, Park, & Calhoun, 1998), as the individual in effect "relearns" the self in the process of con-structing an adequate account of his or her transformation (Attig, 1996, 2001).

The second form of narrative disruption occurs when people's own at-tempts at meaning making are marginalized by the hegemonic influence of a dominant story, one that effectively subjugates them to a preemptive and non-preferred identity (Neimeyer, 2000; White & Epston, 1990). Often such dom-inant narratives originate in broader cultural discourses, but the narratives can come to "colonize" and constrain the sense of self of vulnerable persons or groups. One prominent example is the construction of "disordered" identities through practices of psychiatric diagnosis, in which the individuality of the patient can disappear beneath the universal label of the disorder (Szasz, 1974). Although the conferred identity of "manic-depressive," "schizophrenic," or "op-positional defiant" is itself a social construction (Raskin & Lewandowski, 2000), it is nonetheless real in its effects, marginalizing the person's own voice while granting authority over his or her life to powerful others (Foucault, 1970). The appropriate response to a dominant narrative of identity—whether as-cribed to persons on the basis of their presumed disorder, race, gender, sexual preference, or conduct—is *resistance*, viewed as "performing beyond" the dic-tates of their ascribed role. For example, narrative therapists support persons in first *externalizing* the dominant narrative (e.g., anorexia), as a precondition to understanding its "real effects" on their relationships with themselves and others (White & Epston, 1990). Therapy then helps draw attention to those exceptional actions and decisions that contradict or enlarge the dominant story (e.g., the anorexic's acts of self-nurturance rather than self-monitoring and re-straint), eventually contributing to a more (inter)personally satisfying self-narrative.

Although the implications of this constructivist/narrative account have been extensively elaborated in research and practice focused on individuals and families (Monk, Winslade, Crocket, & Epston, 1996; Neimeyer, 2001c; Ro-senblatt, 2000), it has been less adequately extended to work with broader communities. Yet it strikes us that similar processes of narrative disintegration and domination occur at this broader social level, particularly in the context of conflict and its "resolution" by the state. It is to the task of widening a narrative perspective to address this domain that we now turn.

Conflict as Problem, Conflict as Resource

By any standard, the Western criminal system is in crisis. Spiraling crime rates, prison overcrowding, and increasingly frequent reports of police brutality are matched only by general pessimism about the success of criminal "rehabilitation" (Braithwaite & Pettit, 1990; Haney & Zimbardo, 1998). And yet, despite accumulating evidence that current criminal procedures have done little to improve the lot of either offenders or the society at large, the Western penal system has remained curiously immune from critical deconstruction, with the notable exception of the efforts of Foucault (1970) and a handful of critical legal theorists (Anderson, 1990). Instead, our dominant "grand legal narrative"—that crime disrupts the social order and calls for a cultural and punitive response—is rarely questioned. Conflict, in this view, is a threat to the social contract, a problem to be contained or eliminated. The inadequacy of contemporary legal proceedings to bring about this utopian state of affairs rarely produces calls for a second-order change in the system but instead contributes to a more intensive application of the status quo. As a result, the fundamental premises of the penal system go unexamined and "reform" efforts address incidental procedures rather than core assumptions of the existing paradigm.

In sharp contrast, the Norwegian sociologist Nils Christie (1977) challenged the basic premise of Western criminology in his classic article "Conflicts as Property." "Highly industrialized societies," he argued, "do not have too much internal conflict, they have too little" (p. 1). When the state enters conflicts between persons as the dominant party "it is the conflict itself that represents the most interesting property taken away, not the goods originally taken away from the victim or given back to him. In our type of society, conflicts are more scarce than property, and they are immensely more valuable" (p. 7).

Western society, according to Christie, is currently under the sway of a grand legal narrative organized around a *retributive paradigm*. Metaphorically, it is as if the scales of justice place the offense in one tray (weighted by the criminal's degree of intentionality) and seek to assign a punishment of equal weight to the other. In contrast, consider how a local conflict might be handled in an enlightened household, as when a 6-year-old has taken some money from her mother's purse. Depending on the context, the incident might simply be ignored or the parents might attempt to explore the meaning of the event by engaging the child in conversation. Although they might jointly craft different narratives regarding the significance of the act and the appropriate family response to it, the critical point is that most families would regard the problem as something that is within their province, not as a violation of the "public order." Handled optimally, such episodes provide opportunities not for retribution but for moral growth.

Why then, we might ask, do most people take it for granted that a theft, say, by a 22-year-old should be handled quite differently?[4] In our legal system, crimes are not treated as conflicts that involve two (or more) parties—as in the family example earlier—but as conflicts between one of the parties and the state. Ironically, this retributive paradigm actually compounds the victimization of wronged parties (Christie, 1977). First they have been subjected to some form of loss or violence, and then they are deprived of any real say as to what should happen regarding what might be one of the most important events of their lives. In a typical courtroom proceeding, for example, the victim's role is simply to supply evidence under highly constrained (and rehearsed) circumstances, just as the defender is carefully coached in his or her own disclosures to limit self-incrimination. Under these circumstances, it is the *conflict itself* that is "stolen," robbing its rightful owners of any opportunity for a morally developmental dialogue, as well as mutual negotiation of the transgression and appropriate response. Instead, the offense is defined and emplotted within the grand narrative of the objective legal order, and outcomes of the story (in the form of proportional punishments) are authored by authorities uninvolved in the original conflict.

What might happen if conflicts were returned to their rightful owners, rather than purloined by the criminal justice system or other powerful social institutions and professions? Christie emphasizes the importance of open dialogue in cases of dispute in order to negotiate norms for right and wrong, for moral and immoral conduct, and for progressive conflict resolution. Conflict in this view has high value in engaging interest and commitment and in respecting locally grounded stories, rooted in concrete episodes, in keeping with a narrative trend. Drawing inspiration from Christie's (1977) analysis, recent workers in the criminal justice system in Australia and elsewhere have begun to develop an alternative approach to conflict, one organized around a *restorative paradigm* rather than a retributive one. Restorative justice can be defined as "a process whereby all parties with a stake in a particular offense come together to resolve collectively how to deal with the aftermath of the offence and its implications for the future" (Braithwaite, 1997, p. 5). As such, it is centrally concerned with "restoring social relations . . . in which each person's rights to equal dignity, concern, and respect are satisfied" (p. 5). We will briefly describe and illustrate the growing set of practices gathered under the "restorative justice" umbrella (McCold, 1997), which both resist the domination of the traditional grand legal narrative of Western cultures and help restore personal and communal coherence to the disrupted self-narratives of the conflicted parties. To do this we will situate restorative justice procedures within a framework of narrative processes, suggesting how they (1) assist persons in finding an authorial voice, (2) invite meaningful co-authorship of life narratives by ensuring the participation of both protagonists and supporting characters, and (3) recruit a relevant audience for the performance of a new narrative that transforms the conflict. First, however, we offer a comment on the effects of the dominant legal narrative on victims.

The Dominant Narrative and Its Victims

From the point of view of the dominant legal narrative, a seemingly persuasive rationale for denying victims more substantial participation in the justice system is their presumed motive for "revenge." Supposedly, in this view, victims would tend to militate for harsh punishments for offenders, just as offenders are motivated to seek as light a sentence as possible. This implies that courtroom outcomes that leave one party highly satisfied would leave the other highly dissatisfied. In the view of the dominant narrative, these contradictory interests impede the necessary objectivity of legal proceedings and thus require the imposition of an external order.

It is not difficult to find statements that on face value seem to support the view that victims will favor rather strict punishments. In Norway there was recently a case in which two young girls, aged 8 and 10, were brutally murdered by two young men. The mother of one of the girls is reported to have said, "I do not demand any revenge. As mother of one of the victims, however, I ask for due respect for the slaughtered girls. By due respect for us as human beings I ask for a strict punishment" ("Mor ber," 2000). Note that in accord with the dominant paradigm "revenge" is discounted as a motive, but balance (due respect), so to speak, requires a strict punishment when the crime has been very serious. After cases of murder in the United States it is quite frequent to see the relatives asking for the most severe punishment, the death penalty.

Our question now is whether experiences from conferencing support the view that there is a general tendency for victims to require strict punishment. Or might it rather be the case that when this occurs the victims are in a sense under the "spell" of the dominant legal narrative in society? In contrast, crime victims who participate in a group that constructs its own story about a happening might react quite differently. We thus question whether the antagonism of victim and offender motivation—against which the dominant system seemingly guards—is a necessary given and suggest that it might represent an ironic outcome of the retributive paradigm itself. As evidence for the latter possibility we would cite conceptually replicated empirical research on the "transformative justice" project described here, which suggests that an alternative system for dispute resolution can lead to very high levels of satisfaction on the part of both victims and offenders (Trimboli, 2000). It is this possibility that we will explore through the lens of narrative theory in the remainder of this chapter.

Transformative Justice Australia (TJA): Restorying Conflict and Loss

Surveying the broad context of world cultures, it is not difficult to find alternatives to the retributive narrative outlined earlier. Whether or not they have a formal concept of crime, members of all cultures experience conflicts, and most non-Western communities have developed indigenous procedures for dealing with such conflicts. To the extent that such communities have not been colonized by the Western system, these procedures may be seen as cultural resources, just as biodiversity in the Amazon constitutes a genetic resource for the rest of the world.

One such development took its inspiration from the native Maori of New Zealand, whose custom of treating problems with young persons in the extended family and tribe provided a model for the 1989 Children, Young Persons and Their Families Act. Formulated in response to a long-standing critique of dominant Pakeha (Western) procedures for dealing with young offenders, the act attracted the attention of nearby Australian authorities who were contending with similar juvenile justice problems. Thus in 1990 John McDonald, Principal Adviser on Juvenile Justice to the New South Wales (NSW) Police Commissioner, led a delegation to New Zealand to study the effects of the novel legislation. On the basis of his recommendations a pilot program called Effective Cautioning Using Family Group Conferencing was started together with David Moore, Coordinator of Justice Studies at Charles Sturt University, and Terry O'Connell, Sergeant of Police. The early work was evaluated by Moore and Forsythe (1995). The approach has developed steadily over the last decade, evolving into a unique restorative justice paradigm referred to as Transformative Justice Australia (TJA)[5] (Moore & McDonald, 2000, 2001).

In a nutshell, the aim of a conference is to transform the negative emotions that characterize the relation between parties to positive emotion, to foster a shift from conflict to cooperation.[6] A familiar recipe for achieving this entails (1) separating people from the problem, (2) focusing on interests, not positions, and (3) inventing options for mutual gain (Fisher & Ury, 1981). The difficulty that arises, of course, in the case of interpersonal conflict is that the other party is, by definition, the problem and will usually be seen as driven by malign motives. Furthermore, adversaries will cling to their positions, precluding any possibility of mutual gain (Moore & McDonald, 2000, pp. 109–

111). Thus special procedures are required to construct a stage for progressive transformation of the conflict, rather than the recriminating and retributive discourse that characterizes the dominant Western system of justice.

The overarching principle of conferencing is to understand the harm that has been done and to discover what can be done to repair the harm and prevent similar harm in the future. In criminal cases the harm will usually involve theft or assault, although in other contexts, such as the workplace, disputes might also entail sexual harassment, a breach of safety procedures, or being bypassed for promotion. Whatever the specific issue, at a general level conferencing fosters dispute resolution through a three-step procedure, which consists of preparation, the conference itself, and follow-up. We will briefly outline each of these steps as a prelude to considering the restorative functions of conferencing as a special case of performed narratives.

Preparation

Much of the success of conferencing depends on the thoroughness of preparation for it. In keeping with Christie's (1977) skepticism toward "expert" intervention, TJA emphasizes the centrality of laypeople themselves in resolving conflicts. However, in the preparatory stage expert facilitators play a useful role in ensuring that (1) both parties to the conflict are represented, (2) each is supported by relevant figures, and (3) the general principles of conferencing are explained to all participants. The most important of these principles include clarity, transparency (the importance of not having hidden agendas), and a respectful stance toward all participants (Moore & McDonald, 2000). Of the three main facets of preparation, the most crucial and difficult is the recruitment of a supporting network, particularly for the offender, who is at risk of ostracism and vilification. Thus special efforts must sometimes be made to turn weak links within the (offender's) network into strong links, as a means of reintegrating him or her into a community of concern (Granovetter, 1973).[7]

Conferencing

The primary task for the facilitator during the conference itself is to ensure that participants follow deliberative democratic procedures (Moore & McDonald, 2000). This is quite distinct from the usual interpretation of democracy as a system in which all have an equal right to vote on who should rule (representative democracy) or on what outcome should prevail (referendum). These more typical democratic forms can too easily degenerate into simple suppression of a minority or even a revolving tyranny, the avoidance of which is an important aim of deliberative procedures. Instead, care is taken to ensure that everyone concerned with the conflict is able to attend and speak, that all ideas are considered, and that no one is censored or allowed to dominate through position or personality. Of these norms of participation, equality, deliberation, and nontyranny, the last is hardest to ensure—a respectful stance is taken toward everyone regardless of their behavior. When such conditions are met, a consensual agreement will usually follow.

The conference itself can be roughly described as having five phases. The first involves introducing everyone and explaining the purpose of the meeting. The second entails clarification of what happened and how everyone feels about it. The third phase affords an opportunity for apologies, ushering in a fourth phase of discussion about how the harm might be repaired or future harm prevented. Finally, the conference ends with the signing of an agreement, after which food and drink are served in a ritual of joint celebration.

The second phase encompasses a carefully thought out sequence, in which the person primarily responsible for the harm (the offender)[8] tells what happened, how he or she feels about it, who he or she thinks has been primarily affected, and in what way. During the preparation stage this person would have been identified—as this is not always clear in workplace disputes—and his or her agreement secured to begin the discussion. In criminal cases this second phase is an important step in getting the offending agent to "own" the harmful action. The facilitator then naturally turns to the victim or one primarily affected to get his or her own story and associated feelings and reactions, followed by the accounts of the supporters of the affected person. This not only affirms the victim but also brings forth the harm to the broader family or community (e.g., the children of a parent who has been robbed). Finally, supporters of the offending agent have their say, frequently offering a testimonial that the agent is basically a good person but condemning the act. Stated in other words, the sinner is accepted, but not the sin.

The third phase commences when the facilitator turns to the responsible agent and asks something to the effect of, "Now that you have heard everyone, is there anything you'd like to say to[the offended party]?" This sets the stage for an apology or, alternatively, a concerted attempt to come to terms with what the harmful acts represent. The conference will then move toward repairing what can be repaired within the community and deciding upon collective steps to prevent future harm, often prompted by a question to the injured party about what he or she would wish to see happen. Finally, an agreement is reached and signed, eventuating in a closing ritual of social mingling and celebration.

Paralleling these phases will be certain changes in the emotional climate of the conference, which will move from the "hard" negative affects of contempt, anger, and fear to the "softer" negative affects of distress and shame. Particularly significant in this latter phase is the emergence of "collective vulnerability" (Moore & McDonald, 2000), in which a shared sense of life's tenuousness and fragility emerges for the group as a whole. Eventually, the emotional climate shifts toward interest and excitement as an agreement is negotiated, and joy and hope emerge during the social mingling that follows.

This capsule summary might suggest that the process of conferencing is more orderly than is typically the case. Quite often there will be several interruptions, and multiple themes that pertain to the harm that was done may require attention. Moreover, in keeping with Tomkins's (1962, 1963) theory of emotion, it is assumed that there is an intrinsic and healthy urge to freely access negative emotions as a critical step, clearing them away and facilitating cooperation. The staging of the social ecology of the conference supports this goal by seating the 15 to 25 participants in a circle, none higher than any other, eliminating tables, and discouraging note taking and other behaviors that would serve to increase social distance. Thus the physical space is arranged to prompt the performance of a new and more restorative narrative, assisted by the emotional interactions and contagion that exemplify TJA conferences.

Follow-up

Because a conference sets the stage for the performance of a new narrative that concerns the conflict, it is important that facilitators check at some agreed-upon future point to make sure that the agreement reached has been honored. The confirmation that this is the case further consolidates the new and preferred story and affirms the community of persons involved in the original conferencing. However, discovery that an agreement has been abrogated might suggest the relevance of an additional conference to renew progress, or some other suitable intervention. For example, one conference involved a young drug addict who was caught for theft from an older woman. In the course of the "supportive" testimony by his social network, the grandmother who raised the offender offered the comment that "he's a little shit. He lies faster than he breathes!" His father, recently released from jail, added, "He's a shitbag, just like me." The effect of these remarkable statements—so discrepant from the usual story line in conferences of "a good person who has done bad"—was to arouse the sympathy of all parties for the boy as the victim of a very sad home environment. As a result, the older woman decided that she did not want anything as compensation for her loss but simply wanted the boy to write her a letter each month to let her know how his life had been. But upon follow-up, the police who visited him found he had not written the letter, for a good reason—the boy was illiterate! So the police interviewed the boy about his month and wrote a report for the woman, thus helping the youth maintain the spirit of the accord.

In a narrative perspective, a conference at bottom deals with how a group jointly constructs its own account of socially harmful acts and their aftermath for the story's central and supporting characters. Like prototypical stories, a conference is organized along a dimension of time: what happened (the past), how various actors feel about it now (the present), and what they want to happen next (the future). Far from being a scripted performance, it is an emergent product of group action, one whose outcomes can rarely be anticipated in advance. Adding to the unpredictability of the outcome is that the story that emerges from the group interaction has all the qualities of a "polyphonic" novel (Bakhtin, 1984), a narrative written in many voices, each of which presupposes, appropriates, and transforms the others (Neimeyer, 2000). Unlike the simple morality tales offered to children, however, the resulting group story will probably not have clear villains and heroes but instead engender a greater humility and tolerance for the vicissitudes of life on the part of all participants. We will now consider three primary dimensions of this narrative work, offering a more detailed case illustration of each.

Finding a Voice: A Complicated Bereavement

The reweaving of life tapestries that have been torn apart by tragedy requires narrative work on many levels. On the level of story structure, it requires attempts at "reauthoring" the traumatic event through use of some combination of structural features. These include the narrative's setting (the "where and when" of the story) characterization (the "who" of the story, and attributions of their motives), plot (the "what" of the story, including relevant events), theme (the "why" of the story, its explanatory underpinnings), and fictional goal (the "wherefore" of the story, its projected end point) (Neimeyer, 2000). By configuring an account through the explicit (and more commonly implicit) manipulation of these features, the narrator of a tragedy can position him- or herself as a victim or hero in a sort of morality play and find social validation for this (sometimes constraining) identity (Neimeyer, 2000; Wortham, 1999). Alternatively, a narrator and audience can use these same structural resources to work toward a new telling of the tale, one that opens fresh possibilities for characterizing relevant figures in it, finding new thematic significance in the account, and reaching toward new possible outcomes.

Perhaps a still more fundamental feature of narrative work is the finding of an authorial voice, especially when one or more narrators of a shared account have been silenced by dominant narratives of their experience (Neimeyer, 2000; Neimeyer & Levitt, 2001; White & Epston, 1990). For example, bereaved persons are often disenfranchised in the sense that their unique grieving is invalidated or disregarded by their social world (Doka, 1989). Phrased in narrative terms, the story of their loss finds no social support in the response of a relevant audience but instead meets with a kind of empathic failure on the part of other actors in the social system (Neimeyer & Jordan, 2001). This outcome is particularly likely when either the form of the grieving (e.g., as intense or prolonged) or the griever (e.g., viewed as responsible for the loss) fails to conform to the approved dominant narrative of grief recovery endorsed by the culture (Neimeyer, 2001b). Under such circumstances, the account of the loss can become a circular monologue, one that struggles unsuccessfully to achieve a new and more liberating telling.

The processes of finding a fresh authorial voice and working with narrative features of setting, characterization, plot, theme, and goal can be illustrated by a dramatic restorative justice conference that followed a highway fatality.[9] Approximately three years earlier, Jill, then 21 years old and in treatment for depression, had been driving while drinking and hit and killed a pedestrian, Pat, age 16. Pat's body was badly mutilated in the accident, and she died within hours of admission to the hospital. Jill herself was knocked unconscious in the collision and awoke in the same hospital two days later. Following her recovery she was brought to trial and sentenced to five years in jail. It was in the course of her incarceration that the conference was arranged.

In addition to Jill, the other (living) leading character in the drama was Jack, Pat's father. A prominent and high-ranking executive, Jack had been consumed by intense and angry grieving for the three years that followed his daughter's death. Accordingly, he had done all in his power to "secure justice" for his Pat's "killer," both during the courtroom proceedings and in later reviews of Jill's case by the prison board. By keeping the case "alive" in the eyes of the media, Jack had effectively blocked Jill from earning any privileges during her incarceration, even though she had been a model prisoner. Asked for his account during the preparatory phase of the conferencing, Jack characterized his daughter in the most flattering terms, as a social and academic "star," beautiful, and loved by many. In contrast, he characterized Jill in the most derogatory fashion possible, as a psychiatric patient, unintelligent, lower-class, on drugs, an unwed mother—in short, the sort of person who ruined the lives of others. Above all, his anguish was palpable in the preparatory interviews, forcing the interviewer to struggle to keep from joining in his tears. For Jack, the aim of the conference was clear: to make his daughter's killer feel some of the raw pain that his daughter had suffered and that now consumed him. This same consuming grief made it difficult to recruit supporting figures for the conference from Jack's social world, as many people had withdrawn from his life, unable to deal with his prolonged and agonizing mourning. Therefore, only his wife and one friend accompanied him to the meeting.

Preparatory work with Jill disclosed that she felt apparent contrition for the accident and had wanted to apologize to Jack and his family but had been prevented from doing so by her lawyers. As was true for Jack, Jill and her family had suffered disenfranchisement by their social world following the collision, though more through a process of ostracism associated with blaming Jill for the tragedy. However, several of the ostracized family members agreed to accompany Jill to the conference, including her mother, uncle, and siblings and their partners. With the facilitator, observer, and Jack's contingent, this brought the total number of participants to 15, and it was this group that filed into a conference room in the prison to take their places in a circle of chairs, facing one another for the first time since the trial.

When Jack arrived for the conference, he dramatically placed a large and beautifully framed photograph of his daughter directly opposite Jill, as if in silent accusation of her for her crime. Still, Jill managed to open the meeting as agreed upon with her own account of the plot sequence of the tragedy, filling in events that followed her being knocked unconscious by drawing upon the reports of others. When asked by the facilitator how she thought Jack and his family had been affected, she conjectured that "they would be sad and angry" but added that she really didn't think she could say. When Jack's wife was invited to respond, she described Jill as callous and propounded a shocking thematic explanation of the accident: Jill had deliberately killed Pat in a quarrel about a boy. This accusation caused real distress to everyone in the room and prompted Jill and her sister to deny this in the most strenuous terms. Eventually, Jack's wife seemed to accept this and went on to talk movingly about how much her daughter had meant to her.

When the facilitator asked Jack to speak about his first reactions to news of the accident, he began a vitriolic attack on Jill, declaring that she should be the one in the grave. Choked with emotion, Jack drew on excruciating details of the accident and the condition of his daughter's body, establishing a setting for his account that drew others into the telling. As Gardener (1983) observed about good fiction, "It's physical detail that pulls us into the story, makes us believe or forget not to believe . . . [creating] a rich and vivid play in the mind" (p. 30). Absorbed by the gut-wrenching account, virtually all listeners were moved to tears by Jack's narrative.

Jack's friend, as well as Jill and her family, listened responsively to his telling and supplemented the story with their own points of view and voices. One such elaboration of the theme was triggered by Jack's angry accusation that Jill's uncle was partly to blame for the accident, as he had seen his niece inebriated earlier on that fateful night and cautioned her about but did not prevent her from driving in that condition. This led to a somewhat philosophical discussion between Jack and Jill's uncle about the nature of causality, in which the uncle kept a level tone and introduced several useful reflections about the complex nature of chance and responsibility. Although this thematic elaboration did not negate Jack's emotional assault, it did not feed into an escalating exchange of recriminations or defense, setting the stage for a different form of interaction.[10]

At one point in the conference Jill said that she was losing her place in all of this. She then spoke directly to Pat's picture, saying she wished that horrible night had never happened and that she wished Pat could be there with them. Jill continued in a pleading, apologetic voice, acknowledging the unfairness of the tragedy and saying she wished it was she who had died. Concluding her moving monologue, she turned to Jack and said earnestly, "I hope some good comes from tonight for you."

Jack seemed transformed by this performance. Much of his anger dissolved into a primary sadness, and he cried and held his wife's hand for the first time in the evening, as she put her arm around his shoulders as he sobbed. This emotional shift was further modulated by a moving disclosure by the fiancé of Jill's older sister, who spoke compassionately of the suicidal death of a friend and the father's inconsolable grief in its aftermath. The young man went on to talk about how he wished he could do something to make life easier for Jack and his family but knew he could not. He concluded by declaring his love for Jill, his inability to forget what had happened to Pat, and his struggle to look for some good in the bewildering vicissitudes of life. This made a tremendous difference for Jack, who seemed to grasp for the first time that others had suffered as intense and seemingly senseless a wound as he had.

But perhaps the critical turning point of the conference came when Jack passed around a graphic photograph of the scene of the accident that had been taken by the police, providing a vivid portrayal of the disaster that all participants had in common. As the photo slowly made its way around the room, a reverential silence fell over the group, punctuated only by the occasional sob of a participant. This, in the words of the facilitator, was the point of the emergence of "collective vulnerability," experienced as a shared physical deflation. As the community of conference participants joined in the poignant recognition of the frailty and brevity of life, their new sense of coherence was cemented.[11] With shared sadness but conviction, the group then turned toward forging an agreement.

What emerged from this discussion was a remarkable new partnership: Jack and Jill would join together to create a school-based program to prevent drunk driving, in which both would participate as speakers. With this new and progressive goal in view, the atmosphere shifted to one of solemn celebration as hugs and tears were exchanged all around. At the follow-up point a year later, Jack was much happier with life than before the conference and had stopped advising against prison privileges for Jill. For her part, Jill was carefully rebuilding her relationship with her young daughter, in preparation for her release and resumption of active parenting. Most fundamentally, each had moved from a thin characterization of the other in what Buber (1958) might call "I–it" terms to a much richer and more reciprocal "I–Thou" recognition of the other's humanity. Supporting this shift was the consolidation of a new narrative forged and formalized in the conference, one that brought forth new relational identities for its central characters. By giving voice to the disenfranchised losses of Jack, Jill, and their families and social network, the conference helped restore coherence to their lives, both individually and collectively.

Encouraging Co-Authorship: Lebs versus Aussies

A distinctive feature of restorative justice conferencing is the communal construction of narrative—no one voice predominates over the others; no single point of view holds sway. Instead, each utterance by each participant presupposes, responds to, and overlays the previous utterances of others, opening new dialogical possibilities in the construction of their collective identity (Bakhtin, 1984; Tappan, 1999). The result can be viewed as a metanarrative in which regressive story lines are typically challenged by resourceful co-authoring voices, often shifting the performance into fresh and more hopeful directions. This form of liberating co-narration can be illustrated by a brief account of a conference that followed an outbreak of fighting in an Australian high school that had prided itself on its peaceful relations between different ethnic groups of students.[12]

The fighting had erupted during an open-book test, stimulated by the shortage of necessary books in the classroom. Pushing soon turned to punching, as "Lebs" (immigrant students of Lebanese descent) and "Aussies" (native-born students of Western European background) tangled, and various bystanders got the opportunity for a "free kick." More or less arbitrarily a total of 8 boys (more Lebs than Aussies) were suspended. At the ensuing conference, 6 of these boys were present, together with parents, siblings, and some teachers, bringing the total number of participants to 25.[13]

When the parents were invited to tell how they had been affected by the conflict, one Aussie father expounded a remarkable theory. "The problem with you Lebanese," he declared, "is that you fight like a pack of dogs. Aussie boys fight one-on-one, not like you, where a whole pack attacks one boy." This characterization triggered real consternation and angry interruptions, but the father continued to hold forth. A necessary condition for improvement, he argued, would be for the Lebs to "learn to fight the proper way," like the Aussies. However, he conceded contemptuously that this was unlikely, as the "dog-fighting was in the genes of the Lebanese."

At that point, an older sister of one of the Lebanese boys became especially upset and addressed the facilitator both verbally and nonverbally with the message, "You can't let this go on." Restraining himself, the facilitator simply nod-ded back to her to signal "it's up to you to say what you feel must be said." The essence of her response to the group can be summarized as follows: "Where are we now? We have come here to find out what can be done to prevent further fighting and make this school a peaceful place. But now we are no better than the boys when they were fighting. We must set a good example and stop fighting among ourselves, and concentrate on what can be done to improve the situation at the school."

This earnest plea made many of the adults feel shame, and the emotional climate almost immediately turned from conflict to cooperation. Creative goal setting soon followed, eventuating in an agreement that (1) the teacher in the conflicted classroom would be offered support in managing disruptive behav-ior, (2) the older boys at the conference would actively prevent the younger boys from fighting, (3) the school would offer an apology to three parents who felt their sons had been unfairly selected out for punishment, and (4) the participating boys would meet with school officials to talk about how to make the school a safer place. A follow-up by the Department of Education con-firmed that the conference had made a significant difference in the peacefulness of the school, and the level of violent behavior fell dramatically.

This illustration underscores the importance of nontyranny in the con-ference process, as well as the value of keeping the facilitator from occupying an editorial role in connection with the emerging group narrative. The facil-itator and observers afterward agreed that an active attempt to silence the belligerent Aussie father would have produced resistance or at best grudging compliance, rather than the necessary cooperation. Likewise, they agreed that none of them could have formulated a more apt response to the father's dom-inant narrative of ethnic inferiority than that offered by the Lebanese sister and the attempt to adopt such an editorial role would have sent the message that the group was unable to handle its own affairs. Thus the deliberative democratic procedures that characterize a conference might be analogized to a narrative composed by the very characters who enact it and who are capable of reflexive revision of its theme and goals when it encounters developmental obstacles.

Recruiting an Audience: Transcending Abuse

Constructivist literature on the self-narratives of trauma survivors often focuses on the incoherence introduced into the person's autobiography by the trau-matic event (Polkinghorne, 1991; Sewell, 1997) and the suspension of ex-periences that cannot be emplotted within the orderly progression of the per-son's previous life story (Neimeyer & Stewart, 1996). Although the loss of continuity with self is important, overemphasizing this personal dislodgment risks marginalizing the social dislocation that typically accompanies and sustains it. Thus just as a story requires a reader or listener as well as a narrator, self-narratives find validation (or invalidation) in the response of a relevant audience (Neimeyer, 2000; Tappan, 1999). We believe that conferencing provides a unique window on this social dimension of the narration of identity.

An example of this arose in the case of Cathy, who from the age of 12 had been sexually abused by a man named David who lived in her home.[14] Like many victims of long-term abuse, Cathy reported that she had lived in a kind of "vacuum," reduced to seeing the world through David's eyes. Finally, as a young woman she mustered the courage to disclose her abuse to the police, which led to David's guilty plea and a sentence of three years' imprisonment. Sadly, however, the ending of the abuse did little to improve Cathy's distant relationship with her parents, who had long been absent from her life. As a result of her isolation from a community of concern, she was effectively "frozen" in the identity of a victim of sexual abuse (despite years of therapy), with all of the powerlessness and diminished self-worth that this implies (Harter, Alexander, & Neimeyer, 1988).

After several attempts on Cathy's part to arrange a "victim–offender" meeting, she was finally referred to Terry O'Connell, who prepared her for the conference by emphasizing the importance of involving her family in the meeting. Facing her fears of being "rejected" by them, Cathy consented to their inclusion, and her parents as well as her sister were eventually persuaded to come. Likewise, David's family, including his wife and three grown sons, accompanied him to the meeting. The attendance of several friends of both families brought the total number of participants in the 5-hour conference to 29.

Unfortunately, at no point in the conference did David accept responsibility for his behavior, but instead he maintained that he was as much a "victim" as Cathy. Nonetheless, Cathy courageously held her ground, disputing his claim that he had the misfortune of "falling in love with a young woman"— she was 12, she declared unambiguously, not 18. There was therefore no touching scene of apology and forgiveness—simply revulsion on the part of other participants at David's recalcitrance. For Cathy, however, the conference was transformative. As she later stated:

I'm free. . . . Deceit and corruption officially ended that night. I'm free to perceive, decide and behave in a way appropriate to myself and not to the perpetrator of my life.

Everything has changed because I have changed. Before the conference [my friends and family] didn't know how to behave towards me. Terry was good at making my parents see things from my point of view. My father changed—now he shows me courtesy. . . . The conference allowed the best of humanity to come out. I felt renewed, a rebirth. I'm not the same person after this.

The joyful conclusion of the conference underscored Cathy's personal transformation. Summarizing the support and social mingling that character-ized this occasion, she noted: "There was euphoria at the end, hugging all over the place. David's wife hugged my father. [His sons] hugged my sister. I had been emotionally scared of them, [but] one of them asked me to keep in touch, and gave me a hug. I never expected that. Other people came to tell me that they also had been abused, both men and women."

Indeed, one of two therapists in attendance who had worked with Cathy remarked following the meeting, "I did not sleep last night. I think I will have to go back to the drawing board. I could not have achieved half of what this conference has, even if I worked for the next ten years."

The outcome of Cathy's conference illustrates the liberating power of con-ferencing, even when one of its main protagonists resists reformulation of the conflict between them. In a narrative perspective, this healing potential resides in large part in the changed relationship between the transformed protagonist as author and the other participants as audience, who collectively can validate a new and preferred sense of self. Cathy's story brings to mind the South African *ubuntu* spirit: "I am because you are" or "my humanity is tied up to your humanity" (Llewelyn & Howse, 1999, p. 5). Reciprocally, the emergence of this preferred identity makes possible more satisfying relationships with friends and family, bootstrapping both self and system toward greater levels of coherence and integration. In this way, conferencing catalyzes agentic self-development at the same time that it fosters the construction of community, bridging the sometimes oppositional relation of these two domains as portrayed in constructivist and social constructionist thought (Neimeyer, 1998).

A Closing Coda

Writing in a true social constructionist vein, Christie (2000) observes:

> Crime does not exist. Crime is created. First there are acts. There follows a long process of giving meaning to these acts. Distance in-creases the tendency to give certain acts the meaning of being crimes, and the persons the simplified meaning of being criminals. In other settings—family life being one of several examples—the social con-ditions are of a sort which creates resistance against perceiving acts as crimes and persons as criminals. (p. 22)

From this point of view it follows that acts labeled as crimes, in a truly hu-manistic framework, should "become a starting point for real dialogue, and not for an equally clumsy answer in the form of a spoonful of pain," again quoting Christie (1981, p. 11). In this chapter we have argued that the social construction of crime in Western cultures reinforces a dominant narrative of conflict as an offense against the state and the appropriate societal response as one of retribution. We have suggested that this hegemonic response to conflict has several socially constructed but nonetheless real effects. These include the silencing or constraint of the voices of the affected parties, which deprives them of a socially sanctioned opportunity to attribute coherent meaning to the problematic act in any terms other than those of the retributive justice narrative. As a result, conflicted parties struggle to assimilate the significance of the often-traumatic event into their life stories and all too frequently do so by simply adopting the dominant self-narrative of being a "criminal offender" or "victim." Ultimately, both identities are stigmatizing and disempowering and neither suggests a progressive narrative that leads toward their development as moral agents.

At another, more social level, the dominant retributive paradigm in criminal justice also undermines a sense of community. Ultimately, the state, as the offended party, is an abstraction with which no "I-Thou" relationship is possible. Thus displaced to an abstract civic sphere, conflict loses its transformative power for local communities, where a more immediate and emotional encounter between offender and those affected can catalyze useful change. In this sense the loss of coherence that can characterize the self-narratives of conflicted parties is ironically compounded at a communal level, as local networks are balkanized into disputing factions, respectively seeking evasion of responsibility or revenge. The narration of conflict is thereby preempted by authorities, and living communities suffer a loss of the social coherence necessary to participate in morally developmental dialogue.

It is our view that restorative justice conferencing usefully challenges both trends and that narrative theory provides a useful lens through which to view its operation. At a *literal* level, conferences are all about narratives, as the affected parties attempt to give voice to their unique accounts of their conflicts and losses and struggle together to negotiate shared meanings in the emotionally resonant atmosphere of a facilitated encounter. In the course of doing so, conference participants instinctively draw upon narrative forms and features—which include story setting, characterization, emplotment, thematic attribution, and projection of goals—in order to establish certain moral positions for themselves and attribute (usually quite different) positions to others. However, the polyphony of voices effectively prevents the tyranny of any one and fosters the development of "unique outcomes" or "sparkling moments" (White & Epston, 1990) that could not be envisioned in view of the starting positions of any of the participating parties.

At a perhaps more figurative level, conferences also represent *performed* narratives, enactments of positions in a social drama that may only be hinted at in the literal accounts offered by their participants. Here, too, the narrative structure of the conference evolves across the encounter, shifting from the simple "good/bad," "offender/victim" logic that defines its starting point toward a more complex universe of moral meanings that underscores our collective vulnerability. In the course of this transformation, participants are given the opportunity to claim new and more developed moral identities not merely with their words but also with their deeds. Thus the conference context itself and the follow-up period that it establishes provide a stage and an audience for the performance of a more coherent personhood and a more cooperative community. We hope that our attempts to illuminate and illustrate the narrative dimensions of this activity give encouragement to others who seek to understand, and perhaps facilitate, the human engagement with conflict and loss.

Notes

The two authors contributed equally to preparation of the manuscript. The authors also wish to express their appreciation to David B. Moore for his thoughtful comments on an earlier version of this chapter.

1. Compare also www.transcend.org, an international network created by Johan Galtung.

2. If we were to give a definition of narrative, it would involve the construction of a story that entails the meaningful sequencing of events and typically involves actors, animated by intentionality, who are undertaking some action toward a stated or implied end. Parenthetically, we might note our shared view that narrative does not exhaust the range of individual or collective meaning-making activity. Indeed, people have many non-narrative forms of symbolic ordering, which include mathematics (no trivial symbol system in itself!), logic (e.g., reasoning from antecedents to consequences), and architectural and design elements (e.g., the formal "statements" made by government buildings or the arrangement of a courtroom or classroom). Even the construing of meaning, in its irreducible form of differentiating and integrating various elements of experience (Kelly, 1955/1991), is at most prenarrative in this sense, carving up the world of events in a way that then provides "raw material" for the construction of narratives by their users. Thus we see narrative as simply a significant subset of human symbolic activity, though no less important for that reason.

3. It is interesting that this liberating effect of performance was emphasized by George A. Kelly in his "fixed role therapy," in which a client was invited to enact a carefully scripted fictional identity for a fixed period of time, unbeknownst to other actors in his or her social life (Kelly, 1955/1991). Although clients explicitly "de-role" following the enactment, they typically carry over aspects of the

"make-believe" identity that prove viable, along with a sense of their capacity to re-create themselves on an ongoing basis through future performance (Neimeyer, 1993).

4. Note that there is a gray zone from approximately 10 to 18 years of age, which reflects cultural debates that concern the age at which young people can be considered "fully responsible for their actions." We do not wish to enter this debate but simply to point out that two fundamentally different paradigms seem to be operative on either end of this adolescent ambiguity—indeed, the difficulty shifting from one to the other during adolescence suggests a curious contradiction in the dominant paradigm.

5. See also the Web site www.tja.com.au.

6. The TJA approach relies heavily on Tomkins's (1962, 1963) theory of emotion, which David Moore discovered through Nathanson's (1992) presentation of the theory. Emotional processes are generally ignored or seen as nuisance factors in the retributive paradigm.

7. The crucial role of recruitment of supporting actors in conferencing was underscored in a conversation between one of us (FT) and J. Braithwaite: "What," I asked, "if there were no persons who could be found to support, say, a given drug addict arrested for theft? What if there were no resourceful family members, no supportive friends?" Braithwaite was adamant in rejecting the underlying premise and viewed this problem as simply an indication of the need to be more thorough in preparing the conference. In cases in which at first blush no support network could be found, conferencing could be especially valuable. Careful questioning, he contended, would always reveal someone, perhaps a sports coach remembered after ten years or a sister who lived far away. In New Zealand airfare will even be paid for the sister.

8. We will occasionally use the legalistic term *offender* for the sake of brevity, although stigmatizing terminology is typically avoided in conferences, much as the term *patient* is avoided in narrative therapy (Monk, Winslade, Crocket, & Epston, 1996).

9. This account draws on extensive case notes written immediately after the conference by McDonald, its facilitator, and Moore, an observer. The story was further fleshed out through conversations of both men with one of the authors of this chapter (FT). As with other case illustrations that appear in this chapter, names and identifying information have been altered to respect participants' privacy.

10. The tendency of people who have suffered adversity to seek meaning through a causal search is a frequently noted process in the psychology of loss (Neimeyer, 2001b). As illustrated in this case, such a search can take various forms. On the one hand, observers may seek to identify a single "big cause" of the tragedy, using a simple attributional logic that places responsibility squarely with one person or factor (Nisbett & Ross, 1980). On the other hand, affected persons may try to reverse fate, by engaging in a kind of "counterfactual thinking" that ruminates on "what-if" possibilities that would have produced a different outcome. Both processes were evidenced in the conference discussed here, as stepping-stones toward the recognition of a much wider web of causal responsibility for the disaster. This

expanded conception of cause and effect paved the way for the emergence of collective vulnerability discussed later.

11. It is worth noting that the sense of connection thus established also seemed to reach out to embrace Pat herself. Following the conference, the facilitator and observer asked Jack if there was a part of him that sought, in passing around the photograph of the accident, to reconnect with his daughter through Jill, perhaps abetted by her "prayer" to Pat's picture earlier in the conference. After reflecting for a moment, Jack answered, "Yes." This underscores the vital role of reaffirming, rather than relinquishing, bonds with those we have loved and lost as a central dynamic in reconstructing meaning in the course of grieving (Attig, 2000; Klass, Silverman, & Nickman, 1996; Neimeyer, 2001a).

12. Again, McDonald served as facilitator, with both Moore and one of the authors (FT) observing.

13. It is worth noting that this approaches the upper limit of participants in a conference, which ideally should range from 15 to 30 members. Groups of this size help ensure that the group will include useful resource persons, like the Lebanese sister described later, without becoming unwieldy or too large to permit each person a say.

14. This summary draws on the report of O'Connell (1997) as well as an interview one of the authors (FT) conducted with Cathy in 1998.

References

Anderson, W. T. (1990). *Reality isn't what it used to be.* New York: Harper & Row.

Arciero, G., & Guidano, V. (2000). Experience, explanation, and the quest for coherence. In R. A. Neimeyer & J. C. Raskin (Eds.), *Constructions of disorder* (pp. 91–117). Washington, DC: American Psychological Association.

Attig, T. (1996). *How we grieve: Relearning the world.* New York: Oxford University Press.

Attig, T. (2000). *The heart of grief.* New York: Oxford University Press.

Attig, T. (2001). Relearning the world: Making and finding meanings. In R. A. Neimeyer (Ed.), *Meaning reconstruction and the experience of loss* (pp. 33–53). Washington, DC: American Psychological Association.

Bakhtin, M. (1984). *Problems of Dostoevsky's poetics.* Minneapolis: University of Minnesota Press.

Braithwaite, J. (1997). *Restorative justice: Assessing an immodest theory and a pessimistic theory.* Retrieved from the Australian Institute of Criminology Web site: http://aic.gov.au. March 13, 1998.

Braithwaite, J., & Pettit, P. (1990). *Not just desserts: A republican theory of criminal justice.* Oxford: Oxford University Press.

Buber, M. (1958). *I and thou* (2d ed.). New York: Charles Scribner's Sons.

Christie, N. (1977). Conflicts as property. *British Journal of Criminology, 17,* 1–14.

Christie, N. (1981). *Limits to pain.* Oxford: Robertson.

Christie, N. (2000). *Crime control as industry: Towards Gulags, western style.* (3rd ed.). London: Routledge.

Davis, C. G., Nolen-Hoeksema, S., & Larson, J. (1998). Making sense of loss and benefiting from the experience: Two construals of meaning. *Journal of Personality and Social Psychology, 75,* 561–574.

Doka, K. J. (1989). *Disenfranchised grief.* San Francisco: Jossey Bass.

Edwards, D., & Potter, J. (1992). *Discursive psychology.* Newbury Park, CA: Sage.

Fisher, R., & Ury, W. (1981). *Getting to yes.* London: Arrow.

Foucault, M. (1970). *The order of things.* New York: Pantheon.

Galtung, J., & Tschudi, F. (2000). Crafting peace: On the psychology of the TRANSCEND approach. In J. Galtung & C. G. Jacobsen (Eds.), *Searching for peace: The road to TRANSCEND* (pp. 206–227). London: Pluto.

Gardner, J. (1983). *The art of fiction.* New York: Vintage.

Goffmann, E. (1959). *The presentation of self in everyday life.* New York: Doubleday.

Granovetter, M. (1973). The strength of weak ties. *American Journal of Sociology, 78,* 1360–1380.

Haney, C., & Zimbardo, P. (1998). The past and future of U.S. prison policy. *American Psychologist, 53,* 709–727.

Harter, S. L., Alexander, P. C., & Neimeyer, R. A. (1988). Long-term effects of incestuous child abuse in college women. *Journal of Consulting and Clinical Psychology, 56,* 5–8.

Hermans, H. J. M. (2002). The person as a motivated storyteller. In R. A. Neimeyer & G. J. Neimeyer (Eds.), *Advances in personal construct psychology* (vol. 5, pp. 3–38). Westport, CT: Praeger.

Holzman, L. (2000). Performance, criticism and postmodern psychology. In L. Holzman & J. Morss (Eds.), *Postmodern psychologies and societal practice* (pp. 79–92). New York: Routledge.

Janoff-Bulman, R., & Berg, M. (1998). Disillusionment and the creation of values. In J. H. Harvey (Ed.), *Perspectives on loss: A sourcebook* (pp. 35–47). Philadelphia: Brunner Mazel.

Kaufman, J. (Ed.) (2001). *Loss of the assumptive world.* Philadelphia: Brunner Routledge.

Kelly, G. A. (1991). *The psychology of personal constructs.* New York: Routledge. (Original work published 1955)

Klass, D., Silverman, P. R., & Nickman, S. (1996). *Continuing bonds: New understandings of grief.* Washington, DC: Taylor & Francis.

Llewellyn, J. J., & Howse, R. (1999). *Restorative justice: A conceptual framework.* Retrieved from the Law Commision of Canada Web site: www.lcc.gc.ac/en/papers/hose.html. September 24, 2000.

McCold, P. (1997). *Restorative justice: An annotated bibliography.* Retrieved from www.restorativejustice.org/RJ_Anotated_Bibliography.htm. April 25, 1999.

Milo, E. M. (1997). Maternal responses to the life and death of a child with developmental disability. *Death Studies, 21,* 443–476.

Monk, G., Winslade, J., Crocket, K., & Epston, D. (1996). *Narrative therapy in practice.* San Francisco: Jossey Bass.

Moore, D. B., & Forsythe, L. (1995). *A new approach to juvenile justice: An evaluation of family conferencing in Wagga Wagga.* Centre for Rural Social Research, Charles Sturt University, Wagga Wagga, NSW.

Moore, D. B., & McDonald, J. (2000). *Transforming conflict.* Sydney: Transformative Justice PTY.

Moore, D. B., & McDonald, J. (2001a). Community conferencing as a special case of conflict transformation. In J. Braithwaite & H. Strang (Eds.), *Restorative justice and civil society* (pp. 130–148). Cambridge: Cambridge University Press.

Mor ber om streng straff. (2000, September 14). *Aftenpost,* p. 7.

Nathanson, D. (1992). *Shame and pride, affect, sex, and the birth of the self.* New York: Norton.

Neimeyer, R. A. (1993). Constructivist approaches to the measurement of meaning. In G. J. Neimeyer (Ed.), *Constructivist assessment: A casebook* (pp. 58–103). Newbury Park, CA: Sage.

Neimeyer, R. A. (1995). Client-generated narratives in psychotherapy. In R. A. Neimeyer & M. J. Mahoney (Eds.), *Constructivism in psychotherapy* (pp. 231–246). Washington, DC: American Psychological Association.

Neimeyer, R. A. (1998). Social constructionism in the counselling context. *Counselling Psychology Quarterly, 11,* 135–149.

Neimeyer, R. A. (2000). Narrative disruptions in the construction of self. In R. A. Neimeyer & J. Raskin (Eds.), *Constructions of disorder: Meaning making frameworks for psychotherapy* (pp. 207–241). Washington, DC: American Psychological Association.

Neimeyer, R. A. (2001a). The language of loss. In R. A. Neimeyer (Ed.), *Meaning reconstruction and the experience of loss* (pp. 261–292). Washington, DC: American Psychological Association.

Neimeyer, R. A. (2001b). *Lessons of loss: A guide to coping.* Philadelphia and London: Brunner Routledge.

Neimeyer, R. A. (Ed.) (2001c). *Meaning reconstruction and the experience of loss.* Washington, DC: American Psychological Association.

Neimeyer, R. A., & Jordan, J. R. (2001). Disenfranchisement as empathic failure. In K. J. Doka (Ed.), *Disenfranchised grief* (pp. 235–251). San Francisco: Jossey Bass.

Neimeyer, R. A., & Levitt, H. (2001). Coping and coherence: A narrative perspective on resilience. In C. R. Snyder (Ed.), *Coping with stress: Effective people and processes* (pp. 47–67). New York: Oxford University Press.

Neimeyer, R. A., & Mahoney, M. J. (Eds.) (1995). *Constructivism in psychotherapy.* Washington, DC: American Psychological Association.

Neimeyer, R. A., & Stewart, A. E. (1996). Trauma, healing, and the narrative emplotment of loss. *Families in Society, 77,* 360–375.

Neimeyer, R. A., & Stewart, A. E. (2000). Constructivist and narrative psychotherapies. In C. R. Snyder & R. E. Ingram (Eds.), *Handbook of psychological change* (pp. 337–357). New York: Wiley.

Newman, F., & Holzman, L. (1993). *Lev Vygotsky: Revolutionary scientist.* London: Routledge.

Nisbett, R., & Ross, L. (1980). *Human inference*. Englewood Cliffs, NJ: Prentice Hall.

O'Connell, T. (1997). Dawn or dusk in sentencing. In P. Healy & H. Dumont (Eds.), *Conferencing and community empowerment*: Rediscovering the Human Face of Justice (pp. 141–165). Ottawa: Canadian Institute for the Administration of Justice.

Polkinghorne, D. E. (1991). Narrative and self-concept. *Journal of Narrative and Life History, 1*, 135–153.

Raskin, J. D., & Lewandowski, A. M. (2000). The construction of disorder as human enterprise. In R. A. Neimeyer & J. D. Raskin (Eds.), *Constructions of disorder* (pp. 15–39). Washington, DC: American Psychological Association.

Rosenblatt, P. (2000). *Parent grief: Narratives of loss and relationship*. Philadelphia: Brunner Mazel.

Sewell, K. (1996). Constructional risk factors for a post-traumatic stress response following a mass murder. *Journal of Constructivist Psychology, 9*, 97–108.

Sewell, K. W. (1997). Posttraumatic stress: Towards a constructivist model of psychotherapy. In G. J. Neimeyer & R. A. Neimeyer (Eds.), *Advances in personal construct psychology* (vol. 4, pp. 207–235). Greenwich, CT: JAI.

Sewell, K. W., Cromwell, R. L., Farrell-Higgins, J., Palmer, R., Ohlde, C., & Patterson, T. W. (1996). Hierarchical elaboration in the conceptual structure of Vietnam combat veterans. *Journal of Constructivist Psychology, 9*, 79–96.

Szasz, T. (1974). *The myth of mental illness*. New York: Harper & Row.

Tappan, M. B. (1999). Authoring a moral self: A dialogical perspective. *Journal of Constructivist Psychology, 12*, 117–132.

Tedeschi, R., Park, C., & Calhoun, L. (Eds.) (1998). *Posttraumatic growth: Positive changes in the aftermath of crisis*. Mahwah, NJ: Erlbaum.

Tomkins, S. S. (1962). *Affect, imagery, consciousness: Vol. 1. The positive affects*. New York: Springer.

Tomkins, S. S. (1963). *Affect, imagery, consciousness: Vol. 2. The negative affects*. New York: Springer.

Trimboli, L. (2000). *An evaluation of the NSW Youth Justice Conferencing scheme*. Retrieved from the New South Wales Bureau of Crime Statistics and Research Web site: www.lawlink.nsw.gov.au.boscar1.nsf/pages/media120600. August 16, 2000.

Viney, L. L. (1991). The personal construct theory of death and loss. *Death Studies, 15*, 139–155.

White, M., & Epston, D. (1990). *Narrative means to therapeutic ends*. New York: Norton.

Wortham, S. (1999). The heterogeneously distributed self. *Journal of Constructivist Psychology, 12*, 153–171.

PART V

*The Neural Substrate of Narrative
and Consciousness Realization
(or The Naturalist Model)*

10 Empirical Evidence for a Narrative Concept of Self

John Bickle

Narrative concepts of self have influential recent defenders (Dennett, 1992; Flanagan, 1996). The sense of self under scrutiny is supposed to be the full-blown, philosophically interesting one: the selves that we persons value so highly. We are supposed to take the literary reference literally: "narrative structure" is intended as more than a suggestive metaphor. Owen Flanagan states this point clearly: "The sort of connectedness that constitutes a normatively acceptable self or life is the sort that makes for a contentful story that involves an unfolding rationale for the shape it takes" (1996, p. 67). This approach is not intended to deflate the importance we attach to self. Despite being the creation and expression of a story, our selves are assumed to be causally efficacious for behavior and cognition. Again, Flanagan writes:

> The self in this sense, what I call "self-represented identity," is a causally efficacious part of the whole system, and it affects both the cognitive content and the qualitative character of new experiences. The causal efficacy of the representation of a self is fairly obvious when a person is actively engaged in self-representing. It is also plausible to think that once a complex model of the self has been constructed and is in place, it exists as a complex dispositional structure in the brain and is often involved in structuring experience. (p. 70)

In this essay I first present empirical evidence that supports a narrative concept of self. Partly this evidence is from cognitive psychology, but primarily it comes from remarkable images of the functioning brain. So those (like me) who prefer concepts that enjoy more support than armchair reflection provides can embrace a robust, philosophically interesting sense of self. However, the empirical details also suggest that accounts of our selves' causal efficacy are pieces of narrative fiction. The measurable brain activity hypothesized later as generating and expressing our (narrative) selves does not exert significant control over neural regions that subserve cognition and behavior: at least not in the way that the neurally realized self-generating narratives claim it does. Thus each of us is self-deluded about the extent of our self-control. Put tersely: we are deluded selves. This empirically supported hypothesis carries fascinating consequences. I'll close this essay by developing one that pertains to moral training.

Psychologist Bernard Baars nicely describes "that little inner voice" that occupies so much of our waking consciousness:

> Most of us go around the world talking to ourselves. Just by noticing it more, we can come to realize how often we talk to ourselves in the privacy of our minds, sometimes addressing a completely imaginary jury—of professional peers, family, or you, the reader—in a sort of simulated reality . . . We are a gabby species. . . . Inner speech is one of the basic facts about human nature, one that takes only a minute to demonstrate. It seems to be utterly basic to the human condition. Most of us seem to spend far more hours per day talking to ourselves than to other people. (1997, p. 75)

Baars proposes an experiment: try silencing your inner voice for as long as you can. Perhaps some can exceed his report of about five seconds on self-imposed inner silence, but my experience is that I only become aware that my inner voice has resumed *after* it is speaking again. In this continuous inner speech, we have the beginnings of a narrative account of the self that "answers questions about who a person is, what that person aims at and cares about" (Flanagan 1996, pp. 69–70). It is an entity created and expressed by the narratives of the little inner voice that occupy so much of our waking consciousness.

We can next inquire into the neural basis of these internal narratives. In doing so, by the preceding hypothesis, we are inquiring into the neural basis of our valued self-representation. Psychologist Alan D. Baddeley (1993) first published a remarkable image of a functioning brain during controlled quiet inner speech. Before I present and discuss this image, I will describe the imaging technique employed: positron emission tomography (PET). PET's biophysics is now understood (see, e.g., Posner & Raichle, 1994, for a good nontechnical introduction), but confusions about it remain among non-neuroscientists. PET subjects receive injections of water or sugar molecules labeled with unstable radionuclides (substances that possess a greater ratio of protons to neutrons). Two common compounds are water molecules labeled with oxygen-15 and deoxyglucose molecules labeled with fluorine-18. The first is used to measure amount of regional blood flow, the second to measure amount of regional glucose metabolism. Since both blood flow and glucose metabolism correlate directly with levels of neuron and glial cell activity, PET provides an accurate (albeit secondhand) measure of cellular activity across neural regions.

The excess protons in the labeled molecules convert into neutrons by the normal physical process of radioactive decay. Positron emission (release of positively charged electrons) results from this conversion. Emitted positrons collide with electrons. Each collision releases two photons traveling at opposite (180°) trajectories. Detectors located around the biological tissue being imaged (e.g., around the subject's head) respond to these emitted photons. When two photons simultaneously reach detectors oriented 180° degrees to each other and connected in a coincidence circuit, the site of the positron–electron collision can be localized at present to a spatial resolution of less than 1 mm. The number of collisions localized to a particular region measures either amount of blood flow through or glucose metabolism within it. Sophisticated algorithms and computer graphics then construct the colorful PET images in which color of the region reflects its activity level. Computer graphics simulate cuts at various three-dimensional orientations through the image (hence the term *tomography*). This enables researchers and clinicians to compare activity generated in a variety of neural regions during a particular task.

Temporal resolution for PET is less impressive: at present, only around one minute per image. However, this current physical limitation can be overcome somewhat through use of two analytic techniques: image *subtraction* and *averaging*. The subtracted image results from the PET image generated during performance of the experimental task minus one generated during performance on a carefully chosen control task. The values subtracted are activity measures in specific spatial regions during both tasks. The subtracted image reflects the areas and amounts of activity specific to the experimental task (relative to the control task). (One nice feature of this method is that subjects can serve as their own controls.) A number of subtracted images from the experimental-control combination can then be averaged. The values averaged are activity measures in specific regions of the subtracted images. Image subtraction and averaging washes out any activity that is idiosyncratic to a single performance or to a single individual if subtracted images are averaged from a number of subjects. The resulting averaged images are the ones typically published.

Baddeley (1993) first published such a PET image, one of a number of similar images developed in a study by Paulescu, Frith, and Frackowiak (1993) (but not published in their paper). Paulescu and his colleagues were investigating the neural location of the phonological component of Baddeley's (1986) model of working memory. "Working memory" refers to our capacity to hold information temporarily on line for use in cognition and behavior. Examples range from rehearsing a telephone number while dialing to imagining a sequence of chess moves. Paulescu, Frith, and Frackowiak's (1993) experimental task had participants use inner speech to remember sequences of consonants presented visually. Participants were not permitted to speak out loud during the task. Experimenters used two other tasks to control for both visual and motor involvement in the experimental task (and hence to isolate the phonological working memory component in the subtracted PET images). One was a purely visual working memory task that involved matching Korean characters. None of the subjects read Korean, so inner speech about the target stimuli during the short delay periods was absent. The other was a purely subvocalization working memory task (rhyming) without phonological content. The resulting subtracted and averaged PET images thus revealed activity specific to phonological working memory with subvocal rehearsal (relative to the control tasks), that is, activity specific to inner speech without spoken verbal expression.

The fascinating result is that activity in the classic language areas is specific to inner speech. The anterior bright spot (in Baddeley's published image) reflects activity in Broca's area (Brodmann's areas 44 and 45). Damage to this region yields Broca's aphasia, a speech production deficit. Patients can comprehend but cannot produce verbal utterances. The posterior bright spot overlaps somewhat with Wernicke's area (Brodmann's area 22). Damage to this region yields Wernicke's aphasia, a speech comprehension deficit. Patients have no trouble producing verbal utterances. But their speech is described classically as "word salad" and they poorly comprehend others' utterances (as indicated by their verbal and nonverbal responses). Neurological assessment and imaging studies have also revealed that other areas active in Baddeley's image, particularly in the left supramarginal gyrus (Brodmann's area 40, the primary posterior site of activity), are only active when subjects listen to spoken words rather than acoustically similar pure tones (Posner & Raichle, 1994). Thus in terms of brain areas activated during quiet inner speech, humans are both *producing* and *comprehending* their own overtly linguistic utterances. We just aren't offering them up for public consumption.

Combining Baars's (1997) observation about the ubiquity of human inner speech with this imaging result yields empirical evidence for a narrative concept of self. The self, in the normative "self-representation" sense that has interested philosophers, is created and expressed by the narratives generated by constant activity in the brain's language production and comprehension regions. Some of these linguistic productions are bound for verbal expression, but most are limited to internal comprehension. This hypothesis is a piece of neurophilosophical theory. But the data just scouted provide an intriguing start toward its empirical defense.

Interesting questions arise immediately: Do aphasias extend to quiet inner

speech? Are Broca's aphasics deficient in the production of internal monologues? Does the inner speech of Wernicke's aphasics constitute "word salad"?
Do they fail to comprehend their own inner linguistic productions? The fact
that neuropsychological syndromes such as unilateral neglect invade memory
as well as sensory representations (Bisiach & Luzzati, 1978) suggests positive
answers to these questions. Inner and outer speech seem to employ the same
neural regions. If damage to them is reflected in outer speech deficits, it seems
reasonable to suppose that these deficits invade inner speech as well. And if
the self we know and love is the creation and expression of continuous quiet
inner speech produced by activity in the human brain's language regions, then
what sorts of selves do aphasics create and express? None at all, if the aphasia
is severe enough?

Fascinating as these neuropsychological musings are, let's set them aside
as topics for further work and next consider the contents of these continuous
self-constructing linguistic productions. What kind of self do they create and
express? Clearly, they create and express a causally efficacious self-image: one
of a self not only in causal control of important cognitive, conscious, and behavioral events but also aware of exerting this control. I've suggested that we
call it the Elaborate Practical Reasoning self-image, on the model of Rodin's
famous statue, *The Thinker* (Bickle, Worley, & Bernstein, 2000). Consider a
mundane example: one's self-as-decision-maker. Consciously I face a choice.
What happens next? I experience my self engaged in "all things considered"
idea brainstorming. I experience my self considering the relevance of these
ideas for current, foreseeable, and even imaginary situations. I experience my
self constantly revising and rethinking both ends and means. Finally, I experience my self making a conscious decision about what to do and then initiating
the appropriate action chain. This self-image is so familiar that its description
seems pedantic. It is our common experience of self-in-control. A similar image
is found in our phenomenology of a wide range of self-involved activities: strategy planning, intentional behavior, action execution, meaningful conversation,
and on and on.

Although we often don't notice this, our little inner voice chatters away
in the preceding situations. I stare into my closet on Friday morning and my
little inner voice commences: *Paisley shirt or the canary one? Canary. But gotta
dress up Monday so canary one today means doing laundry over the weekend.
Paisley!* And I reach for the paisley (or is it: *As* I reach for the paisley? Or
even: *After* I've begun reaching for the paisley? I'll say more about confabulation and the timing issue later). If our selves are generated by these sorts of
internal speech productions and comprehensions, as I'm urging here, the self-
image that gets generated is that of the self-in-control. That is exactly the sort
of self-representation created and expressed by the contents of the quiet inner

monologues produced prior to (and during and maybe even after!) the planning, sequencing, and motor executions that comprise everyday cognitive and behavioral events.

But a moment's sober reflection reveals how limited this self-in-control has to be for the bulk of our cognition and behavior. The vast majority of our intentional actions are more "ballistic" than the Elaborate Practical Reasoning model suggests. In Dennett's (1991) picturesque definition, ballistic actions are "unguided missiles": once initiated, their trajectories can't be halted or altered by reflective feedback. Most of our intentional actions have this character. Consider another mundane example: your intentional act of grasping the meaning of this sentence. How much Elaborate Practical Reasoning was involved? Most of our cognitive and conscious events are like this example. Our deliberative intentional actions are far rarer than the ballistic ones that occur constantly. The same point holds about conscious sequences. Psychologists have known of the messy, arbitrary, start-and-stop, hop-and-skip nature of our conscious streams since William James expressed the point more than a century ago: "Like a bird's life, it [consciousness] seems to be made of an alternation of flights and perchings" (1890, p. 269). Even our explicit consciousness rarely stays on target for very long. Folk wisdom and our sometimes unshakeable convictions to the contrary, human behavior and cognition are only rarely the outcome of Elaborate Practical Reasoning. (Incidentally, the preceding quote from James [1890] is followed by the intriguing sentence: "The rhythm of language expresses this, where every thought is expressed in a sentence, and every sentence closes with a period." The tie between [inner] speech, consciousness, and the self was suggested in psychology long before there was neuroimaging to develop and confirm it!)

With our empirically based account of the narrative self, we can even begin to make sense of the actually quite limited scope of our selves-in-control. Anatomical and physiological facts about the neural regions whose activity creates and expresses our selves hold grave consequences for the veridicality of these inner speeches, and so also for the image of the self-in-control they generate. Although it has been known for some time that neurons in the language regions project (via associational fibers) to a wide variety of cortical and subcortical regions (e.g., Crosby, Humphrey, & Lauer, 1962), they don't project to the neurons in those regions that do the bulk of information *processing* there. There are very good evolutionary reasons for this lack. Speech production and comprehension are subject to tremendous time pressures. For example, reflect on how quickly you comprehend an utterance and produce a reply during a heated discussion. To succeed under these time pressures, the language production and comprehension regions can only be privy to a limited amount of information processing that occurs elsewhere in the brain. What they need is access primarily to the output of the brain's other information-processing networks.

This limited access makes the language regions privy to decisions reached in other cognitive networks, yielding the capacity to report these (and comprehend those reports) in inner and outer speech. But it doesn't overburden the language regions or slow them down so that they miss production and comprehension deadlines. Their constant activity also doesn't clutter or gum up processing in the other brain networks with extraneous inputs irrelevant to the specific tasks subserved there.

In addition, the expressive capacity of linguistic representations (the outputs of the brain's language production regions) provides a reason that these neurons enjoy little causal influence over those in other brain networks. In terms of bits of information conveyed per time unit, the informational content of linguistically coded representations is orders of magnitudes less than the activity-vector representations in parallel neural networks (Churchland, 1995). Even the information that streams into the language regions from just the output neurons of other brain networks cannot be squashed effectively into real-time producible and comprehensible sets of sentences. Huge amounts of information get lost in the parallel-to-serial input-output functions implemented in the language regions. Neurons in other cognitive regions, trading on information coded in parallel-implemented activity vectors, also have limited use for information coded in sequential linguistic form, other than as quick synopses (reports) of what is going on elsewhere in the brain. Hence in terms of both their underlying anatomy and physiology, the inner narratives that create and sustain our selves are relatively impotent over information processing in other neural regions.

The general picture that emerges from these biological facts is of limited-access language systems that summarize and then broadcast a highly edited snapshot of the outputs of the brain's cognitive processing networks. Occasionally these reports get bound over for external verbal expression. Together the language regions produce and comprehend a narrative about processing that takes place throughout the cognizing brain. Some of these linguistic constructions compose the (relatively rare) Elaborate Practical Reasonings that occupy short stretches of our conscious streams. Collectively they create and express the image of our selves-in-control. Folk psychology mistakenly elevates stretches of Elaborate Practical Reasoning narratives to the status of norm for cognition and consciousness generally and mistakenly assumes that their contents report actual causal events in the production of cognition and behavior. However, given the limited access enjoyed by the language regions to neural networks that subserve specific cognitive and behavioral tasks, these narratives are actually outright fabrications, as is the self-in-control they create and express. The linguistic contents of these inner narratives about the self's causal control are false; the causal effects they attribute to deliberations and exhortations are pieces of fiction that don't square with the known anatomical and biological facts. Cognitive processing is occurring throughout cortex (and sub-cortically). But activity in the brain's language regions, and hence the neurally realized narrative self, neither accurately reflects *nor causally affects* very much of what is going on.

To elaborate further on the point just sharpened and to see some con-sequences it implies, we need to investigate further the anatomical and phys-iological properties of the neural regions involved. Can activity in the language regions (that generate the image of the causally efficacious self-in-control) be *dissociated* from that in regions known to subserve plan formulation and (sub-sequent) motor commands to execute the plans?. The latter activities are cru-cial steps in the neural processes that generate cognitive behavior. Neuro-psychologists have known since the earliest reports of the infamous case of Phineas Gage that anterior, dorsal, and lateral regions of the frontal lobes sub-serve these functions. (Gage was the nineteenth-century railroad worker who had a steel tamping rod blown through his skull. He somehow survived the accident but suffered a complete personality change. The accident and sub-sequent lesioning destroyed virtually his entire anterior frontal cortex, including the orbitofrontal portion. Harlow [1868] speaks about Gage's planning defi-cits.) Planning and motor execution deficits are now a widely accepted feature of frontal syndromes and are not associated consistently with clinical damage to any other region (in the absence of dementia or consciousness disorders) (Fuster, 1997). Formulating and successfully executing a plan requires a prior representation of its conceptual scheme or strategy, anticipation of the con-sequences of each step, and the preparation needed to execute each step in the proper sequence. The last component involves a form of "motor memory" or "action schema" that also seems to be represented and executed in the fron-tal lobes. Prefrontal damage that invades the dorsolateral convexity impairs both "motor set" representations and their enactment (Fuster, 1997).

The neuropsychological literature on planning and execution deficits in frontal patients is voluminous. But consider just a sampling, to get their general flavor. Kolb and Milner (1981) found that following localized unilateral frontal lobotomies, patients are poor at planning and executing sequences of facial movements and expressions. However, they can recall and reproduce normally individual expressions and movements in the sequence. Shallice and Burgess (1991a) found that frontal patients were impaired significantly on the "dinner party" task, which requires formulating and carrying out multistep problem-solving strategies (shopping for a variety of items in accordance with a set of simple procedural rules). Frontal patients were extremely inefficient compared to normals and to other neural pathologies, constantly violated the rules, and often failed to complete a majority of the component errands. Yet they were not impaired in explaining (verbally!) the individual component errands or the procedural rules. Frontal patients have also shown significant deficits in solving the Tower of London puzzle, a strategic planning task that requires subjects to move three different-colored blocks across three different-sized pegs according to a few simple rules. Depending on the starting and target configurations of the blocks on the pegs, there will be an optimal solution to the puzzle (in terms of the number of block moves required). Subjects are told the optimal number of steps and are asked to solve the puzzle in that many. Finding the optimal sequence requires planning a series of subgoals (configurations of blocks on pegs) to reach the final goal. Subjects must visualize the proper sequence of steps to target configuration and then execute that sequence. (However, as Shallice and Burgess [1991b] reveal, some studies of frontal patients with the Tower of London puzzle have yielded inconsistent results.) Prefrontal patients also do poorly on a variety of maze puzzles, often with motor requirements, and disorders of specifically goal-directed motor tasks are common in frontal patients generally (Fuster, 1997). All this is consistent with the widely accepted planning and (motor) execution deficits of frontal syndromes.

Neuropsychologists often seek *double dissociations* as a method for inferring localization of function (Kolb & Whishaw, 1996). To argue that a specific function is localized to a particular neural region, it is not enough to show only that lesions to that region produce a deficit in that function. One must also show that lesions to other regions fail to produce a similar deficit. Often we can proceed by matching a pair of neural regions (say, A and B) and a pair of functions (say, reading and writing). Suppose that lesions to A produce impaired reading but normal writing capacities, while lesions to B produce impaired writing but normal reading capacities. Then regions A and B would be said to be *doubly dissociated*. A textbook example involves two cases of surgically induced lesions in humans (for tumor removal) (Kolb & Whishaw, 1996, pp. 184–186). One patient, who underwent a left temporal lobectomy, was impaired on standard verbal memory tests but normal on nonverbal memory tests. Another patient, who underwent a right temporal lobectomy, was impaired on the same nonverbal memory tests but normal on the verbal memory ones. The two neural regions are doubly dissociated with respect to these functions.

We can express my point using this concept. I am claiming that the (non-language) frontal regions and the language regions are doubly dissociable with respect to the functions of (1) planning and (motor) sequence execution and (2) generating the internal narratives that create and express our selves-in-control. The anatomical connectivity sketched earlier substantiates this claim, but so does ordinary phenomenology. We can all recall instances from our own lives where our inner narratives (and sometimes even our outer verbal expressions) said one thing while we did another. Equally, we all know individuals (and may well be individuals) whose self-representations might be quite normal while their planning and motor executions are deficient, and vice versa. If my account of self sketched earlier is correct, then given the restricted anatomical connectivities between the two regions neuropsychological dissociations aren't surprising.

The likelihood of such dissociations suggests another way that the internal narratives (and hence the image of the self-in-control that they generate) can be fictitious. These internal narratives might be *confabulations*. *Confabulate* is a semitechnical term in the neurological and neuropsychological literatures that means "to invent or make up," with the connotation that the subject believes his or her utterances. For example, anosognosics ("denial" patients), who clearly cannot see or move a limb, will readily answer questions about visual displays or move to grab falling objects with their paralyzed limb, thereby "denying" their deficit. They will also readily make up reasons for why they trip over large objects ("it's too dark in here") or let the glass crash to the floor ("you held back my arm") (Ramachandran et al., 1996). Global amnesics, who can't recall previously performing a task, will attribute their good performance on preserved learning tasks after training to a general aptitude for such tasks (Squire, 1987). The confabulations will be appropriate to the situation and delivered within the time dimensions of ordinary nonconfabulatory verbal responses. All of these features of clinical confabulation—falsity in light of overwhelming evidence, offered readily and expediently, uttered sincerely, and appropriate to the situation at hand (at least with regard to considerations that folk psychology deems appropriate)—seem to be present in these neurally realized internal deliberations and narratives about behavioral causes. Our delusional image of self-in-control might be as natural an outcome of normal activity in the language regions as delusions of still being able to see or move a limb are for certain types of cortically induced blindness and paralysis. The neurally realized internal narratives that generate and express our selves-in-control need not be thought of as deliberate make-believe or attempts to "keep a good face forward."

Let me emphasize explicitly that we are not (necessarily) talking here about a clinical pathology. The restricted extent to which neurons in the language regions project to and receive projections from neurons in the frontal regions that process plan formation and motor execution could make these dissociations a normal occurrence. (It is not as though a fiber [axon] bundle the size of, e.g., the corpus callosum connects these regions!) Still, it is possible to overemphasize the possibilities of widespread dissociations between these regions. Clearly we can and do formulate plans and execute motor sets in response to verbal commands. And for most of us, most of the time, our behaviorally implemented plans and motor commands coincide with our internal and external speech productions and comprehensions. The question at issue, however, is about the *actual causal antecedents* of the frontal lobe activity that implement planning and motor execution. It is here that the anatomical and physiological facts count against the extent to which both folk psychology and lazy phenomenology attribute causal efficacy to our internal narratives about a self-in-control.

The possibility of comparing the timing of internal narrative onset vis-à-vis activity in the frontal regions to a particular task is intriguing. If we could somehow get an effective measure of when the internal narratives begin that generate the image of self-in-control and of when frontal activity begins that implements plan formation and motor set execution, we might learn something very interesting about the extent to which the former causally affects the latter. Such a study need not suffer from the methodological worries that have haunted attempts to get such timing data since Benjamin Libet (1985) claimed to have found that subjects' conscious decisions to flex one hand at the wrist lagged nearly one half-second behind the onset of the motor "readiness potential" measured from scalp electrodes. (For a good sampling of methodological worries, see the peer commentaries published alongside Libet's 1985 target article.) Armed now with an empirically defensible neurophilosophical theory about the neural regions that subserve the self-generating internal narratives we might be able to bypass problems about measuring the onset of subjective experiences and move directly to measuring the onset of the underlying neural events. Methodological problems would remain, but they would be of the standard sort encountered in evoked-response potential (ERP) or neuroimaging studies.

For what it is worth, I wouldn't be surprised to learn that the frontal planning and motor execution activities occur prior to the onset of internal speech activity that creates and expresses our selves-in-control. Such a result would further the case for the confabulatory nature of our internal narratives and selves-in-control and would raise in earnest the timing questions I floated earlier in this essay. But at present, this possibility remains entirely speculative.

All these issues come together to suggest an interesting practical question that has to do with a normative human activity: moral training. It has been a common theme in Western ethical thought that training people to become better moral reasoners will make them better moral agents. Much ethical training takes place in a behavioral vacuum. Think of the sorts of ethics classes now mandatory for students in particular disciplines (e.g., medical ethics, professional ethics, legal ethics, business ethics, engineering ethics, and the like). Whether these are organized around applying ethical theories or on a purely "case studies" basis makes no difference to my point. On either approach, students learn how to discuss (!) ethical issues specific to their discipline and to talk (!) through possible solutions. The assumption, of course, is that these acquired *narrative* skills will readily translate into ethically preferable planning and behavior. But is this assumption justified? This common sort of moral training teaches people to produce and comprehend more sophisticated moral narratives. According to my theory sketched here, this will make them better moral selves. But if these narratives and the resulting self-in-control image are as causally inefficacious and doubly dissociable from activity in the other frontal regions that actually subserve planning, motor execution, and hence behavior, then *improving the moral aspects of persons' narrative selves won't make them plan and act better.* There are more direct and efficient routes for altering activity in the neural regions that subserve planning and motor execution than through the language regions. Ethical training in a behavioral vacuum (other than speech production and comprehension) is likely not to have much effect on people's behavior, if the account offered here is on track. Better to get people to practice planning and executing the specific motor sequences desired, rather than training them to construct more sophisticated moral narratives (if we as a society can't yet stomach rewiring brains more directly).

Aristotle was thus prescient when he wrote about ethical training, more than twenty centuries ago, that

> as a condition for having a virtue, however, the knowing counts for nothing, or rather for only a little, whereas the other two conditions [he must decide on virtuous actions, and decide on them for themselves; and he must do these actions from a firm and unchanging state] are very important, indeed all important. And these other two conditions are achieved by the frequent doing of just and temperate actions. . . . It is right, then, to say that a person comes to be just from doing just actions and temperate from doing temperate actions; for no one has even a prospect of becoming good from failing to do them. The many, however, do not do these actions but take refuge in arguments, thinking that they are doing philosophy, and that this is the way to become excellent people. In this they are like a sick person who listens attentively to the doctor, but acts on none of his instructions. Such a course of treatment will not improve the state of his body; any more than will the many's way of doing philosophy improve the state of their souls. (1105b, 1–18, from Irwin 1985)

One must perform the appropriate actions repeatedly to acquire the moral virtues. Theory and argument—narratives, both internal and verbally expressed—won't suffice. Our increased knowledge of the diverse neural mechanisms that underlie speech production and comprehension on one hand and planning and motor execution on the other puts us a step ahead of Aristotle toward understanding why theory and arguments (narratives) are less efficient for inculcating virtue than is practice (actually performing the planning and acting). Aristotelean virtue ethics has made a comeback in recent moral philosophy. But no one (to my knowledge) has urged it on neuroscientific grounds!

Often persons' actions and moral narratives are correlated closely. But given the anatomical, biological, and neuropsychological facts sketched in the second half of this essay, the neural regions that subserve these distinct cognitive functions can become dissociated (in nonpathological cases). Even the most consistent among us sometimes act in ways that contradict their sincere assertions. But if our ultimate goal of moral training is to affect behavior (and what else could it be?), then we would achieve this end more efficiently by working to reorganize directly the (mostly) frontal lobe mechanisms of planning and motor command and execution. Working on these mechanisms through the indirect and (relatively) sparse connections from the speech production and comprehension regions, and thus through the (relatively) causally inefficacious narrative self that activity in these regions creates and expresses, is not the best way to proceed. If the neurally grounded account of the narrative self presented here is on the right track, then the old refrain "do as I say, not as I do!" gets effective moral training exactly wrong.[1]

Note

1. Marica Bernstein pointed out to me the account's negative consequence for this old adage.

References

Baars, B. (1997). *In the theater of consciousness*. New York: Oxford University Press.

Baddeley, A. D. (1986). *Working memory*. Oxford: Oxford University Press.

Baddeley, A. D. (1993). Verbal and visual subsystems of working memory. *Current Biology, 3*(6), 563–565.

Bickle, J., Worely, C., & Bernstein, M. (2000). Vector subtraction implemented neurally: A neurocomputational model of some sequential cognitive and conscious processes. *Consciousness and Cognition, 9,* 117–144.

Bisiach, E., & Luzzatti, C. (1978). Unilateral neglect of representational space. *Cortex, 14,* 129–133.

Churchland, P. M. (1995). *The engine of reason, the seat of the soul*. Cambridge, MA: MIT Press.

Crosby, E. C., Humphrey, T., & Lauer, E. W. (1962). *Correlative anatomy of the nervous system*. New York: Macmillan.

Dennett, D. C. (1991). *Consciousness explained*. Boston: Little, Brown.

Dennett, D. C. (1992). The self as center of narrative gravity. In F. S. Kessel, P. M. Cole, & D. L. Johnson (Eds.), *Self and consciousness: Multiple perspectives* (pp. 103–115). Hillsdale, NJ: Erlbaum.

Flanagan, O. J. (1996). *Self expressions: mind, morals and the meaning of life.* New York: Oxford University Press.

Fuster, J. M. (1997). *The prefrontal cortex: Anatomy, physiology, and neuropsychology of the frontal lobe* (3d ed.) Philadelphia: Lippincott-Raven.

Harlow, J. M. (1868). Recovery from the passage of an iron bar through the head. *Publication of the Massachusetts Medical Society, Boston, 2,* 327–346.

Irwin, T. (Trans.). (1985). *Aristotle's Nicomachean Ethics,* Indianapolis: Hackett.

James, W. (1890). *The principles of psychology.* New York: Holt.

Kolb, B., & Milner, B. (1981). Performance of complex arm and facial movements after focal brain lesions. *Neuropsychologia, 19,* 514–515.

Kolb, B., & Whishaw, I. (1996). *Fundamentals of human neuropsychology.* New York: Freeman.

Libet, B. (1985). Unconscious cerebral initiative and the role of conscious will in voluntary action. *Behavioral and Brain Sciences, 8,* 529–566.

Paulescu, E., Frith, D., & Frackowiak, R. S. J. (1993). The neural correlates of the verbal component of working memory. *Nature, 362,* 342–345.

Posner, M. I., & Raichle, M. E. (1994). *Images of mind.* New York: Scientific American Library.

Ramachandran, V. S., Levi, L., Stone, L., Rogers-Ramachandran, D., McKinney, R., Stalcup, M., Arcilla, G., Zweifler, R., Schatz, A., & Flippin, A. (1996). Illusions of body image: What they reveal about human nature. In R. Llinás & P. S. Churchland (Eds.), *The mind-brain continuum* (pp. 29–60). Cambridge, MA: MIT Press.

Shallice, T. & Burgess, P. (1991a). Deficits in strategy application following frontal lobe damage in man. *Brain, 114,* 727–741.

Shallice, T., & Burgess, P. (1991b). Higher-order cognitive impairments and frontal lobe lesions in man. In H. S. Levin, H. M. Eisenberg, & A. L. Benton (Eds.), *Frontal lobe function and dysfunction* (pp. 125–138). New York: Oxford University Press.

Squire, L. R. (1987). *Memory and brain.* New York: Oxford University Press.

11   Sexual Identities and Narratives of Self

Gillian Einstein
Owen Flanagan

Locating the Self

Philosophical ideas about identity, about what makes an individual human, the same person over time, might come profitably into conversation with scientific knowledge about how the sense of oneself might be subserved by certain brain and bodily processes.

The philosophical literature on personal identity has in large measure followed John Locke's (1690/1975) lead in thinking that what distinguishes the identity of a plant or a cockroach, for example, from the identity of a person is that although all three possess biological continuity and organic integrity, only a person possesses semantic, autobiographical memory. Locke conceived of the concept of "person" as a *forensic* concept, a term of art that captures and accounts for what it is that makes a person, but not a plant or ordinary animal, a moral agent, a creature to whom we sensibly apply moral and legal concepts of good, bad, responsible, and irresponsible.

A cockroach, like a plant, possesses biological continuity and organic integrity. But a cockroach may lack consciousness, and even if it has some sort of sensory consciousness, it presumably lacks semantic, autobiographical memory altogether. Although there may be "something-it-is-like to be a cockroach" for the cockroach, assuming a cockroach possesses some sort of sensory consciousness (Nagel, 1974), no cockroach can hold the story of its life in its head, let alone share it with its fellow cockroaches. Likewise a member of the species *Homo sapiens* is not automatically in virtue of being, what Locke called a "man," a person. Human beings are persons only insofar as they can hold in their heads, and tell, the stories of their lives. Locke's view is *cognitivist*. Personhood is constituted by the ability to remember the things one has done and the things that have happened in one's life.

Neither an infant nor a comatose human being is a person on this view, although an infant might become a person and a comatose human might once have been a person. The extent to which an amnesiac is a person would be a matter of degree, depending on how amnesiac he or she is. At first glance, this might be thought to be a disadvantage of the Lockean view. But it is actually an advantage given his aims, since we do not, in fact, think of infants or comatose humans as moral agents, and amnesia can mitigate against finding a human responsible for some act. Of course, the fact that some individual human—or even a nonhuman animal—is not a full-blooded Lockean person does not mean he or she is not worthy of moral respect. Insofar as the concept of personal identity is designed by Locke to capture what it is that makes for the proper ascription of the full range of moral concepts to creatures, it is memory continuity of the sort that enables creatures to remember, tell, and retell what has happened to them and what they have done that is almost certainly a necessary condition.

However, possession of autobiographical memory is not sufficient for personhood, so conceived. A psychopath might have the right sort of memory but lacks certain knowledge capacities or control capacities: he or she lacks knowledge of right or wrong and/or can't rationally control what he or she does. Likewise, children with good autobiographical memory might not be held morally accountable because they fail to some extent to satisfy the knowledge or control conditions—although, unlike the psychopath, they eventually will do so.

In any case, Locke's view focuses on the way we tie attributions of personal sameness—to ourselves and to others—to a high degree of declarative, episodic, semantic, autobiographical memory. For Locke, personal identity is tied not to mere bodily continuity and not even to a sense of ongoing somatosensory continuity and connectedness. Personal identity requires cognitive memory of things that have happened to me and things I have done.

It is not particularly surprising that Locke gave short shrift to feelings, the emotions, moods, and the sense of one's body. After all, he was writing in the aftermath of Descartes. And although Locke claimed that his account did not depend on what Antonio R. Damasio (1994) calls "Descartes' Error," the "abyssal separation of mind and body"—that is, it did not depend on the assumption of mind-body dualism—Locke was certainly influenced by the widely held idea that conscious linguistic capacities are distinctively human, whereas emotions and the sense of one's body are part of our animal nature.

Whatever the advantages of the Lockean view are for capturing a necessary condition of moral agency or moral personhood (i.e., the capacity to hold the story of one's life in one's head and to utilize it in the projects of self-knowledge, self-control, and the like), if it is taken as providing an adequate account of what goes into our sense of self, even as providing an adequate analysis of how the narrative self is constituted and constructed, it has a serious downside.

The sense of oneself as the person one is, is constituted not just by cognitive memory components but by conative components as well or by an admixture of cognitive and conative components. If I say I generally feel happy, I have not reported something that has happened to me or something I have done. I am telling you about a general way I feel. And the way I feel is at least as important to my identity as what has happened to me and what I have done.

The best place to look in the philosophical literature for a theory that emphasizes the conative components of personhood, now broadly conceived, is in William James's famous account of the stream of consciousness (1890). James's account is developmental in a way Locke's is not, and although James gives a robust account of mature adult narratives, he ties the capacity to tell the story of one's life to basic features of the conscious stream, features shared by other animals. Whereas Locke writes after Descartes, James writes after Darwin. And it shows.

Any creature possessed of a stream of consciousness and thus quite possibly a human infant (and many mature nonhuman animals), possesses a feeling of personal sameness in virtue of having a conscious sense of its bodily flow, its corporeal continuation. I am partly and importantly constituted by how I feel, by how it feels to be me. I have a sense of my own experiential continuity—I am the site, as it were, of a continuous stream of consciousness that is, in some large measure, a stream of feeling-myself-to-be-the-organism-I-am. The thread of continuity that makes for a sense of self requires consciousness, a first-personal sense of phenomenological flow. But it need not be linguistic.

In several papers, written toward the end of his life, James suggests that the sense of the self as continuous and continuing is rooted in the ongoing bodily awareness of breathing. That the sense of self is rooted in a sense of oneself as a being-that-breathes may seem like an odd thing for a philosopher to say. But James, as always, was on to something. He recognized that a key feature of identity involves experiencing some sort of somatosensory connectedness to oneself—a feeling of the flow, a sense of the stream. Furthermore, he realized that tying the general concept of the self too closely to linguistic memory would be chauvinistic. It would require denying that infants, prelinguistic toddlers, and all non-language-using animals possess a sense of self. Antonio Damasio presents a modern-day version of this idea in the form of the "protoself," or the preconscious collection of neural activities that map the physiological presence of the organism *for* the organism (1999). Some such collection of themselves unconscious neural activities might well be sufficient—

once they reach a certain level of robustness—to produce at least a dim and inchaote sense of oneself as a distinct continuous creature. Daniel Stern (1985) has produced a similar view of the development and emergence of the sense of self from a more psychodynamic perspective.

The sense of oneself as a continuous biological being that breathes, that feels, that possesses some sort of sense of itself as an integral being is not something that goes away once one becomes able to tell a "Lockean narrative." James talks of the "fringe" of consciousness, the shadow or, as he called it, the "penumbra" that invariably accompanies the stream. For linguistic creatures, such as *Homo sapiens*, the emotions, feelings, moods, and sense of our selves as male or female, compassionate or knavish, may often be penumbral. But since we have words for these things, they can be, and often are, brought into view and become part of the narrative we can tell to ourselves and possibly share with others. Putting aside the possibility that the differences between Locke and James can be accounted for in terms of their somewhat different aims—Locke sought an account of the person suited to moral and forensic purposes; James, one that would capture the full range of meanings of the concept of the self—there is much to be gained from focusing on what they had in common, namely, the belief that their aims were best satisfied by getting at whatever it is that subserves the first-personal feeling of continuity. This much suggests the possibility that both views, Locke's resolute cognitive-linguistic view and James's "feeling-of-and-for-the-body" view, capture something important about identity. Indeed, holding both views in mind can be helpful in considering the conflicting intuitions we have about identity and selfhood in important real-life cases.

Imagine two college-age children home for Thanksgiving discussing a trip to visit Granny, who has advanced Alzheimer's disease. As A. is preparing to go off to visit Granny, B. asks, "Why are you going to visit Granny? Granny is 'no longer home.' She doesn't even know who you are." A. agrees but insists, borrowing a phrase from Thomas Nagel (1974): "Well, that's true. But Granny is still conscious. She is a shadow of her former self, but there is still 'something-it-is-like' for Granny to be Granny." Neither A. nor B. doubts that Granny is still conscious, that she possesses some sort of sense of self. They disagree, we might say, about whether that sense is robustly Lockean. For A. this matters; for B. it matters less.

There is a host of different ways degradation of the nervous system can cause major or minor disorders in the sense of personal sameness or continuity and in third-person ascriptions of sameness and continuity. Examples of how the physical ability to generate one's narrative are affected by the removal of the hippocampus to eliminate intractable epileptic seizures, the destruction of neurons by alcohol as in Korsakoff's, or the accumulation of tangles and the death of neurons in the brains of Alzheimer's patients that destroy memory in different ways are instructive. In terms of the role that being able to generate a personal narrative plays in how much one appears to others, and to oneself, to be the same person he or she was prior to disease onset or at some very recent stage of the disease, such cases reveal important understanding.

There are also patients who have viral and bacterial infections that cause the degeneration of fine nerve fibers, interfering with interoception and proprioception, so that in extreme cases an individual loses the sense of his or her body. Such individuals have lost some sort of normal contact with an important aspect of themselves. The same is true, but to a lesser extent, of patients with certain kinds of parietal lesions who sincerely deny that their arm paralyzed from a stroke does not move. All individuals with disconnections from their bodies or parts of their brains that generate narrative or subserve normal somatosensory consciousness suffer identity disorders. Close observation will lead us to make subtle distinctions about what the identity disturbance consists in—from phenomenological, behavioral, and neurobiological points of view—and what kind of continuity or connectedness, if any, is maintained. Identity, on any plausible view, is a matter of degree (Flanagan, 1992, 1996).

In this section we have been discussing identity in terms of broad categories of memory connections and feelings of continuity that come in degrees. We now join these philosophical ideas with biological analysis of what might underlie the sense of self.

Taking Embodiment Seriously

The current naturalistic consensus within philosophy of mind and cognitive neuroscience holds out hope that philosophical analyses and neuroscientific analyses can be mutually beneficial and illuminating (Churchland, 1986; Flanagan, 1992, 1996, 2000). A credible naturalistic analysis should allow a collaborative analysis between neuroscience and philosophy to bring us to a better understanding of issues of self as well. This collaboration could entail a brain-only view of the mental states of the human organism, or it could include the rest of the body in the analysis of the self. The latter is preferable because it is becoming more and more clear that the brain and the rest of the body work in tandem to create mental states, the sense of one's self, and personal narratives.

The belief that underlies a naturalistic theory of mind is that the nature of conscious mental life will not be revealed just by looking for brain correlates. It is not that physicalism or materialism is false. It is just that the brain is not all that matters. The rest of the body does, too. Narratives of some mental phenomena will require more than information about the brain; they will require information about the whole body. A sense of the whole body is certainly required for a narrative to emerge about the sexual self.

The whole-body view has been most carefully explicated in the realm of the emotions (Damasio, 1994, 1995, 1999), but in this essay we posit that other aspects of the self—such as the sexual self—are rife with interactions between body and brain and set the stage for a narrative that requires thinking about the whole organism.

We have chosen the topic of the narrative of the sexual self because it is not only underdiscussed in the scientific and philosophical literatures but also interesting and, even with our relatively primitive state of knowledge about sex, phenomenological-neurobiological-biochemical correlations and interactions can be articulated. Understanding how a personal narrative is generated from the interaction of different body systems—which include the brain—and culture will also yield some general lessons about the sorts of empirical relations and explanations we might expect as mind-science progresses.

For the naturalist, the sense of self must be cashed out in physical terms. But there is more to the physical than the neural. In this respect, it is important to consider that whole-body explanations may present a challenge to certain orthodox modes of explanation in cognitive neuroscience. Most of the work that currently is receiving attention in cognitive neuroscience involves the use of brain imaging, especially MR, fMRI, PET, and MEG. These are powerful tools. But just because a certain area, say the amygdala, lights up when a person is in a state of fear does not establish that fear is a state of the amygdala or of the amygdala alone. Likewise, the areas of the brain that light up when a person is doing visual or linguistic or memory tasks may well be implicated in the performance of the tasks under study. But it is way too early in the game to know whether the lit-up area is, in fact, the very cognitive event being studied, rather than part of some larger, more complex set of physical processes that taken together constitute the event in question (see Uttal, 2001).

Although most cognitive neuroscientists will, when queried, admit that more may be going on than what is lit up, they often mean no more than that more fine-grained analysis is needed of the lit-up area. They don't normally mean that more of the body than what is lit up in the brain might figure importantly in the explanation of the event under study.

However, a small group of cognitive neuroscientists—Joseph E. LeDoux (1996), J. Allan Hobson (1994), and Antonio Damasio (1994, 1995, 1999) come to mind—have suggested that an important role is played in moods, emotions, and dreams by hormones released by glands outside the brain, for example, adrenaline in the case of fear. Bruce S. McEwen, a neuroendocrinologist, suggests that hormones are the periphery's way of bringing environment into the brain (McEwen, Davis, Parsons, & Pfaff, 1979). Even if hormonal changes are initiated in the brain, this establishes absolutely nothing about the sufficiency of the neural event for the event in question, say, describing oneself as feeling annoyed, happy, or sexy.

LeDoux's work is instructive here. He has shown that the nucleus of the amygdala mediates fear. But he thinks this mediation gets adrenaline flowing and involves complex commerce between visual cortex (where for example, the sight of the ferocious beast is processed), thalamus, association cortex, and adrenal glands.

Where then is the fear? The answer is not clear, but this much is: The fear is not just in the amygdala. The fear is in the person, all over the place in the body. This perhaps is not the best way of putting the point, but it is better than the answer that the fear is in the amygdala.

While brain imaging is an area of intense investigation with regard to properties of mind, it is important to remember that even as a marker of what is happening in the brain, it is not yet very sensitive to neurochemistry, nor to the study of very small populations of neurons. MRS (S = spectrography) is exceptional in that it detects activation of different kinds of neurotransmitters. It, or one of its descendants, will be a very important tool once all parties acknowledge that the study of neuron firings without attention to the activity of neurotransmitters leaves the story of the mind-brain dramatically incomplete. For example, one cannot understand schizophrenia and depression without a picture of the brain chemistry. Likewise, it will be difficult to understand how people are feeling about sex—their own and having it—without having a map of the distribution of estrogens, androgens, prostaglandins, glucocorticoids, and on and on. Probably even happy and sad, up and down, high and low will require an understanding of the relative density of neurotransmitters before, after, and during the moment of recognizing the emotional state. But more important, for our purposes, no brain-imaging techniques are sensitive to the anatomy, physiology, or biochemistry of the body as a whole.

A nice example of how and why the whole body matters is this: Almost all work on biological clocks so far has related to two different nuclei in the brain stem, this largely because these nuclei are implicated in sleep and dreams. The standard inference is that the brain stem contains and regulates the body's two clocks. This is an incomplete explanation at best. First, even the clocks that control sleep and dreams are dependent on what is happening outside the brain—in the external world or in other parts of the body—in particular, on messages the visual cortex gets about light and about metabolism. Second, there is good evidence that some organisms, including humans, contain a bunch of clocks—spread, as it were, all over the place (Campbell & Murphy, 1998; Plautz, Kaneko, Hall, & Kay 1997). Any narrative about being sleepy thus has to take into account how it feels to have the sun on one's skin, sweating (or shivering) due to the heat (or cold) of the day (night), and sensations from the ebb and flow of testosterone concentrations controlled diurnally.

The Sexual Self

One arena in which both the brain and the rest of the body can be combined in the production of the narrative self is that of human self-consciousness, in general—or the ongoing sense of oneself as an individual with a unique identity. Rather than taking on the biological underpinnings of one's whole sense of self, which is too big of a problem, we approach self-consciousness as divisible. For example, one has a sense of oneself as a father, a son, a religious being. But one could be a son without being a father, a father without being a religious being, and, if orphaned during infancy, a religious being and father without the sense of what it is like to be a son. Among these important senses of oneself is the sense of oneself as a sexual being.

This must be so. Think of how ardently people feel about their gender identifications and sexual orientations. We have stories we tell about having always felt a certain way or having always been attracted to a certain type of person. We have styles of dress developed over a lifetime that show or do not show our bodies off in a certain way. We think of ourselves as liking sex in the afternoon or three times a day, only in our fantasies, or not at all—or only to make children. People undergo surgery, hormone treatment, and divorce in order to align how they feel and identify with the way they look. These stories are part of who we are, what we've experienced, and set the stage for future actions. This is not to say that these tastes and self-views are established at birth, have a genetic basis, or are entirely culturally determined (Stein, 1999). By saying the whole body plays a role in the story we tell about our sexual desires and identifications—our sexual self-consciousness—we are not taking the position that there are fixed categories or "natural kinds" for these things (Hacking, 1990). Rather, we are saying that the narrative that we construct about our sexual selves cannot be generated without a feeling for one's full bodily being. Why is this so?

Consider these two aspects of our sexual selves: (1) sexual orientation, what sex or sexes one experiences sexual desire toward; and (2) gender identification, what sex or sexes one sees oneself as belonging to. These are, first of all, types of self-consciousness that have been postulated to have groups of neurons—or brain nuclei—that mediate their expression. These nuclei are under the influence of hormones and experience early in development. And the hormones that both are generated by and play a role in modulating the activity of these brain regions affect every other system of the body: the heart, bone, breast, muscle, pancreas, testes, and so on. While we often think of sex as a *behavior* that leads to procreation or as a *genotype* that leads to a particular *phenotypic expression*, it also includes the interaction of behavior, genotype, and phenotype to influence how one is disposed to engage in sex acts (sexual orientation) and how one views oneself (gender identification). Thus another important component of the sense of self in the robust sense that fills one's being with feeling and that fills one's mind with stories involves gender identification and sexual orientation. These attributes of sex are what we are calling *sexual self-consciousness*.

It will become clear that just as is the case with the neurobiological circuits for an emotion such as fear, the neurobiological circuits for sexual self-consciousness will certainly incorporate brain mechanisms. In very much the same way that emotions involve both autonomic and cognitive neural systems, sex in all its different aspects requires the endocrine system as well as cognitive systems. Because of the intimate connections between the sexual brain (e.g., the hypothalamus), the cerebral cortex, and the rest of the body via the pituitary and hormone systems, a complete explanation of our sexual selves will require reference to multiple body systems, as well as responses to the environment, and complex, ongoing, and, possibly idiosyncratic social experience.

A sense of the whole body is required to make a story about sexual orientation and gender identification. However, although the body's boundaries may constitute a reasonable boundary for certain purposes, even the whole body is not explanatorily sufficient for all purposes. As we have just said, how one feels about or thinks about one's sexual self involves the social world, culture, and history. But if these things partly constitute how we feel about ourselves as sexual beings, then a full explanation for our sexual sensibilities needs to go not only beyond the brain to the rest of the body but also into the world. (People who work in the area of gender studies often sketch explanations of sexual identity that incorporate the world beyond the body—the world spoken of by sociologists, anthropologists, and historians.) Given our purposes here, making the case for including the whole body in the explanation (as opposed to the whole world) will have to suffice.

The Body, the Brain, and the Sexual Self

At the very least, then, we must consider the interplay between the endocrine system and the brain in the development and maintenance of the story of our sexual selves. How does this work?

The interplay between the brain and the endocrine system starts early in development—as early as the initial development of the sexual phenotype. The presence of two X chromosomes or an X and Y chromosome in the cells of an embryo sets in motion events that ultimately affect the development of the brain. These neural effects are determined by the production of estrogens or androgens, which depend normally in turn on the presence of either female or male gonads. At about the sixth week of gestation, the primordial gonads have formed from a gonad that is undifferentiated between female and male. Developing simultaneously is an undifferentiated structure called the urogenital groove, the progenitor of the external genitalia. So, we begin undifferentiated.

However, events are set in motion that start the process of differentiation. At this point, if an individual is an XY a gene is switched on and this gene produces a protein called testicular determining factor, or TDF, which instructs the testes to begin development. It is not clear whether the switch that turns on the Sry gene is on the X or Y chromosome, but if it is activated, the primordial gonads develop into testes. At this point, however, the gonads begin to differentiate by the development of supporting (Sertoli) and hormone-producing (Leydig) cells and the activation of the sets of tubes that are the progenitors of the internal genitalia, Mullerian and Wolffian ducts. In the absence of TDF (that is, in XX embryos), the indifferent gonad differentiates into an ovary, the Wolffian ducts degenerate, and the Mullerian ducts develop into the oviducts, uterus, and cervix. Tissue around the urogenital groove becomes the clitoris, labia, and vagina. Thus the development of the female phenotype depends on the absence of TDF and the consequent absence of androgens during perinatal life. The development of the male phenotype depends upon the presence of TDF and the consequent production of androgens early in life.

Understanding the developmental series of events that are set in motion by the genotype clarifies how sex, including our sense of our sexual selves, comprises multiple components and is separable into genotypic sex, phenotypic sex, and gender identification/sexual orientation. Any arrangement of the different components of genotype and phenotype can affect the latter in various ways. When they are aligned, genotype, phenotype, and brain biology all work together to reinforce one's story as one sex or the other, one sexual orientation or the other. The XX genotype leads to a person with ovaries, oviducts, uterus, cervix, clitoris, labia, and vagina—a phenotypic female. The XY genotype leads to a person with testicles, epididymis, vas deferens, seminal vesicles, penis, and scrotum—a phenotypic male.

The brain is shaped during development by the same influences as the rest of the body. Just as the indifferent gonad becomes clitoris and labia or penis and testes, "indifferent" brain regions, at least in animal models, are shaped by the influence of different hormones at different times of development. The brain region that seems most sensitive to these influences (though no brain region is immune) is the hypothalamus, a group of diffuse nuclei in the middle of the brain near the region where the nerve fibers from the eye enter the brain, just above the stalk of the pituitary. In rodents, this brain region is replete with anatomical differences between female and male as well as functional links to mating behavior in males and cycling/maternal behavior in females. In humans, studies of neurons in this region from the brains of male-to-female transsexuals and those of heterosexual males have revealed that a group of neurons in a subregion called the bed nucleus of the stria terminalis is smaller in males who experience themselves as females (male-to-female transsexuals) than in males who feel themselves to be male (Swaab & Hoffman, 1990). This nucleus is the same size in male-to-female transsexuals and females. There are also neuronal groupings here that may be related to sexual orientation. In a region of the anterior hypothalamus, there are neuron groupings that are different between gay and straight males. One such cell grouping, the interstitial nuclei of the anterior hypothalamus (INAH), has four subdivisions (1–4), with subdivision 3 being different in size between gay and straight males (LeVay, 1991). The suprachiasmatic nucleus of the hypothalamus is also different in size between females, heterosexual males, and homosexual males (Swaab & Hofman, 1990).

The strength of these examples aside, it is a long stretch to say that because the mean size of a group of neurons is different statistically, those anatomical differences mediate behavioral differences. So, just because the INAH3 is more often smaller in gay than straight males does not mean that that nucleus is somehow *responsible* for gay behavior; in fact, there are examples of gay male brains with INAH3s that are the same size as those of straight males. No one has demonstrated that neurons in the INAH3 are involved functionally before, after, or during any component of gay male behavior. However, these brain differences point the way to understanding that many different aspects of sexual behavior and sexual self-consciousness may be mediated by neurons that are exquisitely sensitive to the endocrine system.

While we know little about how hormones influence brain development in humans, there is the suspicion that they do, because many brain regions in rodents are extremely sensitive to androgens and estrogens secreted by the endocrine system, especially during brain development. For example, administering testosterone to females and depriving males of testosterone by castrating them just after birth change the size of different brain nuclei in female and male rats. In addition, differences in the brain's exposure to these steroids are thought to create the structural differences between females and males. For example, there is a greater number of synapses on spines in the preoptic region of the hypothalamus in normal female rats than in the equivalent region in males. However, depriving males of testosterone by castrating them within 12 days of birth increases the density of these synapses to female levels, whereas administration of testosterone to developing females leads to a reduction of preoptic spine synapses to male levels.

Another example of how testosterone can influence differences between females and males is in a group of neurons in the hypothalamus called the sexually dimorphic nucleus, or SDN. The SDN is significantly smaller in females than in males. However, the SDN in male rats can be reduced in size to that of the female by castration within the first two weeks after birth. Similarly, the size of the female SDN can be increased to that of the male by early administration of androgens (Gorski, Harlan, Jacobson, Shryne, & Southham, 1980). These studies, as well as many others, demonstrate clearly that the development of sexually dimorphic structures in the rodent brain is under the control of circulating steroids secreted by the testes, ovaries, and adrenals.

In general, the establishment of such brain dimorphisms in rodents is generated by different levels of hormone circulating at different times in females and males (males have an early surge of testosterone and females a later surge of estrogens). The active agent in both cases is actually estradiol. Although testosterone is popularly considered the "male" hormone and estrogen the "female" hormone, testosterone is converted to estradiol once it has entered the relevant neurons. Thus it is an estrogen that acts inside neurons to stimulate sexually dimorphic patterns of neuronal circuitry as a result of its higher concentration in developing males. Female gonads do not produce a fetal surge of estradiol similar to the male surge of testosterone. Were levels higher, estradiol would act in females to produce the neural circuitry of the male brain— perhaps this is what happens in the brain of an XY woman with androgen insensitivity. (For more detailed discussion of the cases and experiments described in this section, see Einstein, 2000.)

When phenotype, including brain phenotype, matches genotype, phenotypic females and males have behavioral circuits and circulating hormonal levels that match. Societal expectations for that phenotype and the external world's reaction also match. Since the subjective perception of one's sex, gender identification, is reinforced by biology and culture and that perception satisfies the standard norm, things seem "normal." When genotypic and phenotypic sex are not aligned as expected, a complex array of types of sexual self-consciousness and stories can emerge. In such cases, what one believes oneself to be and how one is treated by others can clash. One comes into conflict with expectations—cultural and religious—and sometimes with oneself.

The Continuing Narrative

So far, we have argued that the non-neural body shapes the brain during development and these brain circuits, in turn, mediate the body's response and sense of self after development. It is important to emphasize this last point. The non-neural body's effect on the brain doesn't end with development. We know that, again in animal models, hormones act on brain circuits throughout life. Dramatic examples of the continued effects of steroids on the brain throughout life can be observed in the sexual brain, the hypothalamus, and in the cognitive brain, the cerebral cortex. For instance, among cells in the rat hypothalamus that secrete vasopressin and oxytocin, neural connections change markedly after parturition. In females prior to pregnancy, these neurons are isolated from each other by thin cell processes (astrocytes). Under the influence of the hormones that prevails during birth and lactation, the glial processes retract and the oxytocin- and vasopressin-secreting neurons become electrically coupled by gap junctions. Whereas these neurons fire independently before the female gives birth, after birth, during lactation, they fire synchronously, releasing pulses of oxytocin into the maternal circulation. These surges of oxytocin cause the contraction of smooth muscles in the mammary glands and, hence, the milk let-down response (Modney & Hatten, 1990).

Another change in the brain circuits of adult rats associated with parenting behavior is the altered representation of the ventrum (chest) in the somatic sensory cortex of virgin and lactating female rats. As determined by electrophysiology, the representation of the ventrum is approximately twice as large in nursing females as in nonlactating controls. Moreover, the receptive fields of the neurons that represent the skin of the ventrum in lactating females are decreased in size by about a third. Both the increase in cortical representation and the decrease in receptive field size show that parenting behavior can be reflected in changes of cortical circuitry in adult animals (Xerri, Stern, & Merzenich, 1994).

Also, some of this hormonal release is not controlled and generated by neuronal initiative at all but rather by the "periphery" via the endocrine organs themselves or via endocrine tumors. For example, the implantation of the egg triggers the secretion of human corionic gonadotropin (β-HCG) by the corpus luteum. β-HCG maintains progesterone secretion during pregnancy. Since it has lutenizing hormone-like functions it may well act on and be acted upon by the same neuronal circuits that are affected by lutenizing hormone (Speroff, Glass, & Kase, 1994). In this same vein, the removal of the major estrogen-secreting glands, the ovaries, often results in fatigue and depression, which leads women who have this surgery to complain of "not feeling like themselves." Finally, steroid- and catecholamine-secreting tumors provide strong examples of how the periphery can affect the central nervous system. Pheochromocytomas, tumors of the adrenal medullary tissue, secrete androgens, estrogens, and catecholamines (types of neurotransmitters), which leads patients to present with fatigue and anxiety; adrenal tumors secrete large amounts of Adrenal Corticotropin Hormone (ACTH), which results in some patients presenting with major depressive order, language and memory impairments, and even psychosis (Rubin & King, 1995). Neurotransmitters and hormones secreted by these tumors are so powerful, they override the brain's control of the organ's secretions.

Eventually, just as experience enables us to generate emotional response internally that then gives rise to the classic autonomic responses (pupillary constriction, increased heart rate, increased muscle tone), experience with the many different aspects of sex can eventually establish a sense of it that is also generated internally and then expressed through the autonomic sexual responses (increased heart rate, erection, production of the secretions of the vaginal wall). Sexual desire—the object of one's desires—may ultimately depend a great deal on an internal generation of the feeling that is mediated by both memory, perception, and hormones. Thus the action of the endocrine system on the brain during development and beyond has the potential to establish one's sexual self-consciousness as well as to modify and affect the story of one's sexual self throughout life.

Permutations and Combinations of the Sexual Self

The narrative of the sexual self is shaped, then, by the interplay of genes, hormones, and culture over time. There are many ways in which genotype, phenotype, and gender/sexual orientation might not be aligned according to convention. These combinations of the different aspects of sex clearly illustrate how different stories about sexuality might be generated, as well as how different stories about sexuality might engender different sexualities. The reasons for their not aligning according to expectation can be genetic. For example, there are individuals who are XO (Turner's syndrome), XXY (Klinefelter's syndrome), and XYY, with each of these having their own phenotype. The category that comprises all of these variations (as well as others) taken together is called intersexuality. When calculating the incidence of intersex births, if the situational definition is "how often physicians find themselves unsure which sex to assign at birth' " the number is approximately once in every fifteen hundred live births. However, this is a number that ranges widely, since it requires a definition of "standard" female and male phenotype and that number will vary according to cultural norms. This suggests that even beyond the stricter categories of Klinefelter's syndrome, Turner's syndrome, AIS (Androgen Insensitivity Syndrome), 5-alpha-reductase deficiency, and congenital adrenal hyperplasia, there are permutations and combinations of genes, hormones, and environment, that make the total number of biological/behavioral possibilities very large. The permutations and combinations can powerfully affect identity. Indeed, the stories we tell about our experience of these permutations and combinations are in some important sense constitutive of identity.

Consider, for example, when body phenotype and the subjective perception or story one wants to tell about one's sex don't match up. Here one experiences the transsexual dilemma. Genotypic and body phenotypic males or females may marry someone of the opposite sex, have children, and exhibit gender-typical behavior and suffer great unhappiness because their behavior matches their phenotype but not how they feel about themselves. Many transsexuals now opt for surgery and hormone treatment to make their phenotypic sex more closely match their gender identification and their personal narrative.

Another narrative about sexuality might be told by XY males who are phenotypic females early in life but whose sexual phenotype changes at puberty. As infants and children, these individuals are phenotypic females because they lack an enzyme, 5-alpha-reductase, that converts testosterone to dihydrotestosterone, the agent that promotes the early development of male genitalia. Such individuals develop somewhat ambiguous but generally female-appearing genitalia (they have labia with an enlarged clitoris and undescended testes). As a result, they are usually raised as females and their early gender identification is female. At puberty, however, when the testicular secretion of androgen becomes high, the clitoris develops into a penis and the testes descend, changing these individuals into phenotypic males.

In the Dominican Republic, where this congenital syndrome has been studied in a particular pedigree, this condition is referred to colloquially as "testes-at-12." Such individuals are generally forced to change their gender identity at puberty, and most eventually assume a male role, but it is often not without a struggle and some dire consequences. Early studies reported that there were no problems in the changeover, but the anthropological data would indicate otherwise, and one case is reported in which the XY individual refused to change to a male gender identification, married as a woman, and, when the partner found out that he had married a woman with a penis, he tried to kill his partner (Imperato-McGinley et al., 1991). This example implicates culture as well as the early organization of the brain in the formation of the sexual self. Culture creates powerful pressures on the construction of the narrative of the sexual self—pressures that are sometimes relatively immune to the way one's body speaks.

Other stories might be generated by individuals who are genotypically XY but phenotypically female, due to a defective gene for the androgen receptor, a condition called *androgen insensitivity syndrome*, or testicular feminization. The receptor deficiency leads to the development of the internal genitalia of a male and the external genitalia of a female. Thus people with AIS look like females and self-identify as female even though they have a Y chromosome and are sterile. Since they are generally not aware of their condition until puberty, when they fail to menstruate, they continue to see themselves as female and are experienced by the world as female, and thus their gender identity is externally reinforced. In this case, gender identity matches the external sexual phenotype but not genotype. It is not clear how those with AIS feel about their condition. One very articulate tax lawyer in California who uses the pseudonym Jane Carden, while bitter about never having been told about her status as an XY female and having her testes removed without her consent, nevertheless has never doubted her identity as a female. This syndrome is relatively uncommon—about one in every four thousand births—in spite of this rarity, there are well-known historical examples: possibly Joan of Arc and the woman for whom Edward VIII of England gave up his throne, Wallis Simpson. It is interesting to speculate that such people's stories about themselves as sexual beings may be mixed. This is an area ripe for study.

A powerful and well-known story is that of people whose alignment of the phenotype they desire sexually is their own phenotype (gays). In most cultures someone who is gay learns throughout early life that someone who looks like he or she does should focus his or her sexual attention on a person of the opposite phenotype. However, it matters not how strongly gay persons *know* this; the way they feel and quite possibly their stories do not include attraction to individuals of the opposite phenotype. In an open society, this type of person, if he or she wishes to express his or her sexual self, will seek out members of the same phenotypic sex with which to engage in sexual interactions. Interestingly, many transsexuals are attracted to those who were of their phenotypic sex before they changed it. These individuals do not consider themselves gay.

A final example of how phenoytpe might not match genotype and how the resultant narrative might not be what's culturally expected is women who have congenital adrenal hyperplasia (CAH). Women with CAH have overactive adrenals during development, which cause abnormally high levels of circulating androgens. They have ambiguous genitalia, exhibit "tomboyish" behavior as children, and tend to form lesbian relationships as adults. If we extrapolate from experimental studies with nonhuman animals, high levels of circulating androgens may stimulate steroid sensitive brain circuits to have a male rather than female organization, leading to aggressive play and the eventual choice of a female sexual partner. So we suspect, but don't know for certain, that the levels and timing of circulating hormones during development may sculpt human brain circuits exquisitely sensitive to steroids, thus shaping the underpinnings for much of our sense of ourselves and our personal narratives of ourselves as sexual beings—male, female, gay, straight, transsexual, asexual.

The Narrative of Sexual Self

We have been talking about how the sense of one's sexual self encompasses and incorporates actions of both the brain and the rest of the body. The whole body is involved in the creation of this particular sense of self, as is culture. Furthermore, the preferred personal narrative feeds back and plays a role in the shaping of sexuality—how one desires, whom one desires, how many times a week one wants to experience sex, with what type(s) of partner, and with how many partners.

Just to get a sense of how people with XYY might talk about themselves and how their sense of themselves as sexual beings plays a role in their entire response to the world, let's look at the writing of Dr. Edward R. Friedlander, a 47-year-old pathologist who is XYY. He writes on his Web site:

> I am tall, lean, and physically powerful. At age 47, I still take medicine for acne. I have a temper that I work hard to control. And I've learned to avoid situations that set me off. I have never physically hurt anyone in anger.
>
> I am a macho, fun, well-liked man who enjoys being single and lives clean. Women say I'm good-looking, and a good guy to date.
>
> My big muscles are stronger than they are coordinated, so I've focused on strength sports like gymming and swimming. But I type as fast as most of the secretaries. And I can hammer out a Beethoven piano sonata with reasonable dexterity.
>
> I've got a pectus chest deformity and a wiring problem with my left eye. Cognitively, I'm a little "different" and always have been. But it doesn't bug me.
>
> . . . Now, XXYY boys usually do have serious behavioral and cognitive problems. The extra "Y" in an XYY is obviously not silent. . . . It seems likely that the second "Y" adds a bit more aggressiveness to a man's overall personality. (2001)

A powerful example of how personal narrative shaped by early biology can override phenotype and the culture expectations of that phenotype is the story of John/Joan. In the early 1960s, identical XY twins were born to a Canadian couple. When the twins were 7 months old, due to a narrowing of the opening of the foreskin (phimosis), the parents agreed to have them circumcised. The surgeon performing the operation used an electrocautery knife and burned the penis of one of the twins so severely that it was, in essence, burned off. At the time, the prevailing medical sentiment was that the disfigured twin would be unable to live a normal heterosexual life and thus would be shunned by his peers, generally suffering psychologically through an excruciating childhood and adulthood.

The mother heard of the work involving sex change operations of the eminent sex researcher at Johns Hopkins, Dr. John Money, and placed her child's care in his hands. Money met with the child and parents and advocated that they surgically reassign the child and raise this XY individual as a girl. This the parents did, having the twin's testes removed at 17 months and his scrotum reshaped to resemble a vulva. In Money's accounts, the twin became known as "Joan" and wore dresses. Her parents, in recent interviews, attest to having done everything they could to treat her in a gendered way as female. Although Money's reports in the literature were positive, subsequent interviews with the family, including John/Joan (now John again) himself, indicated that the picture was not as straightforward as portrayed in the medical reports. In their follow-up of the case, Milton Diamond of the University of Hawaii and Keith Sigmundson describe the struggle that Joan underwent with the reassignment from the earliest age. She refused to wear dresses, urinated standing up, always felt that something was wrong, and refused to comply with hormone treatments during puberty. At 14 Joan demanded to know the truth and was told of her circumstances. She reports that rather than being dismayed, she was relieved—that the truth put everything into place for her. She immediately began to take male hormones and underwent surgery to reconfigure herself as a male, having her breasts removed and a penis reconstructed. Eventually, the twin married a female, adopted her children, and lived a conventional life as a father and husband.

This case, rather than supporting the idea that sex and gender identity can be assigned at birth and that the development of a self-narrative depends only on how one is treated and perceived, underscores the notion that "the evidence seems overwhelming that normal humans are not psychosocially neutral at birth but are, in keeping with their mammalian heritage, predisposed and biased to interact with environmental, familial, and social forces in either a male or female mode" (Diamond & Sigmundson, 1997). How the narrative is felt first-personally or is produced for third-personal consumption is hugely dependent on the biology of the whole body.

True hermaphrodites who have the phenotype of both female and male (ovaries, testes, penis, and breasts) have other types of story that include practicing sex as both a female and a male—and not necessarily wanting to have a narrative that does not include both affiliations. The story of Emma, who was a patient of Dr. Hugh Hampton Young at Johns Hopkins, illustrates how stories about sexuality need not be "either/or." Emma was raised as a female and presented to Dr. Young as a female. She had a vagina and a clitoris large enough by today's surgical standards to be considered a phallus (2–3 inches). (S)he experienced sex both by using her clitoris to penetrate other females and by using her vagina to be penetrated by other males. (S)he was married to a male and had female lovers during her marriage. When asked by Young if (s)he would like to simply have a female or male phenotype by having his/her phallus shortened or his/her vagina closed, (s)he said, "Would you have to remove that vagina? I don't know about that because that's my meal ticket. If you did that I would have to quit my husband and go to work, so I think I'll keep it and stay as I am. My husband supports me well, and even though I don't have any sexual pleasure with him, I do have lots with my girlfriend"

(Fausto-Sterling, 2000, p. 43). In this narrative, the female aspects of sexuality were viewed as expedient—who knows in what kind of sexual practices Emma and his/her girlfriend engaged. But, obviously, Emma's sense of him/herself depended on having both a penis and a vagina.

For those born with ambiguous genitalia, however, the narrative is even more confusing. Whereas once they might have had a story that included an identity of themselves as both female and male, intersex individuals today may have been subjected to surgery and hormone treatment throughout life that induced great shame and confusion about what story they can tell about themselves as humans and as sexual beings. A number of Web sites with stories from intersexed individuals attest to this. One story from an intersexed individual trying to reconcile his/her phenotype and feelings with Christianity is put in poetry below:

Regardless of my early life I choose each day to live for Christ.
Yes, I could live for mom and dad, to be the son they thought they
    had.
I could have stood and marked the place a concrete smile upon my
    face.
I could have born the grief and pain, and ended life, gone quite in-
    sane.
For Norman, Carolyn, Roger, Joy, to be a brother, though not a boy.
The part of me you never knew, accused as lies, that life is true.
And though your world demanded "he" each cell of mine was pro-
    grammed "she."

You know I tried, I took a wife, and when she died, amidst the strife
I found the peace that casts out fear from Christ who made me.
    Ever near
He led me to His perfect truth, to understand that, from my youth,
A dozen doctors, maybe two, now all concede to what I knew.
My flaws, my sin, my inner worth are now no longer based on earth.
The self I knew, the self that died, has now in Christ been justified.
Regardless of my early life I choose today to live for Christ. (Anony-
    mous, 2001)

The "Director's Page" from this Web site is also a moving testimony to the struggle to align a story of rejection and sexual mutilation with sexual identity. Writes Deborah Brown, Director of the Intersex Support Group International:

Imagine, if you can, discovering as an adult that your sexual identity
had been altered when you were a baby. The flood of emotional
trauma and self-doubt this imposes is a weight too heavy for some
to bear. . . . There are quite fundamental, yet radical treatment re-

sponses to having malformed parts, spare chromosomes, neonatal surgery, etc., which could ultimately affect not only the person's self image, but society's response. . . . If the child, raised as a girl, who is genetic XY or other chromosome mix, perhaps developmentally affected in the womb by Androgen Insensitivity Syndrome, is never given the opportunity to voice who the person inside them develops to be, we may be sentencing another genetic male to "life as a female with no hope for parole." (2001)

Finally, the story of James Bensen, a 45-year-old scientist, as told by Simon LeVay (2000) highlights the importance to one's overall identity of one's sense of a sexual self. LeVay relates that Bensen was identified as a "normal" girl at birth and then raised as one. In high school it was learned that Bensen did not menstruate, and in college she went to a doctor who determined that she had ovaries but no reproductive tract. She tried having heterosexual vaginal sex, but she discovered that she didn't really have a vagina. Finally, she decided to have her breasts removed and live life as a man. As recounted by Simon LeVay, Bensen says of himself,

The thing that's so hard to describe is the relief . . . I feel it every day, every minute. There's no longer the conflict between my inner self and that outer woman. Years ago, I read about people who changed their sex, and I thought they were some kind of perverts—I'm embarrassed to say that now. But changing sex isn't about sexuality, it's about who you feel you are.

Conclusion: Our Bodies, Our Selves

Our aim has been to join philosophical work on identity to neurophysiological research in order to show that doing so offers resources to enrich our understanding of identity generally and sexual and gender identity specifically. The dominant tradition in philosophical psychology is Lockean. The self or, more technically, what Locke called the person is constituted by the narrative of things that the person has done and the things that have happened to him or her. This cognitive-linguistic view is important. We are language-using creatures with powerful autobiographical memories. But the analysis of what goes into making a self is enhanced significantly if we conjoin the Lockean view with the view, available in William James's writing, of ourselves as creatures who create narratives that are powerfully influenced by feelings we have for our entire bodily being. We are embodied beings with rich emotional and sexual feelings that are incorporated into our narratives. Our narratives contain, as crucial components, not just what has happened to us and what we have

SEXUAL IDENTITIES AND NARRATIVES OF SELF

done but also, just as important, how we feel about our experience, our actions, and our selves and, in the specific cases under discussion, how we experience ourselves as sexual and gendered beings.

We have provided numerous examples of how the "periphery" and the brain affect the narrative we tell about our sexual selves. Whether the periphery initiates the brain response or the other way around is of little consequence for our general methodological and substantive points. The fact is, whatever the order of causation, that the periphery affects the central nervous system, which in turn modulates the peripheral response.

The extent to which neural circuits are modified by hormones and experience is still unknown. But the strong connections of the hypothalamus with cortical structures as well as the direct actions of estrogens on cortical neurons make a circuit that links body with brain. Primary circuits that link the endocrine system with the hypothalamus establish fundamental sexual responses such as ovulation, erection, and perhaps even the early sense of desire. Secondary circuits that link the hypothalamus with the cortex through neural projections and the endocrine system with cortex through humoral hormonal action shape, modify, and eventually initiate sexual responses, as well as responses that are complex interactions between brain/body and environment, such as gender identification and sexual orientation.

Sexual self-consciousness is by no means the only mind state that requires whole-body explanations. We have suggested that emotional and dream states also require whole-body explanations. Upon reflection, the incompleteness of brain-only explanations becomes apparent. What would fear be as an emotional response without the "flight or fight response" or happiness without the relaxation of smooth and striated muscle? What would a dream be without its profound physical affects, affect made possible, in part, by the actions of the very same endocrine system?

Consideration of the whole body in building the narrative of self may seem initially to make the problem of consciousness appear even harder (Chalmers, 1995), by suggesting that the solution to *that* problem will not come from the study of the brain alone—for example, by finding some brain correlate that is what consciousness is. But if figuring out what consciousness is requires taking the whole body into account, then whatever difficulties taking this route involves, it is the way to go if that is where the best answer lies. Is it really plausible to think we can adequately explain a sensory experience simply by determining its neural correlates? Take an experience of "seeing red." It is not remotely implausible to think that it is the interactions between the periphery and the central nervous system that generate a "sense" of red, its different tones, its different shades. It is possible that sex steroids act on primary visual cortical neurons as well as on the hippocampal neurons. If we look and find this to be so, it will expand and complicate the problem of conscious perception, but

230 NARRATIVE AND CONSCIOUSNESS REALIZATION

it may also begin to explain the varying strengths and differences in aesthetic responses: why some compositions "just feel right"; why soft lighting, low music, and checkered tablecloths—all in the perceptual domain—engender romantic response.

Since estrogens are, in essence, growth factors, would we be surprised to discover that the receptive fields of visual cortical neurons expand during times of the menstrual cycle when estrogen levels are high? If this were so, what would happen to visual perception in the postmenopausal woman? Would she complain that her world seemed "less vibrant," "slightly out of focus," "constricted"? Wouldn't this go a long way to begin to explain how it feels to age and why some of the elderly get cranky and/or "tune out?" In short, whole-body explanations may lead us to a better understanding of even how perceptual events play a role in constituting our selves and developing our narrative of self.

References

Anonymous (2001). Under this rock. Retrieved from the Intersex Support Group International Web site: www.isgi.org/isgi/rock.html. December 11, 2002.

Brown, D. (2001). Director's page. Retrieved from the Intersex Support Group International Web site: www.isgi.org/isgi/director.html. December 11, 2002.

Campbell, S. S., & Murphy, P. J. (1998). Extraocular circadian phototransduction in humans. *Science, 279*, 396–398.

Chalmers, D. (1995). *The conscious mind.* New York: Oxford University Press.

Churchland, P. S. (1986). *Neurophilosophy.* Cambridge, MA: MIT Press.

Damasio, A. R. (1994). *Descartes' error: Emotion, reason, and the human brain.* New York: G. P. Putnam's Sons.

Damasio, A. R. (1995). Toward a neurobiology of emotion and feeling: Operational concepts and hypotheses. *Neuroscientist, 1*, 19–25.

Damasio, A. R. (1999). *The feeling of what happens: Body and emotion in the making of consciousness.* New York: Harcourt Brace.

Diamond, M., & Sigmundson, H. K. (1997). Sex reassignment at birth: Long-term review and clinical implications. *Archchives of Pediatric and Adolescent Medicine, 151*, 298–304.

Einstein, G. (2000). Sex, sexuality and the brain. In D. Purves, G. J. Augustine, D. Fitzpatrick, L. C. Katz, A-S. LaMantia, & J. McNamara (Eds.), *Neuroscience* (pp. 645–663). Sunderland, MA: Andrew Sinauer and Associates.

Fausto-Sterling, A. (2000). *Sexing the body.* New York: Basic.

Flanagan, O. (1992). *Consciousness reconsidered.* Cambridge, MA: MIT Press.

Flanagan, O. J. (1996). *Self expressions: Mind, morals, and the meaning of life.* New York: Oxford University Press.

Flanagan, O. (2000). *Dreaming souls: Sleep, dreams, and the evolution of the conscious mind.* New York: Oxford University Press.

Friedlander, E. R. (2001). XYY—stereotype of the karyotype. Retrieved from Dr. Friedlander's Web site: December 2, 2002. www.pathguy.com/xyy.htm.

Gorski, R. A., Harlan, R. E., Jacobson, C. D., Shryne, J. E., & Southam, A. (1980). Evidence for a morphological sex difference within the medial preoptic area of the rat brain. *Journal of Comparative Neurology, 193,* 529–539.

Hacking, I. (1990). Natural kinds. In R. Barrett & R. Gordon (Eds.), *Perspectives on Quine* (pp. 129–141). Cambridge: Blackwell.

Hobson, J. A. (1994). *The chemistry of conscious states.* Boston: Little, Brown.

Imperato-McGinley, J., Miller, M., Wilson, J. D., Peterson, R. E., Shackleton, C., & Gajdusek, D. C. (1991). A cluster of male pseudohermaphrodites with 5 alpha-reductase deficiency in Papua New Guinea. *Journal of Clinical Endocrinology, 34,* 293–298.

James, W. (1890). *The principles of psychology.* 2 vols. New York: Dover.

LeDoux, J. E. (1996). *The emotional brain.* New York: Simon & Schuster.

LeVay, S. (1991). A difference in hypothalamic structure between heterosexual and homosexual men. *Science, 253,* 1034–1037.

LeVay, S. (2000). Male, female, other. Retrieved from www.nerve.com/dispatches/levay/intersex/. December 11, 2002.

Locke, J. (1975). *An essay concerning human understanding,* (P. H. Nidditch, Ed.). Oxford: Oxford University Press, 1975. (Original work published 1690)

McEwen, B. S., Davis, P. G., Parsons, B., & Pfaff, D. W. (1979). The brain as a target for steroid hormone action. *Annual Review of Neuroscience, 2,* 65–112.

Modney, B. K., & Hatten, G. L. (1990). Motherhood modifies magnocellular neuronal interrelationships in functionally meaningful ways. In N. A. Krasnegor & R. S. Bridges (Eds.), *Mammalian parenting* (pp. 305–323). New York: Oxford University Press.

Nagel, T. (1974). What is it like to be a bat? *Philosophical reviews, 83,* 435–450.

Plautz, J. D., Kaneko, M., Hall, J. C., & Kay, S. A. (1997). Independent photoreceptor circadian clocks throughout Drosophila. *Science, 278,* 1632–1635.

Rubin, R. T., & King, B. H. (1995). Endocrine and metabolic disorders. In H. I. Kaplan & B. J. Sadock (Eds.), *Comprehensive textbook of psychiatry* (pp. 1514–1528) (6th ed., 2 vols). Baltimore: Williams & Wilkins.

Speroff, L., Glass, R. H., & Kase, N. G. (1994). *Clinical gynecologic endocrinology and infertility* (5th ed.). Baltimore: Williams & Wilkins.

Stein, E. (1999). *The mismeasure of desire.* New York: Oxford University Press.

Stern, D. (1985). *The interpersonal world of the child: A view from psychoanalysis and developmental psychology.* New York: Basic.

Swaab, D. F., & Hofman, M. A. (1990). An enlarged suprachiasmatic nucleus in homosexual men. *Brain Research, 537,* 141–148.

Uttal, W. R. (2001). *The new phrenology: The limits of localizing cognitive processes in the brain.* Cambridge, MA: MIT Press.

Xerri, C., Stern, J. M., & Merzenich, M. M. (1994). Alterations of the cortical representation of the rat ventrum induced by nursing behavior. *Journal of Neuroscience, 14,* 1710–1721.

Index

a/b: Auto/Biographical Studies (Smith), 90

Abelson, R. P., 60, 61

abstract concepts, 43–44

accuracy, in personal narrative, 5, 119, 120

acknowledging (Cavell literary concept), 133

action, 25–28

Adrenal Corticotropin Hormone (ACTH), 221

adrenaline, 25, 214

adrenals, 215, 224

adrenal tumors, 221

aesthetic responses, 230

affective disorder, 71

affective experiences. *See* emotions

agnosia, 62, 65–66

AIS. *See* androgen insensitivity syndrome

Alzheimer's disease, 71, 212, 213

ambiguous genitalia, 225–27

Améry, Jean, 150, 151–52

amnesia, 63–66
  brain areas and, 63–64, 69, 73
  confabulation and, 204
  personal, 88
  personhood and, 210
  retrograde vs. anterograde, 63–65, 68
  visual memory deficit and, 62, 65–66, 68, 69, 75, 76
  See also agnosia

amygdala, 215

anatomo-politics, 88

Anderson, W. T., 170

androgen insensitivity syndrome (AIS), 222, 223, 224, 228

androgens, 215, 218, 219, 220, 221, 223, 224

Annotated Lolita, The (Appel), 136, 143n.3

anomia, 68

anosognosics, 204

anterior frontal cortex, 202

anterior hypothalamus, 219

anterograde amnesia, 63, 64, 65, 66

anthropology. *See* culture

aphasia, 59, 62, 66–69, 72
  classifications of, 66–67, 198
  damaged brain region and, 198
  inner speech and, 198–99

aphasia (*continued*)
  intact narrative reasoning in, 69–71,
    72, 75, 76
Appel, Alfred, Jr., 136, 143n.3
Aristotle, 206
artificial intelligence, 88
Art of Memory, The (Yates), 87
Asperger's syndrome, 109n.5
assassinations, flashbulb memories for,
  58
association, 89, 91
association cortex, 215
associative visual agnosia, 65
assumptions, 168
At the Mind's Limits (Améry), 151–52
Auschwitz, 149, 151–52, 154, 156
*Auschwitz and After, None of Us Will
  Return* (Delbo), 149, 156
Australia, 172, 173–77, 181–82
authorial voice, 177–81
  dual, 181–82
  dual first-person, 9, 129–43
  ethical consequences of, 130–43
  first-person, 9, 57, 135–37, 162–63
  inner speech and, 196–207
  point of view and, 58, 135–36, 138
  third-person, 138
  unreliable narrator, 130, 135–37
autism, 94–107, 108
  diagnostic characteristics of, 94–95
  neurobiological model of, 95–96
  recovering, 97–107, 108, 109n.5
  variations in, 109n.5
autobiographical memory, 53–108
  agnosia and, 62, 65–66
  anterograde amnesia and, 63–66
  aphasia and, 67–68, 69
  autobiographical reasoning and, 61
  bilingualism and, 59–60
  brain areas involved in, 63, 72–73
  child's appropriation of story as, 31–
    32, 93
  confabulation and, 73, 74
  conscious recall of, 53–54

cued retrieval of, 56
cultural effects on, 61
eyewitness testimony and, 58
failure of. *See* amnesia
hierarchy of, 92
Holocaust experiences' persistence
  in, 153–54
as integration of systems and skills,
  75
meaning making and, 125
narrative as organizer of, 61
narrative reasoning and, 55, 75
neural system damage and, 8, 62–
  74, 76
output vs. input, 119
personal narratives and. *See*
  autobiographical narrative
as personhood marker, 209–11
point of view in, 58
recovered, 58
retrieval of. *See* recollection
retrospective meaning making with,
  123
as selective, 120
self and, 86, 92–108
self as interpreter of, 92
semantic dementia impairment of,
  67–68, 69
somatic markers for key events and,
  90
as specific and concrete, 57
storytelling as shaping of, 47, 93–
  94. *See also* autobiographical
  narrative
systems needed for, 54–55
temporal order and, 72, 73–74, 93,
  124, 126–27
theories of, 60–62
visual imagery as central to, 54, 56–
  59, 66, 69, 75
See also recollection
autobiographical narrative, 4–8, 115–
  27
  accuracy and, 119

by aphasics, 67, 70–71
autism and, 94–107
autobiographical reasoning and, 55, 61
child's development of self and, 7, 25–33, 44–47, 93
cognitive research and, 4–5
coherence and relevance of, 61
cultural narrative and, 22
daily use of, 167
disintegration of, 168
disruption in, 10, 169–86
dominance of, 168
early somatic impact of, 11
as examined life, 127
experience falsification in, 9, 119, 120, 121, 124
fictional narrator of, 129–44
fiction's relationship with reality and, 115–18
hindsight and, 123
of Holocaust survivors, 9–10, 149–64
as illusions, 124
as inner speech, 196–207
interpretation and, 4, 38, 124, 126
meaning making from, 21, 116, 119, 125, 167–69
parent-child construction of, 3, 22, 28, 29–33, 45–46, 93
as personhood marker, 210–11
of preschoolers, 28–29
prompted recall and, 31
protonarrative and, 122–23
pseudo, 9, 129–43
real vs. fictive, 12
selectivity in, 120
self as interpreter of, 92–94
self-consciousness and, 3–4, 29, 45–47, 92–94
sexual self and, 223, 225–30
shared experiential, 29–33
social function of, 168
time and, 9, 61, 93, 124–26

trauma and, 9–10, 12, 177–86
truth and, 5, 117–21, 124, 126–27
uniqueness of own past and, 29–30
See also fiction; storytelling
autobiographical reasoning. See narrative reasoning
autonoetic consciousness, 53–54
autonomic sexual response, 22
awareness. See conscious awareness; self-consciousness

Baars, Bernard, 196, 198
Baddeley, Alan D., 196, 197–98
Bakhtin, Mikhail, 133, 177, 181
Barclay, C. R., 60–61
Barnes, Hazel, 117–18
behavior
    autistic markers of, 95, 109n.5
    metaphors for, 55–56, 77
    physical realities of, 77
    sex as, 217
    systems needed for recollection of, 54–55, 74–75
Bensen, James, 228
bereavement, authorial voice and, 177–78
Bergen-Belsen, 150
Bernstein, Marcia, 207n.1
Bertalanffy, L. von, 18
biases, historical truth vs., 120
Bickle, John, 10, 195–207
bilingual autobiographical memory, 59–60
biography
    cultural mores and, 61
    embryonic sexual development and, 217–18
    fatal flaw in, 116
    See also autobiographical narrative
biological clock, 215–16
biology. See cell biology; neurobiology
bio-politics, 88
Bliss, E. L., 109n.10
Bloom, H., 144n.3

Bluck, S., 55, 61, 73
body
  brain relationship, 213–30
  narrative of self and, 11, 90–94,
    107–8, 108n.2, 211, 213, 228–29
  naturalistic theory of mind and, 213–
    16
  sexual self and, 216, 217–28
Booth, Wayne C., 132–33
bose-einstein condensates, 89
Boston Diagnostic Aphasia
    Examination, 70
brain
  amnesia and, 63–64, 69, 73
  aphasia and, 198
  autism and, 95–96
  autobiographical memory and, 63,
    72–73
  function images. *See* brain imaging
  function localization within, 203
  hormones and, 214–15, 216–17,
    219, 220, 221, 222, 224, 229
  language region, 11, 198, 199, 200–
    201, 202, 204, 206
  mapping of, 87
  memory distribution within, 55, 56,
    68, 74, 76, 87, 90
  memory loss subsystems, 63–64, 68,
    69
  as metaphor for human behavior,
    55–56, 77
  narrative ability localization in, 72
  narrative concept of self and, 10–11
  narrative reasoning distribution in,
    76
  naturalistic theory of mind and, 213–
    15
  non-neural body's effect on, 213–
    30
  processing systems, 89
  quantum indeterminacy and, 89
  recollection systems, 56, 63
  semantic dementia pathologies and,
    68
  sexual development and, 218–19

  sexual self-consciousness and, 217–
    20, 229
  standard cognitive development
    model of, 18, 56
  visual imagery subsystems of, 65–
    66, 68
brain damage. *See* neural damage
brain imaging, 10–11, 72, 74, 196–97,
    214, 215
brain stem, 215
Braithwaite, J., 187n.7
breathing, 211
Brewer, W. F., 60, 62
Broca's aphasia, 66, 71, 198, 199
Broca's area, 198
Broca studies, 87
Brodmann's areas, 63, 198
Brown, Deborah, 227–28
Brown, R., 57, 61
Bruner, Jerome, 21, 25, 60, 62, 94,
    117
Buber, Martin, 181
Buchenwald, 155, 157–64
Burgess, P., 202, 203

CAH. *See* congenital adrenal
    hyperplasia
Campbell, D. T., 23
Carr, David, 123
Carrithers, M., 22, 25
cartoons, 62
catecholamines, 221–22
categorization, 27
causal coherence, 61
causality
  infant understanding of, 42–43
  inner speech and, 199, 200, 201,
    202, 205, 207
  in meaning making of adversity, 187–
    88n.10
  sequences in, 74
Cavell, Stanley, 133
cell biology, 88, 90
Centerwall, B., 144n.6
cerebral cortex, 217, 221

cervix, 218
Challenger disaster, 58
Chatman, Seymour, 138
child development, 17–33, 37–48
  comparative concepts in, 43–44
  conceptual contrast of self and
    others in, 30
  cultural narratives and, 22
  emergence of narrative in, 7, 27–29,
    93
  emergent levels of learning in, 18,
    23–24, 26–27
  emotional interaction and, 42–43
  growing awareness levels in, 19–21,
    23–24, 33, 38–39
  imitation in, 41–42
  intentionality realization in, 26–27,
    38
  language development in, 24, 27–
    28, 32, 33, 38, 40–42
  "little scientists" learning analogy
    for, 39–40
  meaning making in, 40–41
  mirror recognition test as milestone
    in, 20
  personal narratives and, 44–47, 107
  perspective and, 19, 22, 27, 29, 31–
    33, 38
  Piaget's theory of, 38–42
  preverbal gestures in, 40–41
  preverbal sense of self and, 211
  of self, 37–48
  self- and other-awareness in, 31–33
  of self-understanding, 44–47
  stream of consciousness and, 211
  temporality concept and, 24, 27, 29–
    33
  theory of mind and, 26–27, 29
  See also parent-child relations
childhood memories, 66
childhood realism (Piaget concept), 38
Children, Young Person and Their
    Families Act of 1989 (New
    Zealand), 173
chimpanzees, 20, 23

Christie, Nils, 170, 171, 174, 184, 185
clitoris, 218, 223
closed head injury, 64, 71
co-authorship, 181–82
cognitive processes, 53–77
  computer models for, 55, 56
  connectionist, 91
  conscious awareness development
    and, 17–18
  emergent levels construct of, 18
  emotions and, 39, 43–44
  evolutionary model of, 23
  explicit memory and, 54, 55–56
  field vs. observer point of view and,
    58
  inner speech and, 202
  integration of analysis levels and,
    74
  language stages and, 23–24
  levels of knowing and, 19–21, 23–
    24
  meaning making and, 21
  models of, 90–91
  narrative theories and, 60, 93–94,
    195
  neural basis of, 54–74, 90–91
  as ongoing self-organizing system,
    18
  parent-young child narrative making
    and, 22
  personal narratives and, 4–5
  personhood and, 211–12
  Piaget's approach to, 39
  for recollection, 54
  sexual self-consciousness and, 217
  somatic marker hypothesis, 90–91
  standard epistemic model of, 18
  whole-body explanation and, 214–
    15
cognitive self, 209–10
  characterization of, 20
cognitivism, 209
coherence
  autobiographical reasoning and, 61,
    73–74

coherence (*continued*)
  narrative organization of life events
    as quest for, 168
  narrative repair and, 10
  self-deception despite, 126
community
  co-authorship and, 181–82
  conflict repair and, 167, 185
  language users and, 24
  narrative making and, 22, 33, 46,
    47
Company We Keep, The (Booth), 132–
  33
Comparative Literature Symposium
    on Narrative and Consciousness:
    Literature, Psychology, and the
    Brain, 32nd Annual, 53
competition, 39
comprehension, 199, 200
  aphasics' retention of narrative, 70
  tests of, 62, 71–72
computer graphics, 197
computer modeling, 55, 56, 91
concrete concepts, 43–44
conduction aphasics, 66–67
confabulation, 73–74
  aphasic narratives and, 71
  autobiographical causal sequences
    and, 74
  definition/characteristics of, 73, 204
  frontal-lobe damage and, 73
  internal narratives as, 204
  unawareness of, 73, 204
conferencing, 174–86
  ideal group size, 188n.13
  supporting actors in, 187n.7
conflicts, 10, 167, 169–70. *See also*
  transformative justice
"Conflicts as Property" (Christie), 170
congenital adrenal hyperplasia (CAH),
  222, 224
connectionism, 91, 107
conscious awareness, 6, 7, 17–47
  in child development, 19–21, 23–
    24, 26–27, 33, 38–39

internal narrative and, 196–97
new levels of, 19–21
of past conscious state, 53–54. *See
  also* autobiographical memory
sequences in, 200
See also self-consciousness
consciousness. *See* self; self-
  consciousness
consciousness and narrative. *See*
  autobiographical narrative
conscious recall. *See* recollection
constructed memories, fixed vs., 58
constructivism. *See* social
  constructivism
context cues, 70
contextualism, 89
Cook, Kay K., 86, 90
Cornell, D., 96, 109n.8
cortex, 63, 65, 202, 229
counterfactual thinking, 187n.10
Courage, M. L., 20
crib monologues, 31
criminal system, 10, 170–86
critical legal theory, 170
Crosby, E. C., 200
cruising, in child development, 20–21
cued memory, 56, 69, 70
cultural consciousness, 24
cultural narrative, 24, 25
culture
  autobiographical memory and, 61,
    117
  emergence of symbolic language
    and, 24
  function of narratives and, 22
  literary conventions and, 117
  meaning making and, 21, 22
  narrative conventions of, 24, 25,
    61
  sexual self-formation and, 11, 223,
    225

Damasio, Antonio R., 90, 108n.2,
  210, 211, 214
Darwin, Charles, 211

data organization, right-hemisphere
    damage and, 72
data storage, explicit memory as, 54,
    55–56
death
    missed destiny of, 10, 149–64
    restorative justice and, 177–81
death camps. *See* Holocaust narratives
Death of Ivan Ilych, The (Tolstoy), 161
declarative memory, 210
deconstruction, 91, 109n.8
Delbo, Charlotte, 149, 153, 154, 156
denial, 204, 213
Dennett, D. C., 200
depression, 215
depth knowledge, 88
Derrida, Jacques, 109n.8
Descartes, René, 210, 211
details
    aphasic's correct use of, 70
    in flashbulb memories, 57–58
    memory for, 57
developmental disabilities, 71
developmental psychology
    conscious awareness and, 17–19
    differentiation-integration theory, 30
    narrative process and, 5, 93–94
    nonlinear dynamic systems theories,
        18
    Piaget's theory of, 18, 19, 29, 32,
        38–39, 42, 43
    self as end product of stages in, 38
    See also child development
dialogue, 57
Diamond, Milton, 226
diencephalon, 63
differentiation, sex-formation, 218
differentiation-integration, 30
dihydrotestosterone, 223
"dinner party" task, 202
discourse/story distinction, 138
discourse structure, 70
disintegration, of self-narrative, 168
disordered identities, 169
dispute resolution. *See* conferencing

disruption. *See* narrative disruption
dissociations, 203–4, 207, 213
distorted memories. *See* false
    memories
dominant narrative, 169, 183
Dominican Republic, 223
Donald, Merlin, 21, 22, 23, 24, 27,
    32
dorsal frontal cortex, 202
double consciousness, 87
double dissociations, 203
dreams, 4, 214, 229
    storied forms of, 167
dual first-person voice, 9, 129–43
dual voices, 181–82

Eakin, Paul John, 92, 107, 108n.1
early childhood. *See* child
    development
E.B. (conduction aphasic), 67
Ebbinhaus, Hermann, 87
Edelman, Gerald M., 108n.2
Edwin Mulhouse (Millhauser), 116
Effective Cautioning Using Family
    Group Conferencing, 173
egocentrism, 29
eidetic memory, 109n.3
Einstein, Gillian, 11, 209–30
Elaborate Practical Reasoning, 199,
    200, 301
electrons, 197
embarrassment, 20
embodiment. *See* body
embryonic sexual development, 218
emergence, child developmental, 18,
    23–24, 27–29
Emergence, Labeled Autistic (Grandin),
    97–98, 106
Emma (hermaphrodite), 226–27
emotions
    autism and, 95
    cortical/subcortical brain areas
        supporting, 63
    hormones and, 214, 215
    importance in child learning, 42–44

emotions (*continued*)
    life story retelling and, 46–47
    Piaget's separation from cognitive
       development, 39
    somatic marker system and, 90–91
    transformative justice and, 173–74,
       175–76, 187n.6
    vivid memories and, 92
    whole-body view of, 214
empathy, 60, 133
Emperor's New Mind, The (Penrose),
    89
emulation, 23. *See also* mimesis
encoded memory, 56, 63–65, 67
endocrine system. *See* hormones
Engel, S., 28, 30
Enlightenment, 90
episodic cognition, 23
episodic memory, 23, 31, 63, 68, 93,
    109n.3, 210. *See also*
    autobiographical memory
erection, 229
ERP (evoked-response-potential), 205
estradiol, 220
estrogens, 215, 218, 219, 220, 221,
    229, 230
ethical training, 205–6
ethics
    fictional narrator and, 129–43
    of reading, 130, 131–43
    See also moral training
evaluation of narrative, 25
event-based memory. *See* implicit
    memory; semantic memory
events recall
    as autonoetic consciousness, 53–54
    child's narrative construction and,
       45–47
    creation of self and, 118
    without narrative structure, 62
    neural system damage and, 76
    significance and, 125
    visual imagery and, 58–59
events sequences, 25–26, 27, 73–74,
    200

evoked-response-potential (ERP), 205
evolutionary model, 21–24, 211
examined life, 127
expanded natural method, 4, 23
experience
    autobiographical memory
       falsification of, 119, 120, 124
    child's differentiation of own from
       other's, 31–32
    co-construction of narrative with,
       167
    construction of meaning from, 7
    dual coding of, 42–43
    narrative ordering of, 166
    retrospective significance of, 123,
       125
    See also meaning making
explanatory myths, 22
explicit memory, 23, 76
    brain areas for, 63, 64, 68, 69
    function of, 54, 55–56
    loss of, 63–64
eyewitness testimony, 57, 58

Facing (Levinas literary concept), 133
facts, autobiography and, 116, 117
false memories, 31–32, 47, 119, 120
falsification, 9, 119, 120, 121, 124.
    See also confabulation
fantasies, storied forms of, 167
Farah, M. J., 65
fear, 214, 215, 217, 229
female phenotype, formation of, 218.
    See also gender identity; sexual
    identity
fiction
    autobiographical narrative and, 5–6,
       8–9, 11, 12, 116–26
    ethics of reading and, 130, 131–43
    meanings of, 125
    nonfiction and, 9
    polyphonic, 177
    pseudoautobiography and, 9, 129–
       43
    reality and, 5–6, 115–16, 120

as speaking truth, 126–27
on suffering and dying, 160–62
See also storytelling
fictional narrator, 130–43
Field, Joanna, 116
Fireman, Gary, 3–13
first-person narrator
dual nature of, 9, 129–43
of Holocaust experience, 162–63
involvement and, 57
unreliable, 135–37
Fitzgerald, J. M., 61
5-alpha-reductase deficiency, 222, 223
Fivush, Robyn, 28, 45
fixed memories, constructed vs., 58
fixed role therapy, 186–87n.3
Flanagan, Owen, 3–13, 195, 209–30
flashbulb memories, 57–58, 61
flight or fight response, 229
fluent aphasia. *See* Wernicke's aphasia
fMRI, 214
focalization, 130, 138, 139
forgetting, pathological, 88. *See also*
    amnesia
Forsythe, L., 173
Foucault, Michel, 88, 109n.6, 169,
    170
Frackowiak, R. S. J., 197–98
Freeman, Mark, 9, 61, 115–27
free will, 89
Freud, Sigmund, 58, 87
Friedlander, Edward R., 225
fringe of consciousness, 212
Frith, D., 197–98
frontal lobes, 63, 72, 73, 76
    planning/motor activity and, 202–7

Gage, Phineas, 202
Galtung, Johan, 186n.1
gay persons, 219, 224
Gazzaniga, Michael S., 118–19, 120,
    124
gender identification, 216, 217, 223–
    24, 226–27, 228, 229
generate-select-replicate model, 23

genetic code, 89, 91, 96, 218
genetic engineering, 89
Genette, G., 135
genitalia, 218, 223, 224
    ambiguous, 225–27
genocide. *See* Holocaust narratives
genomes, 89–90, 91, 107
genotype, 217, 218, 220, 222
    unmatched with phenotype, 223–
    24
Gergen, K. J., 61
Gergen, M. M., 61
Glass, James M., 105, 109n.10
glucose metabolism, 197
goal structure, narrative, 61
gonads, 218, 220
Gopnik, Alison, 39
Graham, K. S., 69
Grandin, Temple, 97, 106
Greenberg, Daniel L., 7, 53–77
grief, authorial voice and, 177–78
Grosz, Elizabeth, 108n.2
group experiences, 47
group recollection/shared memories,
    61

Habermas, T., 55, 61, 73
habit memory. *See* implicit memory;
    semantic memory
Hacking, Ian, 76, 87–88, 106, 119,
    125–26
Hamlyn, D. W., 43–44, 44
Hanna F. (Holocaust survivor), 151,
    152
happiness, 229
Hardcastle, Valerie Gray, 7, 37–48,
    125
Harlow, J. M., 202
hearsay, autobiography and, 117
Hendriks-Jansen, H., 22
hermaphrodites, 226–27
hermeneutic ethics, 133
heterodiegetic narrator. *See* third-
    person narrator
heterosexual males, 219

hindsight, in narration, 123
hippocampus, 63, 64, 69, 212, 229
historical truth, 3, 120–21
Hobson, J. Allan, 214
Hodges, J., 69
Hoffman, Dustin, 109n.5
Holocaust narratives, 9–10, 149–64
hominids, 23
homodiegetic narrator. *See* first-person narrator
Homo sapiens, 24, 209, 212
homosexuals. *See* gay persons
hormones, 214–15, 216–18, 219, 220, 221–22, 224, 229, 230
How Do We Know Who We Are? (Ludwig), 120
Howe, M. L., 20
How Our Lives Become Stories: Making Selves (Eakin), 92, 108n.1
Hudson, J. A., 28
human corionic gonadotropin (β-HCG), 221
Human Genome Project, 89–90, 91
Humphrey, T., 200
hybrid mind, 24
hypothalamus, 217, 218, 219, 220, 221, 229

identity. *See* personhood; self; sexual identity
identity disorders, 213
idiots savants, 109n.5
illusions, 124
imagery system. *See* visual imagery
imagination, 125, 127, 161
imaging of brain. *See* brain imaging
imitation. *See* mimesis
implicit memory, 23, 109n.3
indeterminacy
of past experience, 125–26
of quantum physics, 89, 91
infants. *See* child development
information processing, 200
data storage and, 54, 55–56
See also knowledge

innate content knowledge, 21
inner speech, 196–207
as confabulation, 204
neural basis of, 196, 203–4
timing of action initiated by, 205
ubiquity of, 196, 198, 199–200
working memory and, 198
insights, 126
intentionality, 26–27, 38
internalization, 19
internal narratives. *See* inner speech
interpersonal conflict. *See* conflicts
interpretation, 4, 38, 124, 126
Intersex Support Group International, 227–28
intersexuality, 222, 225–28
interstitial nuclei of anterior hypothalamus (INAH), 219
intersubjectivity, 27
intrapersonal conflict. *See* conflicts
involvement, 57
isolated events, 62
"I-/Thou" relationship, 181, 185

James, Henry, 48
James, William, 11, 33, 168, 200, 211, 212
Janet, Pierre-Marie-Félix, 87
Joan of Arc, 224
Johns Hopkins University, 225–26
jokes, 62
justice. *See* restorative justice; retributive justice; transformative justice
juvenile justice, 173–77

Kanner, Leo, 95
Karmiloff-Smith, Annette, 39–40
Kauffman, L., 143n.3
Kelly, George A., 186n.3
Kennedy, John F., assassination of, 58
King, Martin Luther, Jr, assassination of, 58
Kintsch, W., 60
Klinefelter's syndrome, 222

knowledge
   brain areas for retrieval of, 63, 69
   levels of, 19–21, 23–24
   long-term storage of, 63
   retrieval of. *See* recollection
   about selfhood, 87–88
   semantic dementia loss of, 68
   storage of, 24, 57, 59, 63, 69, 76
   written language's impact on, 24
Kolb, B., 202
Korsakoff's syndrome, 64, 71, 212
Kosslyn, S. M., 65
Kotre, John, 92, 93, 94
Kulik, J., 57, 61

labia, 218, 223
Labov, W., 25
lactation, 221
landscape of action, 25–26, 27
landscape of consciousness, 25, 26–28
Langer, Lawrence L., 9–10, 127, 149–
   64
language, 59–60
   aphasic's continued abilities with,
      67, 69–71
   aphasic's speech loss and, 59, 62,
      66–69
   autism and, 95, 97, 98
   autobiographical memory and, 59–
      60, 67
   brain region and, 11, 198, 199, 200–
      201, 202, 204, 206
   child development and, 24, 27–28,
      32, 33, 38, 40–42
   components of, 59–60
   cued retrieval of memory and, 56
   developmental stages for, 23–24
   early childhood sense of self and,
      17, 20
   as human capacity, 24, 210, 212
   information processing and, 200–
      201
   inner speech and, 196–207
   invention of written, 24
   involvement dimension of, 57

narrative formation and, 5, 7, 22,
   32
narrative reasoning and, 54, 59, 75
parent-child personal narratives and,
   28, 32
preverbal gestures and, 40–41
preverbal sense of self and, 211
lateral frontal lobe, 202
Lauer, E., 200
learning
   children as "little scientists" analogy
      and, 39–40
   concrete vs. abstract concepts of, 43–
      44
   emotional interaction and, 42–44
   as imitation, 27, 41–42, 97, 98
   Piaget's theory of, 38, 39
   stages of, 23–24, 26–27
LeDoux, Joseph E., 214, 215
left supramarginal gyrus, 198
left temporal lobectomy, 203
Leiris, Michael, 116
lesbians, 224
LeVay, Simon, 228
Levi, Primo, 157
Levinas, Emmanuel, 133
Lewandowski, A. M., 169
Lewin, Philip, 122
Libet, Benjamin, 205
"Life as Narrative" (Bruner), 94
Life of One's Own, A (Field), 116
life scripts, 89
life stories. *See* autobiographical
   narrative; biography
Lincoln, Abraham, assassination of,
   58
linguistics. *See* language
literary conventions, 117. *See also*
   fiction
literary theory, 4, 6, 12
   narrative divisions and, 25
   narrative ethics and, 129–43
   on topic content vs. treatment of,
      131
Literature or Life (Semprun), 157

Locke, John, 209–11, 212, 228
locomotion, child's progressive stages of, 19, 20
logic, narrative, 130–43
Lolita (Nabokov), 9, 129–43
long-term memory, 57, 65
  visual memory loss and, 65–66
Long Voyage, The (Semprun), 157, 159, 161, 162, 163–64
Lucariello, J., 4
Ludwig, Arnold, 120–21, 126
Luria, A. R., 67
luteinizng hormone, 221
lying. *See* falsification

Mado (Holocaust survivor), 153–54
magnetic resonance (MR), 214
making sense, metaphor of, 19
male phenotype, formation of, 218. *See also* gender identity; sexual identity
mammillary bodies, 63
Manhood (Leiris), 116
Maori, 173
Marcel, Gabriel, 123, 124, 125
Martin, Mary Patricia, 137
material self, 86–94, 107–8
maze puzzles, 203
McAdams, Dan P., 4
McCarthy, Mary, 117
McDonald, John, 173, 174, 175–76, 187n.9, 188n.12
McEwen, Bruce S., 214–15
McVay, Ted, 3–13
Mead, M., 33
meaning making, 7, 21–22
  of adversity, 187–88n.10
  autobiographical memory and, 125
  child development and, 40–41
  constructivist approach to, 167
  current vs. retrospective perspective and, 123, 125
  narrative disruption and, 168–69
  narrative truth and, 116, 120, 121, 125–26

personal narratives and, 21, 116, 119, 125, 167–69
poesis and, 125–26
remembering as process of, 92
self-consciousness and, 119
medial temporal structures, 63, 66, 68
medial thalamus, 63
"Medical Identity: My DNA/Myself" (Cook), 86, 90
Meltzoff, Andrew N., 39
Memories of a Catholic Girlhood (McCarthy), 117
memoro-politics, 8, 88–106
memory
  accurate vs. distorted, 119
  child development and, 27, 31
  child's self-narratives and, 45–47
  cognitive processes in, 54–55
  conscious retrieval and, 56
  as fixed vs. constructed, 58
  genetic code as, 89
  group, 61
  historical conceptualizations of, 87–88, 107
  knowledge storage and, 24, 55, 56, 57, 59, 63, 69, 76
  levels of knowing and, 23
  manipulation of, 31–32, 47, 57
  neural networks and, 90–91
  parent-child recollection dialogue and, 31
  perspective in, 58
  psychodynamics of, 87
  representation and, 22
  repression of, 87, 120
  retrieving vs. encoding, 56, 63–65, 67
  sciences of, 87–88, 106–8
  types of, 109n.3
  visual imagery and, 5, 54, 56–59, 60, 62, 198
  See also autobiographical memory; explicit memory; semantic memory; working memory

Memory and Narrative: The Weave of Life-Writing (Olney), 149
memory loss. *See* amnesia
metabolic disorder, 71
metanarrative, 181
metaphors, 62, 77, 91–92, 108
    autism as, 97
    of reading, 132, 133
Miller, P. J., 31, 46
Millhauser, Stephen, 116
Milner, B., 202
mime (performance art), 59, 62
mimesis
    autistic functioning and, 97, 98
    in child development, 23, 24, 27, 41–42
mind
    adult's hybrid, 24
    children's "theory of," 26, 29
    levels of representation in, 21–22
    naturalist theory of, 10–11, 213–15
    personal narrative and, 4, 21, 22, 25
    See also meaning making; self-consciousness
mind-body dualism, 90, 107–8
Mind's Past, The (Gazzaniga), 118–19
mirror recognition test, 20, 23
mnemonics, 57, 87
Money, John, 225–26
monologue, inner. *See* inner speech
Moore, David, 173, 174, 175–76, 187nn.6, 9, 188n.12
moral agency, 210
moral training, 11, 205–6, 207
Moscovitch, M., 69
motivations, 25
motoric imitation, 23
motor memory. *See* planning and motor execution
MR (magnetic resonance), 214
MRS (S = spectrography), 215
Mullerian duct, 218
multi-infarct dementia, 71
multiple personalities, 105, 109n.10
myths, 22

Nabokov, Vladimir, 9, 129–43
Nadel, L., 69
Nagel, Thomas, 212
narrative, 3–7
    beginnings of, 21–22
    communal authorship and, 181–82
    community and, 22, 33, 46, 47
    cultural, 24, 25
    definition of, 186n.2
    disruption in, 10, 169–86
    evaluation and, 25
    event sequence and, 25–26, 27, 200
    expanded natural method study of, 3–4
    inner speech and, 196–207
    interdisciplinary approach to, 4, 5, 6
    language development and, 5, 7, 23–24, 32, 59
    logic of, 130–43
    natural method study of, 3–4, 6, 12
    as prototypical form of human activity, 167
    retrospective meaning and, 123, 128
    sexual identity and, 214–30
    theoretical models of, 12
    truth and, 3, 118–21
    visual memory and, 58–59
    See also autobiographical narrative; narrative reasoning
narrative disruption, 10, 169–86
    two forms of, 168–69
narrative ethics, 130–43
narrative reasoning, 60–62
    aphasic's retention of, 69–71, 72
    in confabulation, 73–74
    context cues and, 70
    definition of, 54, 61–62
    four components of, 61
    language and, 54, 59, 75
    localization of, 76–77
    loss of, 61–62, 71–74
    nonverbal expressions of, 59, 62

narrative reasoning (*continued*)
  properties of, 60
  recollection theory and, 76
  retention of, 69–71
  systems underlying, 54–55, 72, 75–77
  tests of, 62
narrative structure, 9, 61, 124–26
narrative therapists, 169
narrative thought, 61
narrative time, 124–26
Nathanson, D., 187n.6
naturalist model, 10–11, 213–15
natural method, 3–4, 6, 12
Natzweiler concentration camp, 154–55
Neimeyer, Robert A., 10, 127, 166–86
Neisser, U., 61
Nelson, Katherine, 7, 17–33, 93, 107, 109n.3, 125
neocortical pathology, 68, 69
neural damage
  aphasia and, 198
  autobiographical recollection and, 62–74, 75, 76
  double dissociations and, 203
  explicit memory and, 63–64
  localization technology and, 76–77, 203
  narrative reasoning and, 61–62, 70–71, 75, 76
  non-explicit memory systems and, 64–65
  planning/motor execution and, 202–3
  sense of personal continuity and, 212–13
neural networks, 90–91, 107, 201, 229
neurobiology, 4, 6, 7–8, 10–11, 12, 88
  autism and, 95–96
  consciousness and, 89–91, 107

language/information processing and, 200–201
  PET imaging and, 196–97
  protoself and, 211–12
  self-representation and, 10–11, 90–107, 195–207
  sexual self-consciousness and, 217–30
  visual imagery and, 65–66
neurons, 89, 95, 200, 201, 204, 212–13, 215
  PET imaging and, 197
  sexual self and, 216, 219, 220, 221
neuropsychology, 53–77
  autobiographical memory and, 54, 62–74, 76, 92
  dissociations and, 203–4, 207, 213
  frontal patients' planning/execution deficits and, 202–3
  integration of analysis levels in, 74
  narrative reasoning and, 60–62, 72–77
  theories of self and, 90–91
  See also cognitive processes
neurotransmitters, 215, 221
neutrons, 197
Newton, Adam Zachary, 132, 133
New Zealand, 173
Nobody Nowhere: The Extraordinary Autobiography of an Autistic (Williams), 86, 94, 97, 98, 99–107, 108
nonfiction, 9
nonfluent aphasia. *See* Broca's aphasia
nonhuman primates, 20, 23
nonlinear dynamic systems, 18, 19
nonliteral statements, 62
nonverbal narrative, 59, 62

O'Connell, Terry, 173, 183, 188n.14
Olney, J., 149
ovaries, 218, 221
oviducts, 218

ovulation, 229
oxytocin, 221

parallel distributed processing, 89,
    91
parent-child relations
    autism and, 95
    emotional interaction and, 42–44
    imitation and, 41–42
    intentionality and, 26–27
    narrative formulas and, 45–46
    narrative making and, 3, 22, 28, 29–
        33, 93, 107
past, recollections of. See
        autobiographical memory;
        recollection
Patnoe, E., 143n.3, 144n.5
Paulescu, E., 197–98
pedophilia, 130, 131, 135
Peirce, Charles, 109n.8
penal system. See criminal system
penis, 218, 223
Penrose, Roger, 89
personal coherence. See coherence
personal identity. See personhood; self
personal narrative. See
        autobiographical narrative
personhood, 209–11, 228. See also self;
        self-consciousness
perspective
    in autobiographical memory, 58
    child's development of, 19, 22, 27,
        29, 31–33, 38
PET. See positron emission
        tomography
Phelan, James, 9, 129–44
phenomenology, 4, 6
phenotype, 217–18, 220, 222–24
    hermaphrodites and, 226
    unmatched with genotype, 223–24
pheochromocytomas, 221
philosophy, 6, 12, 209–13
phonetics, 59, 60, 69
phonological working memory, 198

photons, 197
phrases, 59
physics. See quantum theory
Piaget, Jean, 18, 19, 29, 32, 38–39,
        42, 43
    core developmental assumptions of,
        38, 39
pictures, 62
pituitary gland, 217, 219
planning and motor execution, 203–7
play, narrative development and, 28
plot, 25
Plotkin, H. C., 23
Poe, Edgar Allan, 155
poesis, meaning making and, 125–26
point of view
    field vs. observer, 58
    narrators as focalizers and, 138
    unreliable fictional narrator and,
        135–36
    See also authorial voice
positivist naturalism, 5
positron emission tomography (PET),
        10–11, 196–97, 214
    workings of, 196–97
posterior cortex, 65
postmodern theory, 108n.1
prefrontal lobe damage, 3202
pregnancy, 221
preschool children. See child
        development
Preston, M. Elizabeth, 136
preverbal consciousness, 40–41, 211
primordial gonads, 218
Prince, Gerald, 138
problem solving, multistep, 202
processing systems, 89
progesterone, 221
proteins, 91, 218
protonarrative, 122–23
protons, 197
protoself, 211–12
pseudoautobiography, 9, 129–43
psychiatric diagnosis, 169

psychoanalytic theory
autism and, 95
autobiographical memory and, 61
historical vs. narrative truth and,
120–21
psychology, 4, 6, 12. *See also* behavior;
child development; cognitive
processes; developmental
psychology; neuropsychology
psychotherapy
fixed role therapy and, 186–87n.3
historical truths and, 120
personal narratives and, 5, 166, 169
punishments, 172

Quantum Self, The (Zohar), 88–89
quantum theory, 88–89, 91, 107
quantum thinking, 89

radioactive decay, 197
Rain Man (film), 109n.5
Raskin, J. D., 169
rationality, 89–91
Ray, John, Jr., 130
reading, ethical engagement in, 130,
131–43
reality
imposition of fictive process on, 5–
6, 115–16, 120
memory's relationship with, 119–
20, 124
reasoning. *See* narrative reasoning
recall. *See* recollection
recollection
of autobiographical memory, 54, 61–
62, 67, 76, 123–24
autobiographical narrative haziness
of, 117
as autonoetic consciousness, 53
brain as substrate of, 56, 63
connectionist, 91
cued, 56, 69, 70
distortion of, 119
in groups, 61
language and, 59–60

mnemonic systems for, 57, 87
narrative reasoning and, 76
neuropyschological data on, 62–77,
87
noncoherent, 62
redescriptions and, 125
retrieval-cue-retrieval process, 56
selfhood and, 87, 92
as synchronous multitasking, 92
visual imagery and, 5, 54, 56–59,
60, 62
See also autobiographical memory;
events recall
recovered memories, 58
relevance, 60, 70
relived events. *See* event recall
"remembered" self, 61, 92
remembering. *See* recollection
Renee H. (Holocaust survivor), 150
representation
ethics of, 133
of events, 24
levels of, 21–22
repressed memories, 87, 120
restorative justice, 10, 171–86
retributive justice, 10, 170, 171, 172,
173, 185, 187n.6
retrieval strategies. *See* recollection
retrograde amnesia, 63–64, 65, 68, 69
retrospective pseudoautobiography, 9,
129–43
retrospective viewpoint, 123, 125
revenge. *See* retributive justice
Rewriting the Soul (Hacking), 87
rhetoric, narrative as, 132
Ricoeur, Paul, 9, 124
right frontal cortex, 63
right-hemisphere damage, 72–73
right temporal lobectomy, 203
Rimland, Bernard, 106
Robinson, J. A., 60
Rodin, Auguste, 199
Roth, Philip, 117
Rubin, David C., 7, 53–77, 119
Russell, R. L., 4

Sacks, Oliver, 97–98, 108n.2
Saying (Levinas literary concept), 133
Scarriano, Margaret M., 106
Schachter, D. L., 119–20
Schafer, R., 61
Schank, R. C., 60, 61, 93
schizophrenia, 71, 103, 215
script, vivid memories and, 92
scrotum, 218
Searching for Memory (Schachter), 119
secondness, 109n.8
selective memory, 120
self, 4
    autism and, 95–107, 108
    autobiographical narrative and, 86,
        92–108, 116–27, 168
    body and, 11, 90–94, 107–8,
        108n.2, 211, 213, 228–29
    child's development of, 37–48
    child's emergence of consciousness
        of, 17–33
    cognitive, 20, 209–10
    as commonality of reference, 108n.1
    connectionist, 91, 107
    as continuous and continuing, 211
    dominant narrative of, 169, 183
    events reconstruction and, 118
    genomic, 89–90, 91, 107
    inner speech and, 196–99
    materiality of, 86–94, 107–8
    narrative concept of, 5, 6, 7, 8–9,
        12, 22, 47–48, 195–207, 209–12,
        228
    narrative disruptions in construction
        of, 9–10, 168–70
    neurobiological support for, 10–11,
        90–107, 195–207
    as quantum phenomenon, 88–89,
        91
    recollection and, 87, 92
    "remembered," 61, 92
    sexual identity and, 11, 214, 216–
        30
    therapeutic "make-believe" and, 186–
        87n.3

self-consciousness, 17–19
    brain-body combination and, 216
    child's personal narratives and, 44–
        47
    child's progressive levels of, 20, 26,
        30–33
    as continuous biological being, 211–
        12
    as divisible, 216
    of fictional narrator, 130, 135–36,
        137
    illusions and, 124
    meaning making and, 119
    mirror recognition test of, 20, 23
    personal narratives and, 3–4, 29, 45–
        47, 92–94
    sexual, 217–30
    of specific experiential history, 30
self-control, 196
self-deception, 126
self-defining memories, 92
selfhood. *See* self
self-in-control, 199–206
self-in-the-now world, 30
self-knowledge. *See* self-consciousness
self-narrative. *See* autobiographical
    narrative
self-representation, neural basis of, 4,
    195–207
self-understanding, 126
semantic dementia, 67–68, 69–70, 75,
    76
semantic memory, 23, 68, 93, 209,
    210. *See also* autobiographical
    memory
semantics, 59, 60, 69
Semprun, Jorge, 157–64
sensory details, 57
sensory experiences, 42
sentences, 59, 62
sequencing of events, 25–26, 27, 73–
    74, 200
serial processing (rational thinking), 89
sexual abuse, 130–31, 183
    recovered memories and, 58

sexual desire, 221, 229
sexual identity, 11, 214, 216–30
sexually dimorphic nucleus (SDN), 220
sexual orientation, 216, 217, 219, 224
sexual self-consciousness, 217
Shallice, T., 202, 203
shame, 20
shared experiential narratives, 29–30
shyness, 20
Sigmundson, Keith, 226
significance, retrospective viewpoint and, 125
silent film, 59, 62
Simpson, O. J., trial verdict, 58
Simpson, Wallis, 224
smiling, 42–43
Smith, Sidonie A., 8, 86–108
Smith, T. S., 60–61
Smith, Thomas, 90
social constructivism, 8, 38, 166, 167, 168, 169, 182, 184
social contract, 170
social-cultural theory
    function of speech and, 24
    meaning making and, 21, 22
social interactionism, 93
social signals, 26
somatic marker hypothesis, 90–91
Somebody Somewhere: Breaking Free from the World of Autism (Williams), 86, 99, 106, 107, 109n.8
soul, 88, 106, 119
speech
    inner, 196–207
    loss of. See aphasia
    working memory and, 197–207
    See also language
Spence, Donald P., 61, 120, 126
Steiner, George, 160
Stern, Daniel, 212
steroids, 221, 229
storage of knowledge, 24, 57, 59, 76
    long-term, 63

story-based memory. See autobiographical narrative
story/discourse distinction, 138
Story I Tell Myself, The (Barnes), 117–18
storytelling
    autobiographical writing and, 117
    child development and, 28, 31–32, 93
    child's life stories and, 44–47
    child's undifferentiated, 31
    comprehension tests and, 62
    in daily life, 167
    goal-directed nature of, 60
    hindsight as advantage in, 123
    specific, concrete details and, 57
    temporal significance in, 125
    See also autobiographical narrative; fiction
stream of consciousness, 211, 212
stria terminalis, bed nucleus of, 219
subjectivity, 87
    autism and, 96–107
suprachismatic nucleus of the hypothalamus, 219
surface knowledge, 88
survivor memoirs. See Holocaust narratives
symbolization, 23, 24
    in childhood play, 28
    infant's awareness of, 26
    narrative and, 186n.2
    shared experiential narratives and, 29–30
    of vivid memories, 92
    See also language
synapses, 90, 219
synoptic seeing, 119
syntax, 59, 60, 68, 69
systems theories, 18, 19, 21, 91
Szasz, T., 169

"Taking It to a Limit One More Time: Autobiography and Autism" (Smith), 94

talking. *See* language; speech
Tappan, M. B., 181, 183
temporality. *See* time
temporal lobes, 63
temporal neocortex, 68
testes, 218, 223, 225
"testes-at-12" syndrome, 223
testicular determining factor (TDF), 218
testicular feminization, 223
testosterone, 219–20, 223
Texas Tech University, 6
thalamus, 215
theme, 60, 61, 74
Thinker, The (Rodin sculpture), 199
third-person narrator, 138
thought
    brain processing systems for, 89
    confabulist confusion and, 73
    narrative as mode of, 60, 62
time
    autobiographical memory ordering of, 72, 73–74, 93, 124, 126–27
    autobiographical reasoning and, 61
    child's consciousness of, 24, 27, 29–33
    coherence in, 61
    fictional reality and, 115
    narrative structure and, 9, 61, 93, 124–26
TJA. *See* Transformative Justice Australia
Token Test, 70
Tolstoy, Leo, 161
Tomasello, M., 26
Tomkins, S. G., 176, 187n.6
Tower of London puzzle, 203
transformative justice, 172–86
Transformative Justice Australia (TJA), 10, 173–77
transsexuality, 219, 223, 224
trauma
    as narrative disruption, 168–69
    shaping of personal narratives and, 9–10, 12, 177–86

See also Holocaust narratives; restorative justice
Trilling, Lionel, 143n.3
truth
    historical vs. narrative, 3, 121
    meaning of, 116, 120, 125–26
    in personal narrative, 5, 117–21, 124, 126–27
Tschudi, Finn, 10, 166–86
Tulving, E., 53
tumors, 221–22
Turner's syndrome, 222

understanding
    reaching new levels of, 19
    tests of narrative, 62
unreliable narrator, 130, 135–37
urogenital groove, 218
Useless Knowledge (Delbo), 156
uterus, 218

vagina, 218
Van Dijk, T. A., 60
vas deferens, 218
vasopressin, 221
vhzivanie (Bakhtin concept), 133
victim-offender meetings. *See* conferencing
visual cortex, 215, 229–30
visual imagery
    in autobiographical memory, 54, 56–59, 66, 69, 75
    conscious recall and, 5, 54, 56–59, 60, 62
    Holocaust narratives and, 150, 152, 154–55
    narrative and, 58–59
    neural substrate of, 65–66
    semantic dementia parallel with, 69
    working memory and, 198
visual memory. *See* visual imagery
visual memory deficit amnesia, 62, 65–66, 68, 69, 76
vivid memories, four features of, 92

voice. *See* authorial voice; inner speech

Vygotsky, L., 19

Waletsky, J., 25

Walkerdine, Valerie, 44

wave/particle function, 89, 91

Wernicke's aphasia, 67–68, 70–71, 72, 198, 199

Wernicke's area, 198

Western criminal system, 10, 170–86

What a Beautiful Sunday! (Semprun), 157

White Gloves (Kotre), 92

whole-body explanations, 214–15, 229, 230

"Why Narrators Can be Focalizers and Why It Matters" (Phelan), 138

Williams, Donna, 86, 94, 97, 98–107, 108

Wilson, Elizabeth A., 91

Wittgenstein, Ludwig, 160

Wolffian duct, 218

Wood, M., 143n.3

words, 59
    comprehension loss of, 68

working memory, definition of, 197–98

Writing or Life (Semprun), 157, 160

written language, invention of, 24

Wulf, H. H., 67

www.transcend.org, 186n.1

X chromosomes, 217–18

XO genotype, 222

XX genotype, 218

XXY genotype, 222

XY genotype, 217–18, 220, 223, 224, 225

XYY genotype, 222, 225

Yates, Frances A., 87

Young, Hugh Hampton, 226–27

Zasetsky (aphasic patient), 67

Zohar, Danah, 88–89